Can War Be Just

Can war be justified? Pacifists answer that it cannot; they oppose war and advocate for nonviolent alternatives to war. But defenders of just war theory argue that in some circumstances, when the effectiveness of nonviolence is limited, wars can be justified.

In this book, two philosophers debate this question, drawing on contemporary scholarship and new developments in thinking about pacifism and just war theory. Andrew Fiala argues that pacifism follows from the awful reality of war and the nonviolent goal of building a more just and peaceful world. Jennifer Kling argues that war is sometimes justified when it is a last-ditch, necessary effort to defend people and their communities from utter destruction and death. Pulling from global traditions and histories, their debate will captivate anyone who has wondered or worried about the morality of political violence and military force. Topics discussed include ethical questions of self-defense and other-defense, the great analogy between individuals and states, evolving technologies and methods of warfighting, moral injury and post-traumatic stress disorder, broader political and communal issues, and the problem of regional security in a globalizing world. The authors consider cultural and religious issues as well as the fundamental question of moral obligation in a world saturated in military conflict. The book includes reflection on lessons learned from the past decades of war, as well as hopes for the future in light of emerging threats in Europe and elsewhere.

The book is organized in a user-friendly fashion. Each author presents a self-contained argument, which is followed by a series of responses, replies, and counter-arguments. Throughout, the authors model civil discourse by emphasizing points of agreement and remaining areas of disagreement. The book includes reader-friendly summaries, a glossary of key concepts, and suggestions for further study. All of this will help students and scholars follow the authors' dialogue so they may develop their own answer to the question of whether war can be justified.

Andrew Fiala is Professor of Philosophy and Director of the Ethics Center at California State University, Fresno. His recent works include *Seeking Common Ground: A Theist/Atheist Dialogue* (with Peter Admirand, 2021), *Nonviolence: A Quick Immersion, Transformative Pacifism* (2020), and (as editor) *The Routledge Handbook of Pacifism and Nonviolence* (2018). Fiala is co-author of a widely used textbook, *Ethics: Theory and Contemporary Issues.* He is the past President of Concerned Philosophers for Peace.

Jennifer Kling is Assistant Professor of Philosophy and Director of the Center for Legal Studies at the University of Colorado, Colorado Springs. She is the author of *Racist, Not Racist, Antiracist: Language and the Dynamic Disaster of American Racism* (with Leland Harper, 2022), *The Philosophy of Protest: Fighting for Justice Without Going to War* (with Megan Mitchell, 2021), *War Refugees: Risk, Justice, and Moral Responsibility* (2019), and the editor of *Pacifism, Politics, and Feminism: Intersections and Innovations* (2019). She is also the Executive Director of Concerned Philosophers for Peace.

Little Debates About Big Questions

About the series:

Philosophy asks questions about the fundamental nature of reality, our place in the world, and what we should do. Some of these questions are perennial: for example, *Do we have free will? What is morality?* Some are much newer: for example, *How far should free speech on campus extend? Are race, sex and gender social constructs?* But all of these are among the big questions in philosophy and they remain controversial.

Each book in the *Little Debates About Big Questions* series features two professors on opposite sides of a big question. Each author presents their own side, and the authors then exchange objections and replies. Short, lively, and accessible, these debates showcase diverse and deep answers. Pedagogical features include standard form arguments, section summaries, bolded key terms and principles, glossaries, and annotated reading lists.

The debate format is an ideal way to learn about controversial topics. Whereas the usual essay or book risks overlooking objections against its own proposition or misrepresenting the opposite side, in a debate each side can make their case at equal length, and then present objections the other side must consider. Debates have a more conversational and fun style too, and we selected particularly talented philosophers—in substance and style—for these kinds of encounters.

Debates can be combative—sometimes even descending into anger and animosity. But debates can also be cooperative. While our authors disagree strongly, they work together to help each other and the reader get clearer on the ideas, arguments, and objections. This is intellectual progress, and a much-needed model for civil and constructive disagreement.

The substance and style of the debates will captivate interested readers new to the questions. But there's enough to interest experts too. The debates will be especially useful for courses in philosophy and related subjects—whether as primary or secondary readings—and a few debates can be combined to make up the reading for an entire course.

We thank the authors for their help in constructing this series. We are honored to showcase their work. They are all preeminent scholars or rising-stars in their fields, and through these debates they share what's been discovered with a wider audience. This is a paradigm for public philosophy, and will impress upon students, scholars, and other interested readers the enduring importance of debating the big questions.

Tyron Goldschmidt, Fellow of the Rutgers Center for Philosophy of Religion, USA

Dustin Crummett, Ludwig Maximilian University of Munich, Germany

Published Titles:

Do We Have Free Will?
A Debate
By Robert Kane and Carolina Sartorio

Is There a God?
A Debate
by Kenneth L. Pearce and Graham Oppy

Is Political Authority an Illusion?
A Debate
By Michael Huemer and Daniel Layman

Selected Forthcoming Titles:

Consequentialism or Virtue Ethics?
A Debate
By Jorge L.A. Garcia and Alastair Norcross

Are We Made of Matter?
A Debate
By Eric T. Olson and Aaron Segal

For more information about this series, please visit: https://www.routledge.com/Little-Debates-about-Big-Questions/book-series/LDABQ

Can War Be Justified?

A Debate

Andrew Fiala and
Jennifer Kling

Routledge
Taylor & Francis Group

NEW YORK AND LONDON

Designed cover image: © guvendemir / Getty Images

First published 2023
by Routledge
605 Third Avenue, New York, NY 10158

and by Routledge
4 Park Square, Milton Park, Abingdon, Oxon, OX14 4RN

Routledge is an imprint of the Taylor & Francis Group, an informa business

ISBN: 978-0-367-40917-3 (hbk)
ISBN: 978-0-367-40916-6 (pbk)
ISBN: 978-0-367-80985-0 (ebk)

DOI: 10.4324/9780367809850

Typeset in Sabon
by MPS Limited, Dehradun

Contents

Land Acknowledgment

We completed this book on the unceded homelands of Indigenous peoples. Acknowledging this is an important step in recognizing the history and the original stewards of these lands. Such recognition is an essential element of working toward justice and peace. We are privileged to have had this opportunity as part of our ongoing pursuit of knowledge—it is important that each of us acknowledges and reflects on that privilege, what it means, and how we can use it to create positive change.

General Acknowledgments

Jen thanks her family and friends, many of whom read elements of the manuscript, talked through its ideas with her, and kept her well-nourished throughout the writing and editing process. She would also like to thank her RA, Romello Valentine, who assisted with the research for, and editing of, this book. Finally, her thanks go out to her students, who always ask the best questions and make the most insightful points. Y'all are amazing!

Andrew thanks friends and colleagues with whom he has talked about peace, violence, and war. He is especially grateful to the scholars involved in Concerned Philosophers for Peace. It was through that group that he first met Jennifer Kling.

We would like to thank the editors of the Routledge Little Debates About Big Questions book series, Tyron Goldschmidt and Dustin Crummett, for their support of this project, as well as two anonymous reviewers for their helpful, in-depth commentary. Books are always group endeavors, and this one is no different—thank you, family, friends, colleagues, supporters, and advisors! Additionally, our thanks go out to the University of Colorado, Colorado Springs, and California State University, Fresno, which have supported us in doing what we love to do.

This book is dedicated to all those who are working to better understand a world shot through with military conflict and war, and what we can, may, and should do in response. We hope this book contributes, in some small way, to a more just and more peaceful world.

Foreword: Can War Be Justified?

The haunting phrase, "Only the dead have seen the end of war," whether first articulated by Santayana or perhaps even Plato, has continued to capture our minds and has resonated with so many people. And it's no wonder; war, in all its terrible manifestations, has traumatically transformed so many lives, lives directly and indirectly affected by war's death and destruction. Whether we consider war as "an act of force to compel our enemy to do our will,"[1] or even the more concise view that "War is cruelty, and you cannot refine it,"[2] we are often led to believe that war is tied in some inseparable way to human nature, and thus is inevitable. But is this necessarily true? Upon reflection, we ought to ask ourselves (1) whether war is inevitable and (2) whether war can ever be morally justified; (3) if war can be justified, then how so; and (4) if war is not inevitable and it cannot be morally justified, should we ever go to war or fight in war?

For over three decades as a soldier, I have directly witnessed war on several occasions, and as a philosopher I have pondered the above questions in some detail. Further, I have taught a generation of young officers to reflect on these questions as they consider their future as Army officers. This topic is both relevant and personal. I deployed with the U.S. Army to Iraq, Afghanistan, and other places, and witnessed both the horrors of the death and destruction of war, and the brutal effects on the local population. But, I have also seen acts in prevention of violence, glimpsed communities who have regained stability, and witnessed incredible acts of humanity. I have taught Just War Theory to nearly 1,000 students and have even served with former students in these conflicts. What I have discovered is that these remain open questions, and the answers aren't mere academic debate; they are playing out in real time in places like Ukraine.

It's an honor to be able to introduce this important work on pacifism and just war. I've had the pleasure of knowing Dr. Jen Kling for many years, since we were students together at the University of Colorado, Boulder. I was, and continue to be, impressed by her critical reasoning, philosophical acumen, passionate pursuit of truth, and her academic humility. An ardent defender of peace, Jen continues to explore the complex topic of war and peace, focusing on those who are so greatly impacted by war yet who have little agency to avoid it, including relevant topics of refugees and displaced persons, as well as protest as a means of change without the resort to war.

This book, a scholarly debate between pacifism and just war theory, furthers Jen's research and advocacy. Her colleague in this journey is Prof. Andrew Fiala, Founding Director of the Ethics Center at California State University, Fresno, and expert on both religious and secular theories of pacifism. Both Dr. Kling and Prof. Fiala recognize that war exists descriptively, but they engage the reader to contemplate whether war is ever necessary or even justified.

The book is as much a dialogue as a debate between learned scholars and is intended for those already immersed in this discussion or those who are new to the debate. Conceived as such, the book is crafted to present both pacifism and just war positions, respective responses, and concise summaries in a logical, rigorously argued yet approachable manner. Helpful to readers or students are section and chapter summaries, but also embedded replies by each author.

Kling and Fiala expertly present the main pacifist and just war positions, and they engage with not only each other's lucid presentations but also the complexities of war from theoretical and philosophical points of view, using recent and more historical examples to enable the reader to better understand each view, recognizing, as Jen mentions, that "we should be cautious of treating historical examples as though they prove our positions, rather than merely illuminating certain aspects of them that we wish to draw out."[3] The breadth of the topics covered is expansive: from different theories of pacifism to militarism, propaganda, individual versus collective views, PTS(D), and the coercive element of war. They walk the reader through a better understanding of the complex relationship between war and peace, nation building, conflict resolution, and prevention of war, and they even touch on war on behalf of the environment.

Kling and Fiala ask us to think of this debate not necessarily between rigid, established theories of pacifism and just war theory, but rather between the complex, nuanced, and often related traditions of pacifism and just war. Kling and Fiala move well beyond simple, absolutist views of war and peace, and they capture two compelling and competing intuitions many share about war: just war is possible; prima facie, wars are never justified.

They both clearly recognize that war—even just war—in practice never seems to live up to expectations. The ad bellum decision to go to war is never clear cut: both sides commit in bello violations, and even when the just side is victorious, the post bellum is messy, costly, and often fails to address the underlying ante bellum causes and context. Perhaps, as Fiala, in quoting Michael Walzer, states: "just war theory 'made war possible in a world where war was, sometimes, necessary'" (Walzer 2004, 3).[4]

Professor David M. Barnes, PhD[5]
BG, US Army, Retired
Dennis, MA

Notes

1 *On War*, Book 1, Chapter 1 (p. 75 in M. Howard's translation).
2 https://en.wikisource.org/wiki/Letter_to_James_M._Calhoun,_et_al.,_ September_12,_1864
3 Chapter 3 reply, p. 11.
4 Chapter 1, pp. 51–52.
5 My remarks are personal views and do not necessarily reflect those of the Department of Defense, the United States Army, the United States Military Academy, or any other department or agency of the United States Government.

Preface

As we are completing this book in spring 2022, a long-simmering war has erupted in Europe. Russian tanks are bearing down on Ukrainian cities. There is talk of war crimes and warnings about a third world war. Ukrainian forces are fighting for survival with varying levels of support from NATO countries, including the United States. War remains a terrifying reality in the world today. The defenders of just war theory will likely look to the Ukrainian defensive war as an obvious example of war that can be justified in the name of self-defense. Pacifists and defenders of nonviolence will likely view the Russian advance as another example of why the world needs to demilitarize and find nonviolent ways of preventing atrocity.

Scholarly debate is a privilege of peace. We are aware that people are bleeding, killing, and dying, even as we debate the deeper question of whether war can be justified. Our minds are focused here on that question. But our hearts are with those who are suffering.

This book is organized as a debate—we prefer to think of it as a philosophical discussion—between anti-war pacifism and just war theory. It is meant for undergraduate students and, more broadly, all those who are interested in arguments about the ethics of war and peace. Because our goal is to bring people into thinking through these topics in a systematic way, we have focused on clarity and ease of exposition, trying to avoid what is sometimes called "insider baseball." There are particular, fine-grained debates within the philosophical and political literatures that we don't go into in detail, because doing so would take us too far afield from our key argumentation. However, we have tried to indicate some of these points of contention with endnotes for the interested reader.

This book also includes an extensive bibliography and additional reading list for those interested in further research.

The book begins with an explanation and defense of pacifism from Andrew Fiala. The first chapter can be read in its entirety to get a picture of the overall pacifist framework. Alternatively, various sections can be read in a non-linear fashion, as the chapter discusses a variety of different arguments in favor of pacifism and against the justification of war, including discussions of active nonviolence.

Chapter 2 is an explanation and defense of just war theory from Jennifer Kling. The chapter presents an overview of just war theory as it is understood today. It incorporates discussion of various just war traditions from around the world as it argues that war can be sometimes justified. The chapter is broken down into sections, some of which focus on explaining contemporary just war theory, and some of which focus on arguments for the occasional justification of war.

Chapter 3 is Fiala's pacifist response to Chapter 2 (i.e., his response to Kling's defense of just war theory). Professor Fiala makes a number of important critiques, some more practical, and some more theoretical in nature. At the end of each critique from Fiala, there is a boxed reply from Kling. The boxed reply, in each case, speaks directly to the pacifist critique raised. With these critiques and interwoven boxed replies, we work to replicate the back and forth of traditional philosophical and political debate in written form.

Chapter 4 is Kling's just war response to Fiala's anti-war pacifism (i.e., her response to what Fiala wrote in Chapter 1). Kling critiques the pacifist position from various theoretical and practical angles. At the end of each critique from Kling, there is a boxed reply from Fiala. The boxed reply, in each case, speaks directly to the just war critique raised. Again, by writing critiques and then immediately including responses to those critiques from the interlocutor, we hope to demonstrate how reasoned argumentation can and should occur, even regarding contentious issues such as these.

Chapter 5 is Fiala's overall summary. This summary includes a discussion of the 20-year war in Afghanistan and the War on Terror. He remarks on the state of the debate between pacifism and just war theory, while summarizing his view of and arguments for pacifism. Readers should look to this chapter for a concise, rich summation of the contemporary pacifist position.

Chapter 6 is Kling's overall summary. She emphasizes the importance of holding to moral standards in a world that all too often falls short of them. She considers the Afghanistan war and ways forward for just war theory in the 21st century, while summarizing her view of and arguments for just war theory. Readers should look to this chapter for a summation of the contemporary just war position, its difficulties, and its hopes.

Given its structure, this book can be used in a variety of ways. While it unfolds as a dialogue or debate that includes replies and responses, it need not be read in a linear fashion. Some readers may, for example, want to jump to Chapter 2 and begin with Kling's justification of war.

The hope is that readers will gain a sense of the ways that pacifism and just war theory are in dialogue with one another. We hope that readers will gain insight into the complexity of the question of whether war can be justified, and the long history of that question. We also hope that instructors without specialized training or knowledge in these fields of study will feel comfortable using this book to teach. That is partially why we emphasize areas of commonality and conflict between the various sides of the debate. It is also why much of the argumentation is self-contained; it is possible to assign sections of the book, out of order, as issues and topics become relevant in a class or course of study. Finally, the dynamic interaction between the authors is meant to serve as an example of how to reason in compact, but comprehensive, ways about serious issues while also introducing and extending new lines of thought.

The Problem of History and the War in Ukraine

The question of the morality of war remains, sadly, a live and difficult issue. In February 2022, Russia invaded Ukraine, a major escalation of the Russo-Ukrainian War (ongoing since 2014). Undoubtedly in the coming years, there will be more wars fought with both old and new and emerging technologies. It is impossible to offer final pronouncements about war and peace from within history.

Given the deadline under which this book was written, we were unable to say anything substantial about issues arising in the context of Russia's increased military aggression. But it is worth noting some of the topics we were unable to address in depth. These include questions about the morality of providing arms to those who are fighting, the continued threat of weapons of mass destruction, the effectiveness of nonviolent sanctions, the need to care for refugees, the role of conscientious objection and protest, and the importance of international norms and laws governing war.

Defenders of justified warfare will tend to support the idea of supplying weapons, intelligence, and other military aid to those fighting against aggression, as the U.S. and European allies have done for Ukraine. But critics of war will warn of the possibility of escalation. The problem of escalation is linked to the problem of nuclear weapons and other weapons of mass destruction. There are significant questions about whether these kinds of weapons could ever be justifiably used in warfare. But large stockpiles of these weapons exist in the hands of Russia, the United States, and other countries. The Russo-Ukrainian war reminds us of the dangerous threat, familiar from the Cold War, of mutually assured destruction. Defenders of war will need to think carefully about the logic of deterrence and the risk of escalation in a world with enough nuclear weapons to destroy the essential ecosystems on which all life on Earth depends.

In response to the 2022 Russian invasion of Ukraine, the international community made quick and extensive use of nonviolent political and economic tools including boycotts, embargoes, and other sanctions. Pacifists typically advocate the use of these tools. But as we've seen in the Ukrainian case, such techniques can often have unintended and severe effects, including the threat of a global food crisis, fuel shortages, and economic repercussions such as inflation. The war in Ukraine has also created a significant refugee crisis, as typically happens when wars break out. This reminds us that the costs of war are not only calculated in deaths and injuries but also in lives and communities that are disrupted and uprooted. Any discussion of the justification of war or its critique will need to think carefully about all of these impacts.

The Russian invasion of Ukraine also prompts us to think about the role of conscientious objection and the more general question of how warfare, and resistance to warfare, are linked to domestic political arrangements. According to media reports, a number of Russian soldiers deserted from the Russian military or refused to fight. Many were arrested or otherwise disappeared. There were also several Russian civilians who spoke out in protest against the war. Many were arrested or silenced in other ways. Pacifists may urge resistance to warfare, protest, and conscientious objection. But the Russian state's response to its citizens reminds us that nonviolent resistance can be difficult and costly, if not deadly.

Finally, one bit of hopeful good news emerged from the Spring 2022 response to the Russian invasion, in terms of an emerging global consensus regarding military aggression and war crimes. Soon after the invasion, the United Nations General Assembly issued a proclamation deploring Russian aggression and demanding the immediate withdrawal of Russian forces. The International Criminal Court also began investigating allegations of war crimes. Admittedly, the emerging global consensus against military aggression and war crimes was not able to prevent the Russian invasion—and Russia predictably rejected the condemnation of the UN and the ICC. But we can hope that as history continues to unfold, international norms and laws will become stronger and countries will continue to join together to create a more just and more peaceful future. We hope that the ideas discussed in the present book can and will contribute to this project.

Andrew Fiala and Jennifer Kling

Part I

Opening Statements

Chapter 1

War Cannot Be Justified

Andrew Fiala

Contents

I'm writing this as the United States is ending its 20-year-long war in Afghanistan. The war in Afghanistan provides ample evidence to support the claim that war cannot be justified. In Afghanistan, more than 150,000 people were killed (Knickmeyer 2021). This includes Taliban fighters, Afghan government forces, and an estimated 47,000 civilians. Nearly 2,500 American soldiers were killed. Trillions of dollars were spent. Millions were displaced, including 2.6 million Afghan refugees (Coi 2021). As the U.S. withdrew in 2022, some people trying to escape from Afghanistan fell to their deaths while clinging to the outside of American planes leaving the country. Along the way atrocities were committed, including probable war crimes committed by the supposed "good guys" in the conflict. American forces tortured prisoners and killed civilians. The

DOI: 10.4324/9780367809850-2

U.S. prison at Bagram was a notorious site of some of these atrocities (so too was the Abu Ghraib prison in Iraq) (Bazelon 2005). Even as the war ended, drones were still killing civilians, including in a widely publicized drone attack at the end of August 2021 that killed seven children (Cooper 2021). And it wasn't only Americans who did these things. American allies also engaged in war crimes (Gossman 2021).

And here we are 20 years later with a return to the status quo ante: the Taliban regime is back in power. Many are outraged by the return of this repressive government. But some ordinary people in Afghanistan are simply glad that the fighting has ended (Bulos 2021). It is true that the terrorist mastermind, Osama Bin Ladin, was eventually killed and that terrorist attacks against the United States have been suppressed. But one wonders whether those limited outcomes could have been achieved with less cost by the creative use of nonviolent means.

Pacifists generally hold that war cannot be justified. But there are no simple answers here. War is a complex human activity that evolves over time. Wars erupt, simmer, and percolate. The causes and personnel shift as wars drag on. So too, do the methods and strategies. The evolving reality of war is true within wars and across the history of warfare. At one time war involved Roman legions marching with spears and chariots. Later there were knights in armor laying siege to castles. In the 20th century, war grew into massive inter-state conflicts using mechanized weapons such as occurred in World War II. In the 21st century, war has evolved into the kind of multifaceted and targeted violence using so-called "smart weapons" that we see in the War on Terrorism. In order to say that war can (or cannot) be justified, we must ask what kind of war, who is fighting, and what are they fighting for. The war in Afghanistan is different from World War II; and these modern wars are different from the medieval Crusades and the ancient Peloponnesian War.

And yet, the prevailing intuition of pacifism is that in general all of this violence is wrong. There are a variety of reasons to think so, which I'll discuss in what follows. Among these reasons are the following:

(1) War produces bad consequences including death, destruction, and dislocation.
(2) War involves bad (evil or wicked) intentions and actions that are intrinsically evil.
(3) War solves nothing in the realm of ideas.

We'll discuss these reasons for thinking that war cannot be justified in what follows. The first point is the kind of claim we'd find in the moral theory that philosophers call *consequentialism*. Consequentialism focuses on measurable harms and benefits in the empirical world. The second point is focused on what philosophers call *deontological* concerns. Deontological considerations focus on intentions, consistency in moral reasoning, and the question of intrinsic value. The third point is connected to a general critique of the logic of war, which tends to hold that war and violence are subhuman ways of solving conflicts. This is the basic idea that "might does not make right." My argument weaves together these concerns and argues that the cumulative evidence of these different approaches leads us to conclude that war is generally not justifiable.

Pacifists are sometimes viewed as naïve and utopian. I worry that this dismissive view of pacifism rests upon a mistaken understanding of pacifism and a simplistic way of understanding the question of whether war can be justified. The caricature of a pacifist sees him (or her) holding up a sign saying simply, "No War!" That pithy statement may be appropriate for a political protest. But philosophy makes things more complicated and more interesting. Some wars are easier to justify than others. Much depends on the nature of the war in question: who is fighting, for what reasons, and with what weapons. The version of pacifism that I defend maintains that most wars are not justifiable, that we should avoid war, and that we should devote ourselves to developing nonviolent ways to resolve conflicts. I reach this conclusion by considering consequences of war, the wrongful actions that are often employed in war, and by thinking about the logic of war. But my thesis—that war is usually and for the most part not justifiable—is cautious. I want to avoid dogmatism and absolutism in my response. Instead, my conclusion is skeptical. I argue that for the most part, the proponents of war have not proved their case. This conclusion arrives by way of "the preponderance of the evidence." My argument is secular, philosophical, and circumspect. It is not grounded in religious belief or in a dogmatic claim about the nature of war or morality. I admit that there may be circumstances in which war could be justified and that there are plausible principles that could be invoked to justify war. But for the most part, actual wars fail to live up to the standards of that theory. My argument could be described as a kind of "conditional" or "contingent" form of pacifism. Describing pacifism in this way keeps the door open to discussions and dialogue with defenders of just war theory.

This chapter has several points of emphasis. I discuss the question of proof, while considering the conceptual field in which pacifism and just war theory are located. I then present several arguments against the justification of war, including both consequentialist and deontological arguments. I examine an area of common ground between those who argue against war and just war theory—with regard to a common argument against the realist idea that the end justifies the means. One significant point is the basic argument against the idea that might makes right, which I connect to a number of problems in thinking about ideology, power, and morality. I also explore pacifism as a critical and transformative theory of ethics and politics that is not only opposed to war but that is also committed to creating peace through creative nonviolence. This includes a critical analysis of militarism, the military-industrial complex, and the problems of moral injury and post-traumatic stress disorder (PTSD). I conclude that the cumulative weight of these arguments points toward a negative answer to the question of whether war can be justified.

1. The Question of Proof

Before turning directly to the argument against war, let's consider the complexity of the conceptual field. To argue against war, we first need a definition of war. So let's stipulate the following:

> **War** is *large-scale, sustained, and direct political violence.*

This definition focuses our attention on those kinds of events that are typically described as war: international wars (sustained violence between nations), civil wars (widespread violent conflict within nations), and terrorist/guerrilla wars and wars against them (sustained campaigns of violent attacks by subnational groups and responses to them in domestic and international settings). This definition sets aside criminal activities and enterprises, episodic violence such as assassination, and domestic violence. These non-war types of violence either lack a political focus or are not widespread or sustained. This definition of war also ignores indirect violence—what is called systematic, structural, or institutional violence. Although pacifists are usually concerned with a critique of all kinds of violence and understand war as only one of the manifestations of violence, the focus of this chapter is the argument against war. With this definition in mind, we can state:

> **Pacifists** maintain that war is wrong, which means that large-scale, sustained, direct political violence cannot be justified.

I've already indicated three reasons to think this might be true: war causes bad consequences, it involves wicked intentions, and it proves nothing in the realm of ideas.

But how would we know that this is true? At issue here is the question of the burden of proof. Who has to prove what in this conversation? Pacifism often begins with a basic intuition that holds that peace is good and that nonviolent means ought to be employed in pursuit of peace (Fiala 2021). The rejection of war follows from this basic intuition. Some versions of pacifism stop there and simply declare that war cannot be justified. But philosophical pacifism digs deeper. A significant philosophical question is who has to prove what, and to what extent.

One version of pacifism—what we might call "prima facie pacifism"—holds that the pacifist intuition is obviously right: war is a *prima facie evil* (which means that on the face of it war appears as evil). This idea need not be dogmatic. It could remain open to the justification of war. But that open-minded approach still holds that war is an anomaly that requires special justification. The basic idea here is that killing is wrong and that people should not go around killing each other. Defenders of just war theory will argue that in some cases this prohibition against killing can be set aside. Pacifists generally argue the opposite. I am sympathetic to prima facie pacifism. The version of pacifism that I defend here holds that it is very difficult (if not impossible) to overcome this prima facie prohibition against war.

And so, with regard to the question of whether war can be justified, some pacifists simply say, "of course not." Some add, dogmatically: "You'll never be able to convince me that war can be justified." We might call that idea "absolute pacifism." But my own argument is more cautious and restrained than that. I think we ought to say: "if you think war can be justified, it is up to you to prove it." And: "the burden of proof with regard to war is very high, since most wars have failed to live up to the standards of just war theory." In other words, a very high burden of proof rests upon the proponent of war. It is her obligation to defeat the pacifist presumption against war. I try to show in this chapter that the preponderance of the evidence points in the direction of pacifism.

I don't think that absolutism and dogmatism are particularly helpful in thinking about ethics. The questions of applied ethics are complicated and involve plural perspectives. This is true of abortion, euthanasia, animal welfare, and other issues. It is especially true with regard to war. History includes a number of passionate defenses of war and intelligent justifications for war. We cannot simply dismiss this by saying, "No war!" Nor should we set the burden of proof so high that we could never be convinced that war could be justified. Some of the basic intuitions of the just war tradition are persuasive (such as the idea that violence could be justified in self-defense or in defense of innocent others). Those intuitions cannot simply be dismissed. The argument is more complicated than that. The point is not that self-defense or other-defense is a dumb idea. Rather, the point is that war typically involves much less moral clarity than its defenders claim it has.

My approach to applied ethics is pragmatic and pluralistic. I want to avoid dogmatism and absolutism. And so, my claim that war cannot be justified is offered as a modest conclusion that follows from a complex argument. My conclusion is that war is typically not justifiable, that the burden of proof for the justification of war is quite high (but not insurmountable), and that for the most part, the preponderance of evidence shows that wars fail to be justified. What matters to philosophers is not merely the conclusion but also the kinds of evidence and the sorts of arguments that are made in favor of and against war. As I stated at the outset, when we look carefully at the consequences of war, the intentions involved, and the logic of violence, skepticism about war is justifiable. War tends to produce bad consequences, it tends to involve wicked intentions, and it rests upon the logical fallacy that might makes right.

Summary

In this section, we have considered the question of who has to prove what. Pacifism begins from the basic intuition that peace is good and nonviolent means are preferred. Pacifists thus set a high standard of proof in the argument against defenders of war. The approach I defend is pragmatic and skeptical. It tries to avoid dogmatism. It holds that war is typically not justified and that defenders of war have to confront a substantial burden of proof.

2. The Complexity of Pacifism

As mentioned above, pacifism is often quickly dismissed as a naïve and utopian theory. But pacifism is not simply an idealistic and overly optimistic point of view. The philosophical literature on pacifism is careful and restrained. And once we scratch the surface of pacifism, we discover that there are a variety of points of view that could be called "pacifist."

Pacifism is a complex idea that includes a variety of concerns and commitments. Pacifism is best understood as an umbrella term that covers a range of values that lie on a continuum. Some of these values are positive and affirmative: pacifists love peace; they value nonviolence; and they aspire to social justice and harmony. But pacifism is often understood as merely a negative doctrine that rejects violence and war. While some kinds of pacifism reject all kinds of violence including violence against animals, this chapter will focus only on anti-war pacifism.

Before going further, let me point out that pacifism does not mean that we must be "passive": pacifism is not passive-ism. The root of the term comes from the Latin word for peace (*pax*). And pacifists have often been quite active—both in their opposition to war and in their advocacy for nonviolent techniques of engaging in social and political change. A caricature of pacifism claims that pacifists simply surrender to violence and refuse to resist. Now history does include some kinds of **non-resistant pacifism**, those who say that violence can never be employed in self-defense or in defense of another. Beyond non-resistance, adherents of **nonviolent resistance** hold that one can resist an attack so long as that resistance does not escalate to the point of using violence. Let's pause to define these terms more precisely.

> **Non-resistance** is the idea that we should not resist harm or "return evil for evil" as it is often put. Historically arguments in favor of Christian non-resistance appealed to an idea stated by Jesus in the Sermon on the Mount, where he says (Matthew 5:38), "Do not resist an evil person. If someone strikes you on the right cheek, turn to him the other also." We find this idea explained by Tolstoy, to cite the most famous example. But versions of non-resistance can also be found in other traditions, for example, in the Taoist idea of *wu wei* (letting things be).
>
> **Nonviolent resistance** is the idea that one may not use violence to resist evil, harm, or injustice but that one may use nonviolent techniques to do so. This idea is associated with the philosophies and strategies of Mohandas K. Gandhi and Martin Luther King, Jr. Strategies of nonviolent resistance were employed by Gandhi and King in movements for equality, liberation, and social justice. These strategies have also been employed successfully even in the face of totalitarian regimes (e.g., in Danish resistance to the Nazi occupation).

We will consider active nonviolence or nonviolent resistance (including the Tolstoy-Gandhi-King connection) in more detail below. For the moment, let's set non-resistance and nonviolent resistance aside and focus on pacifism as a critical or skeptical response to the justification of war. This is what we might call **anti-war pacifism**.

There are varieties of anti-war pacifism (see Fiala 2018a).[1] Consider the following basic distinction between absolute and non-absolute pacifism. Absolute pacifists simply declare that war cannot be justified, while non-absolute pacifism maintains that most wars cannot be justified or that war can only be justified in rare and exceptional circumstances. Absolute pacifism is easy to explain: it establishes a fundamental prohibition against war. But one could be skeptical of war without being an absolutist.

My argument here follows from a skeptical and critical application of just war theory. I argue that most wars fail to live up to the standards of the just war tradition and that it is difficult to know whether just war principles obtain in actual and proposed wars (see Fiala 2004, 2008). We could call this point of view "just war pacifism" or "skeptical pacifism." As I'll argue in what follows, there are good reasons to believe that wars typically do not live up to the standards of just war theory.

This way of describing things makes it clear that pacifism emerges in conversation with just war theory. Indeed, as the debate in this book shows, there is overlap and conversation between pacifism and just war. A crucial question in this conversation is about whether (1) just war theory is a theory for exceptional cases that arises out of a more general background assumption of pacifism or whether (2) pacifism results from an interpretation or application of just war theory. In the first case, we have a kind of non-absolute pacifism that permits exceptions to the general prohibition on war: this is related to what is called "conditional pacifism" or "contingent pacifism." In the second case, we have a theory that is sometimes called "just war pacifism" and which holds that war does not live up to the standards of just war theory (see May 2015; McMahan 2009, 2010; Sterba 2006, 1998; Morrow 2018; Fiala 2014).[2] A crucial question in this debate is how we should organize our thinking about the relationship between pacifism and just war theory. Which has theoretical primacy: the presumption of peace or the idea that war is necessary? And how does this help us understand the burden of proof in thinking about the justification of war? A simple way of putting this is to ask who has to prove what here: must the pacifist prove that war is wrong; or must the just warrior prove that war can be justified?

The question of the burden of proof helps clarify how we might begin thinking about an answer to the question of whether war can be justified. Absolute pacifists will say that war can never be justified: there are no cases in which the burden of proof can be met. Less absolute forms of pacifism will say that war is rarely justifiable, while establishing a high burden of proof for the justification of war. Skeptical pacifism will say that we could never know if the burden has been met; or that ordinary citizens who lack access to information and relevant expertise can never know that the burden has been met. The more permissive response of just war theory shifts the burden of proof, maintaining that it is wrong to assume that war cannot be justified and that it is up to the pacifist to prove that war cannot be justified. As I argued above, the pacifist has a different understanding of who has to prove what.

Summary

In this section, we have considered conceptual and definitional questions regarding the varieties of pacifism. We have also considered the relationship between anti-war pacifism and arguments about non-resistance and nonviolent resistance.

3. Self-Defense and the Domestic Analogy

A general point to make here at the beginning of our discussion is that from the standpoint of pacifism, the larger and more sustained the violence, the more difficult it is to justify. A precise attack that limits violence is easier to justify than a decades-long war that spreads violence, for example. This point is connected to a general question about the difference between personal self-defense and war. Some critics will claim that pacifism is incoherent and ridiculous because it seems to imply that pacifists are not willing to defend themselves against attack. But pacifism in our present discussion is an argument about war and not about personal self-defense. One may believe that one may use limited violence to defend oneself, while still arguing that war is wrong because war is qualitatively different from personal self-defense. In this sense, pacifism of the sort we are considering here is *anti-war pacifism*.

But the connection between personal self-defense and war has often been made in discussions of the justification of war. Typical justifications of war make use of an analogy with personal self-defense, what Michael Walzer (one of the most important contemporary defenders of just war theory) has called "the domestic analogy" (McMahan 2009; Rodin 2002; Walzer 2006). This can be defined as follows:

The domestic analogy: The right to personal self-defense can be extended to a state's right to defend itself against aggression.

The basic idea is that since individuals are entitled to defend themselves using violence, states are also entitled to do so. But this analogy is merely suggestive. Persons have rights, desires, hopes, and fears; states are different. Indeed, the argument about war typically pushes beyond the domestic analogy. This argument has been made by the Christian Saint Augustine of Hippo (354–430) as well as by the humanist author Hugo Grotius (1583–1645) and others who argue that while individuals are morally entitled to use violence in self-defense in limited cases, the state is empowered to use violence in more general ways: not only to defend itself but also to defend the innocent and to administer justice. Grotius explains this by invoking a distinction between private war and public war. He says, "private war extends only to self-defense, whereas sovereign powers have a right not only to avert, but to punish wrongs. From whence they are authorized to prevent a remote as well as an immediate aggression" (Grotius 1901, Bk. 2, chap. 1, para. xvi). This idea has been developed and explained more recently by contemporary authors such as James Turner Johnson and George Weigel, who make a distinction between wars and duels (between public warfare—*bellum*—and private violence—*duellum*) (see Johnson 1981; Weigel 2003). It is important to note here that dueling is illegal these days, while war is not. The idea in ordinary domestic life is that you should avoid violence if possible and that you ought to call the cops or go to court instead of fighting a duel. But in the international arena there are no cops to call or court that can defend a state's rights. And instead of fighting against a single human aggressor (as in the case of a duel), war involves social forces, historical events, and political ideologies. Unlike personal defense, war is intimately connected with the idea of sovereignty and political authority. Political authorities are, on this account, those who are authorized to make war, which is why the just war tradition maintains that only legitimate political authority has the right to make war.

Pacifists often have a different interpretation of political power—one that does not simply assume that there is a right to make war. This helps explain the connection between pacifism and anarchism. Some anti-war pacifists reject the claim that legitimate political authority includes the right to make war. If, as absolute pacifists claim, war is wrong, then those entities/authorities who claim the right to make war are engaged in immoral activity. From this, an anarchist might argue that this proves state authority in general to be immoral: since it claims something immoral as among its fundamental rights.[3]

We will return to the connection between pacifism and anarchism below. But let's turn our attention here to a related point, which is that pacifists generally consider the domestic analogy to be weak. Let's consider the distinction between wars and duels a bit further. Just war theory typically holds that wars can be justified but duels cannot (states can legally fight wars but individuals are no longer legally permitted to fight duels). Pacifists might turn this around suggesting that while a duel (conceived as violence used in personal self-defense) may be justifiable, war is less easy to justify. Consider a typical justification of violence focused on a paradigm example of personal (and other) self-defense. If I am being attacked and my life is threatened, I am justified in using force—including lethal force—to defend myself. This force ought to be narrowly focused on the attacker. I can kill the person who threatens me. But this is true only so long as he remains a threat. Once the threat is reduced, I cannot hunt down the attacker. Nor can I escalate violence and hunt down his friends and family. Nor can I indiscriminately shoot at him as he flees into a crowd. Similarly, in the case of other-defense, if my children or some innocent stranger are under attack, I can use force, including lethal force, in their defense. But the same kinds of narrowly focused restrictions apply. The individual case shows us the importance of restraint and focus. But war is typically not so restrained or focused. The just war tradition stipulates some kinds of restraint. But actual wars typically go beyond those restraints.

Pacifists will point out that war is simply not like self- and other-defense. The more sustained and large scale the violence, the less like personal self-defense the case becomes. The basic idea of war as a matter of national defense claims that citizens (and their children) may be defended against enemy attack. But the goods that are defended or obtained through war also include a variety of abstract political goods that are only indirectly connected to personal self-defense. These abstract political goods include issues related to the stability of borders, the justification of political authority, the so-called "national interest," political identity, patriotism, and national pride. Furthermore, the strategic goals of widespread, sustained political violence are diffuse and complex and, importantly, involve substantial sacrifice on the part of soldiers and the community, who may not be fully informed of these goals and the risks involved (and who may not be unified in agreement about the merit of those goals and risks).

A further problem for the domestic analogy arises when we consider how war is targeted. In the domestic case, violence is supposed to be targeted toward the unjust attacker. But the harms that are caused by large-scale, sustained war tend not to be narrowly focused on a singular attacker. Rather, enemy soldiers may have no clear responsibility for the war (especially if they are conscripted). And bystanders are often caught up in war, which causes collateral damage that includes the deaths of innocents, social dislocation, and environmental harm. It is also worth considering the lasting trauma and moral injury for soldiers and their families—even those fighting in what they believe to be a justified war. This problem arises because, unlike in a case of private self-defense, soldiers themselves often do not fully understand (or agree with) the cause for which they fight; nor do they necessarily believe that enemy soldiers and civilians killed as collateral damage are fully responsible and thus liable to be killed. In general, the justification of war is made more difficult by the problem of imagining the long-term impacts of war, conceiving the structures of responsibility and liability, seeing the totality of the social network of values at play in war, and grounding this justification in a coherent ethical and political worldview.

Summary

In this section, we have considered how war is different from personal self-defense and why it is possible to be opposed to war while still allowing for personal self-defense. This discussion was focused around the domestic analogy.

4. A Controversial Historical Example: World War Two

As mentioned at the outset, war is a complex and evolving historical process. Our judgments about war depend, in part, upon concrete details and actual events. I began by mentioning the end of the American war in Afghanistan. That war was controversial. So too was the American war in Vietnam. Both wars give us a reason for skepticism about the justification of war. But a critic may suggest that those are anomalous cases and that there are other wars that are more obviously justified. So let's begin with a paradigmatic historical example to help ground the argument—one that we will return to throughout: the example of American involvement in World War II. The American fight in World War II is typically viewed as an example of justified warfighting. The Japanese attacked Americans first—at Pearl Harbor. And so, the argument usually goes, American forces were justified in fighting against Japan, in self-defense. The Germans aggressively invaded a number of countries in Europe and systematically murdered people in concentration camps, including the Holocaust of the Jewish people of Europe. And so, a war against Germany was also justified. These initial points of justification make good sense. But the justification of war is not a simple binary choice. War is a historical event that changes over time. Wars have antecedents. They unfold and evolve. And they leave lasting impacts on social and political life. While some response to Japanese aggression might be justified, it is unlikely that the use of fire-bombs and atomic bombs against the Japanese home islands and similar attacks against Germany can be justified. Indeed, a number of non-pacifist scholars have argued that the "good guys" in World War II violated basic principles of justice in war (in the category of *jus in bello*) (see Anscombe 1981; Fiala 2010; Rawls 1999).

We will return to this problem below. But let's note furthermore, that in the background of World War II are complex causal and historical questions that call any simplistic justification of World War II into question. We should consider American colonial adventures in the Pacific, including American power in the Philippines as well as the American and British embargo against Japan that some have argued was used to goad Japan into firing the first shot. We should consider the punishment of Germany after World War I. We should consider the long history of anti-Semitism in Europe and America, as well as racist antipathy toward the Japanese. And we should consider the so-called "Great Game" of power that involved Britain's colonial aspirations in Asia, Russia's desire for power, French colonialism in Africa, and so on, along with the alliances and maneuvers of power unfolding across centuries. This is not to say—as some revisionist historians have—that the American entry into World War II was the result of a secret plan by President Franklin Roosevelt to find an excuse for war (see Morgenstern 1947;

Stinnet 2001). Rather, the point is that the American entry into World War II cannot be understood as a simple and easily justified response to an unpredictable outburst of violence that is either justified or not. The American entry into World War II was the result of complex historical forces that celebrated militarism, that unfolded out of racist and ethnocentric values, and that involved political entanglements that should be subject to critique. The pacifist critique of war and the systems of military and political power that give rise to war point toward a critique of all of this, suggesting that we ought to *take steps before war breaks out* to change the world such that war is not necessary. In this sense, pacifism is not only a theory that rejects war; it is also a theory that seeks to prevent war in the first place. The problem is that in the moment of decision—once hostilities have commenced, when we are considering whether *this* war can be justified *here and now*—a whole network of decisions have already been made and a whole system of values has been put into action. The pacifist critique of war is a radical critique of all of this. It is not simply a rejection of war at the moment of decision; rather, it is a theory that seeks to transform the social, cultural, and political preconditions of war. I return to this below.

Now let me connect this example to the basic argument of skeptical pacifism. I've mentioned three American wars here: the Vietnam War, the Afghanistan War, and World War II. It is fairly obvious that the first two are controversial and morally problematic. If it turns out that World War II is also morally problematic (as we'll consider in even more detail below), then one wonders whether any war can be morally justified. Of course, proponents of war may offer other paradigms. And the details matter. But the strategy of my approach is to argue that there are good reasons to be skeptical of the justification of war. One reason is that the usual paradigm case of World War II turns out to be morally problematic.

Summary

In this section, we introduced a historical example, World War II. This supposed paradigm of a justified war is more controversial than often supposed. We concluded by noting that pacifists generally want to change social and political conditions in order to prevent war.

5.   Consequentialist and Deontological Arguments Against War

Before returning to the general social and political critique of violence and the pre-conditions of war, let's dig deeper into two standard pacifist arguments against war. I consider here two basic arguments that are typically made against war: a consequentialist argument and a deontological or non-consequentialist argument.

(1)   The first argument against war focuses on consequences. A **consequentialist argument against war** holds that war ends up causing widespread destruction and harm. War kills people, disrupts social systems, destroys the environment, and creates instability and terror. The critic of war holds that the negative consequences of war are not redeemed or outweighed by positive consequences.

(2)   The second argument focuses on rights, duties, and intrinsic values. A **deontological argument against war** holds that war involves actions that are inherently wrong. Typically, this kind of argument includes the following sorts of claims. That war demands that soldiers violate the basic moral rule against killing. That soldiers give up their autonomy in service to the state. And that states that make war are fundamentally corrupt insofar as they focus on power at the expense of justice, care, and other positive values.

My argument in this chapter combines elements of both the consequentialist and deontological arguments. My approach here is pluralistic in this regard. When combined, the consequentialist and deontological critiques of war give us good reason to be skeptical about the justification of war.

5.1.   The Consequentialist Argument against War: The Harms of War Outweigh the Benefits

The consequentialist argument against war is an empirical one. Consequence-based arguments must look at the real world and give an account of what actually happens (and what would happen if something was done or not done). This means that consequentialist arguments against war are typically not absolute or dogmatic. Arguments against war articulated in this fashion end up with what is called "contingent pacifism" (see Fiala 2014; May 2015; Morrow 2018). Contingent pacifism declares that war is generally wrong because war generally produces bad consequences. Two caveats must be mentioned at the outset. First, as a non-dogmatic, empirical argument, the consequentialist critique must remain open to the possibility that war could create good consequences that outweigh the bad ones. Second, this argument is limited to the extent that it must engage in cost-benefit analysis that involves speculation about counter-factual possibilities and "what if" scenarios. Despite these caveats, I think there is substantial power in the consequentialist argument: it is not clear that war produces more benefit than harm.

The most obvious negative consequence of war is the death of human beings: both soldiers and civilians. One typical point to make here is about the outrageously staggering death toll of wars in the 20th century. In the 20th century, war became mechanized with the advent of artillery, machine guns, aerial bombardment, missile technology, as well as nuclear, chemical, and other weapons of mass destruction. One estimate of war deaths in the 20th century puts the number of direct "battle deaths" at 40 million (see Pinker 2011, 49ff; White 1999). If we expand our purview to include deaths that are indirectly linked to war (say from famine and other problems caused or exacerbated by war), the number of war deaths in the 20th century quickly escalates upward toward 180 million.

That is a horrifying number of casualties. However, the number must be interpreted in context. Raw numbers provide us with only one way to measure atrocity. If we compare these 180 million people with the 6 billion total people who died in the 20th century, it turns out that the war deaths of this era only account for at most 3% of deaths. Steven Pinker notes that there have been other eras in which war deaths had a much worse statistical/proportional impact. And in fact, the proportion of war deaths in recent wars has gone down—thanks in part to "smart" weapons that target more precisely and to better battlefield medicine. In the 21st century these technological innovations continue to evolve. Soldiers (and civilians) receive better and quicker medical care. Drones, satellite guidance systems, and better intelligence help to target violence. We might also note that in our networked and mediated world, the atrocities of war are now more difficult to cover up—and that some weapons (such as poison gas) are now viewed as inherently evil. In addition, the benefits of nonviolent interaction and global trade have helped us evolve in a more integrated, cos-mopolitan, and peaceful direction.

Pinker uses this kind of analysis to point out that we are actually becoming more peaceful. Nonetheless, for the consequentialist critic of war, the bloodshed of the 20th century seems senseless, atrocious, and impossible to justify. But consequentialist cost-benefit analysis must compare different possible scenarios. Obviously, the best-case scenario would be if there were no war and no killing, all things being equal. That is the ideal toward which pacifism directs us. Unfortunately, in the real world, all things are not equal: there are evil people and outlaw regimes who rape, kill, invade, and commit genocide. A thoroughgoing consequentialist pacifism would have to find some way to measure the negative outcomes of fighting in comparison with not fighting war. It turns out that this is difficult to do, since the counterfactual histories we must construct quickly lead us down bizarre and troubling pathways.

Consider as an example a consequentialist argument based upon a counter-factual history of World War II. What if the United States had refused to enter into World War II? Would there have been less horror if the United States had let Europe succumb to Nazism and had allowed Japan to occupy much of Asia? The national World War II Museum estimates that about 416,000 American soldiers and 2,000 American civilians died in World War II (see World War II Museum, n.d.). If the United States had stayed home, those American would not have died—that is, so long as Japanese and German aggression did not cross over to North America. Now one narrow version of pacifism will hold that what matters is the *consequences for us*. This could be a kind of **egoistic** or **isolationist pacifism**, which is concerned with avoiding war in order to minimize harms for members of our own nation. While this position does occasionally show up in contemporary political discourse, very few philosophical pacifists are only concerned with the damage done on one side of a war. Most consequentialist pacifists are concerned with a global cost-benefit analysis.

So let's dig deeper. What would have happened in Europe and Asia if Japan and Germany had been allowed to conquer? If the United States did not fight and prolong the war (and the Germans and Japanese easily marched to victory in Europe and Asia), it is likely that there would have been fewer German and Japanese casualties (but again—this is merely counter-factual speculation). German deaths are estimated at around 8 million (around 5.5 million military

and another couple of million civilians). Japanese deaths are estimated at around 3 million (of which 2 million were military deaths).
The worst death tolls in World War II were in the Soviet Union (estimated at around 24 million—with the majority of these civilian
deaths) and China (20 million—again with the vast majority of these
civilians). The civilian death toll was caused by direct violence but also
by famine, the siege of cities, and destruction of infrastructure. It
seems likely that large numbers of Soviet and Chinese citizens would
have been killed, even if the United States had stayed out of the war
and the Soviets and Chinese had quickly surrendered to the Germans
and Japanese. And there would have likely been major atrocities
committed against civilian populations. We know, for example, that
the Nazis murdered or allowed to die millions of Jews, as well as
prisoners of war—around 20 million people (United States National
Holocaust Museum 2020). The Japanese were also brutal in their
occupation of China and other Asian countries.

A consequentialist must do some very grim math here and weigh
the costs and benefits in a case like this. And as you can see, such a
calculation is almost impossible to make, as we do not know how
many more would have been murdered by the Nazis or how much
damage a Japanese or Nazi rule would have done to civilian populations. Nor do we know the long-term consequences of
Japanese/German victory on subsequent global history. Despite
these difficulties, a consequentialist would argue that in the case of
World War II the bloody cost of war was not justifiable in comparison with estimates of the costs that would have incurred if the
allied powers had refused to fight.

Before we move on, let's note two challenges to the consequentialist argument. The first is that consequentialists must be
open to the possibility that some minimal violence can be justified in
order to prevent much worse future violence. What if Hitler had
been assassinated in 1932, for example? A consequentialist pacifist
might allow that sort of minimal and targeted violence as a way of
preventing the Nazi rise to power and subsequent mayhem and
atrocity. The second challenge has to do with how we might include
other values in our consequentialist calculus. In the discussion above,
we are only focusing on deaths. But the World War II scenario also
includes threats to liberty, sovereignty, national identity, the potential genocide of peoples, and so on. The challenge for the consequentialist is to formulate a way of doing cost-benefit analysis that
includes these other less concrete values. Would we want to say, for

example, that sovereignty or liberty is such an important good that it is worth the lives of dozens or thousands or millions to defend it? A comprehensive consequentialist argument about war will have to find a way to correlate and compare a number of ethical and political variables. Pacifists also argue that in such a calculation we will have to include those damages that are done to liberty, sovereignty, and identity by war. War changes the nature of domestic social and political reality, as a nation at war may sacrifice civil liberties in the name of social cohesion, for example. We might also include fiscal responsibility and issues related to war-spending, borrowing, and the national debt.

Again, it is difficult to include all of this in a simple consequentialist calculation. But the general conclusion of the consequentialist argument is that the benefits of war do not outweigh its costs. Or as I suggested at the outset of this chapter: "War produces bad consequences including death, destruction, and dislocation."

Before concluding this section let us note that the pacifist critique of war does not merely suggest doing nothing in the face of aggression and atrocity. Rather, pacifists will emphasize nonviolent alternatives to war: sanctions, embargoes, strikes, non-cooperation, civil resistance, etc. A consequentialist critique of war would also have to calculate the effectiveness of these nonviolent techniques in comparison to the possible harm and damage of war. Again, it is difficult to imagine how we might complete such a calculation without engaging in substantial counter-factual speculation. But advocates of nonviolence have pointed out that nonviolence can be effective—and that it has in many cases been more effective than violence. Erica Chenoweth and Maria Stephan conducted a comparative empirical study of violent and nonviolent struggles between 1900 and 2006. This includes the example of Danish resistance to Nazi occupation, which they rank as a "partial success." They conclude, "between 1900 and 2006, nonviolent resistance campaigns were nearly twice as likely to achieve full or partial success as their violent counterparts" (Chenoweth and Stephan 2011, 7). Studies of this sort provide support for consequentialist pacifism. However, we must note that this conclusion is not absolutist: Chenoweth and Stephan only note that nonviolence can be and has been successful. It is not successful in every case. And there are some cases in which war has been effective.

5.2. The Deontological Argument against War: The Intrinsic Wrongness of War

The consequentialist argument is open-ended. It leaves open the possibility that in some cases war can be justified. For that reason, consequentialist pacifism is best understood as a kind of "contingent pacifism": it depends upon the outcomes, harms, benefits, and circumstances. An approach that focuses on the intrinsic wrong of war will offer a more absolute sort of conclusion. One simple way of formulating this idea is to say that it is always wrong to kill people—and *a fortiori* it is also wrong to order or hire someone else to kill on your behalf. Absolute pacifism will simply declare that killing is always wrong. And since war involves killing, war is always wrong. This is the basic idea I stated at the outset: "War involves bad (evil or wicked) intentions and actions that are intrinsically evil."

Of course things are more complicated than the simple declaration that killing is always wrong. And so deontological approaches to ethics do not necessarily lead to simplistic absolutism. One might object, for example, by saying that not all killing is wrong or even that killing could be done without evil or wicked intentions. A critic will say that killing in self-defense should be permitted and that in some cases it is permissible to kill people who threaten life, liberty, and other rights. This justification of killing that allows for defensive killing is used to support domestic police power as well as military campaigns. Such justifications of killing do, however, distinguish between those who are liable to be killed and those who deserve not to be killed. In the just war account, the focus is on the combatant/noncombatant distinction: combatants may be killed, while noncombatants ought not be directly targeted. The doctrine of double effect comes into play here, which allows unintended killing of noncombatants. In less rigorous discussions of this issue, there is also the question of "innocence" (a matter that is more complicated than we often think): the idea is that innocent people should not be directly killed, while those who are responsible for evil things may be targeted.

Even if we accept the possibility of defensive killing, the doctrine of double effect, and an easy way of marking the distinction between combatants and noncombatants, it is still possible to arrive at a pacifist conclusion. The pacifist argument claims that war typically or usually violates these moral limitations on the justification of killing. Absolutists will claim that war always violates these moral limits, while another version of contingent pacifism will claim that war usually (typically or generally) violates these limits. As in the discussion above, the contingent argument depends upon real world and historical detail—and may be open to counter-examples.

The absolutist claim offers a categorical generalization about the wrongness of war. Categorical and dogmatic arguments are open to refutation by counter-examples. The most persuasive counter-example would be an example of a war that only kills those who deserve to be killed—in which there is no collateral damage. A brief glance at real wars indicates that it is difficult to imagine a war in which there is no collateral damage. In most wars, most of the time, innocent noncombatants are killed. Sometimes this is deliberate.

Indeed, in the paradigm case of World War II, American forces deliberately targeted civilians: in the firebomb campaigns used against both Japan and Germany—and in the atomic bombing attacks against Hiroshima and Nagasaki. These were terror bombing campaigns that involved the deliberate choice to target noncombatants. And often these acts of terror were motivated by wicked intentions, including racist stereotypes and outright cruelty. American servicemen fighting in Asia cut off the ears and pulled out the gold teeth of dead and dying Japanese fighters (Dower 1986, Chapter 3). A common refrain at the time (repeated by Admiral Halsey) was that "the only good Jap was a dead Jap" (Dower 1986, 79). And some Americans cheered on the fire-bombing and atomic bombing of Japan with a kind of enthusiasm that Dower describes as genocidal (54).

Now some collateral damage may be justifiable by the doctrine of double effect. But pacifist critics of war will point out that the typical justification of war utilizes a quite permissive version of that doctrine that is sullied by the presence of wicked intentions.

The doctrine of double effect stipulates that some collateral damage (killing of noncombatants) is permitted if it is not deliberately intended and is merely a foreseen but accidental secondary effect of a legitimate action in war.

Two points should be made here. First, a deontological pacifist need not accept the doctrine of double effect. The doctrine of double effect is an idea that seems to fit within a general deontological approach to ethics: it focuses on intentionality (what the warrior *intends* to destroy) and upon a fundamental question about desert (about *who* deserves to be harmed). Consequentialists are less interested in such things. And there is an extensive literature that challenges the basic idea of the doctrine of double effect. For example, Quinn (1989) provides an argument that suggests that the idea of human rights (and Kant's prohibition against using persons as means) provides a limitation on what the doctrine permits: those innocent people killed as collateral damage have a right not to be killed without their consent (see Fischer, et al. 1993; Katchadourian 1988; McMahan 1994; Woolard 2017). On a stringent application of this idea, it is simply wrong (and a violation of human rights) to engage in actions that knowingly kill people who do not deserve to die—even if unintentionally. Second, warfighting typically is not so stringently limited by the concern to prevent collateral damage. World War II case provides an example of actions that deliberately killed noncombatants. Now perhaps this problem is ameliorated by better intelligence and by the use of smart weapons that more precisely target combatants. In the so-called war against terrorism, for example, drones have been employed to deliver more targeted killing. It seems true that smart weapons are better than the mass slaughter of firebombs and atomic bombs. And so, perhaps wars that employ these weapons are easier to justify. But even in the war on terrorism, these so-called smart weapons have created significant harm to noncombatants. The data on this is shrouded in secrecy—but estimates of civilians killed by drone strikes during the past 20 years across the Middle East and North Africa are likely in the tens of thousands.[4] A deontological pacifist would argue that these numbers of civilians killed—even in a supposedly "smart" war—show us that war cannot be justified.

As we conclude this section let me return to the basic deontological claim that war involves bad (evil or wicked) intentions and actions that are intrinsically evil. It is possible to imagine a pure war in which targets are appropriately limited and in which soldiers have noble and pure intentions. But for the most part real wars are not like this. They are motivated by cruelty, hatred, and racial stereotypes. And violence often expands beyond justifiable limits. This is why I conclude that the deontological perspective gives us good reason to be skeptical of the justification of war.

Summary

In this section, we have considered consequentialist and deontological arguments against the justification of war. We have discussed the challenge of weighing out the harms and benefits of war. We have considered the deontological claim that war is wrong because it kills innocent noncombatants, while also thinking about the doctrine of double effect and its critique. I argue that these arguments give us good reasons to be skeptical of war. War often produces bad consequences and it often includes wicked intentions and immoral actions.

6. Other Arguments against War: Autonomy, Democracy, and Pacific Virtue

Before turning to the next section of this chapter, where I examine the history of pacifism and look for common ground between pacifism and just war theory, let me note a further argument against the justification of war. This argument is connected with the deontological critique of war. But it also points toward issues in social and political philosophy, as well as questions that arise in the ethical framework known as virtue ethics. This further critique of war focuses on the structure of command and obedience that is essential to war. A different pacifist argument will criticize such structures as fundamentally immoral. On this argument, war is wrong for two reasons: because (1) in war, some individuals command others to kill or be killed and because (2) some individuals either deliberately subordinate themselves and give up their autonomy or are forced to do so. The first is a problem of command, the second is a problem of obedience. Of course, deontological ethics in its Kantian version does focus on obedience: we are to do our moral duty and obey the moral law. But the pacifist critique offered here will argue that in war, some individuals turn themselves into a means (an instrument) of state action. The soldier who obeys is viewed as a mere tool in the war effort. Individuality is subverted as soldiers are viewed as fungible troops who serve the logic of military force. The pacifist argument here is that it is wrong for volunteer soldiers to give up their individuality in this regard, that conscription is also wrong, and that it is wrong for states (and for the military hierarchy) to treat soldiers as depersonalized military assets.

This argument has been made by Robert Holmes, who argues that there is something inherently undemocratic (and unethical) about war, military service, and the structure of command and obedience that is involved. He writes, "A society that allows some people to order other people to kill, and compels others to respond obediently to such orders, is a free and open society in name only" (Holmes 2017, 140; also see Holmes 2018). This points to a larger worry about the undemocratic values of militarism. Thoreau made this point when he fretted that military service produced "wooden men" who serve the state, "not as men mainly, but as machines, with their bodies" because they are not permitted "free exercise of the judgment of the moral sense" (Thoreau 2000, 669–670).

We must be careful in articulating this kind of critique to note that it is made in solidarity with soldiers. It is not the individual soldier's fault that he is viewed as an instrument of state power. And many soldiers—especially in the contemporary volunteer army—willingly submit to the structure of command out of a sense of patriotism, loyalty, and virtue.

The problem here is a conflict of values. The logic of war is collective: it is about troops, armies, and nations. The collective structure requires that individuals relinquish their autonomy in the name of the greater good. But a different type of morality focuses on the rights of the individual. An individualistic moral theory will be reluctant to affirm collectivism. This way of looking at the conflict of values points toward a larger critique of structures of command and obedience that overlaps with some kinds of anarchism. We will return to the connection between pacifism and anarchism below.

Before moving on, let's note a connection with virtue ethics. As mentioned above, soldiers exhibit the virtues of patriotism, courage, and so on. The virtue ethics tradition is historically related to warrior cultures. In the Greek and Roman traditions, courage and military valor are viewed as virtues. From this vantage point it is virtuous for an individual to soldier to sacrifice himself for the greater good, for the nation, or in the name of courage, valor, and victory. From this standpoint, there is virtue in sacrificing one's autonomy. A different tradition—perhaps we should call this the libertarian tradition—will hold that autonomy is the greatest good and that there is virtue in proudly refusing to submit to another and in refusing to sacrifice oneself for the greater good. In conclusion, we should also note that there are rival virtue traditions, which focus on peacefulness and nonviolence as primary virtues. Thus the pacifist critique of war may also grow out of pacifist traditions—such as can be found in Christian and South Asian religious traditions—that maintain that a good life should be grounded on pacific virtues such as compassion, forgiveness, patience, and love (see Fiala 2018b, 2018c).

Summary

In this section, we have considered a further critique of war that is focused on the loss of autonomy that occurs in war and the problem of command and obedience. I have argued that these arguments give us further reasons to be skeptical of war. War seems to involve a fundamental violation of autonomy. And warrior virtues are in conflict with a more pacific set of virtues.

7. The Pacifist Tradition and the Just War Tradition

This mention of pacifist traditions provides us with a transition point for understanding the common ground that can be found between pacifism and just war theory. Just war theory in the Western world evolved out of the background of Christian pacifism. The next chapter of this book (the argument presented by Jennifer Kling) will explain the just war tradition in more detail. In this section of the present chapter, I will first examine a different tradition, what I call "the pacifist tradition," and its relationship with the just war tradition. Then in the next section, I will examine the argument against realism. Realism holds that moral limits do not apply in war. There are varieties of realism and the word is used in other contexts. So let's stipulate a definition here.

> **Realism:** The idea that moral judgment does not apply in war, which means that "anything goes" in war so long as it is effective for bringing about victory.

Pacifists and just war theorists are united in their rejection of realism. Just war theorists maintain that war can be morally justified in exceptional cases and that there are moral limits within war. Realists deny this. Often realists go further and assume that war is the natural and normal background condition of reality and a feature of human nature: as the early modern philosopher Thomas Hobbes (1588–1679) suggests, the state of nature is a state of war. Pacifists often have a different assumption about reality and human nature, holding that peace is the background condition, the highest good, and a real possibility for human relations. Pacifists also offer a theory of nonviolent social and political change that aims toward peace and requires a unity of means and ends: peaceful means ought to be employed for peaceful ends. Just war theory differs, holding that violent means can be justified. I begin by offering a genealogy of the pacifist tradition and its relation to the just war tradition. These two traditions developed, in the Western Christian world, in conversation with one another (see Ryan 2018). But (as we'll see next), there is also an emerging global tradition of pacifism and nonviolence that includes, for example, Buddhist and Hindu sources and which comes to fruition in the work of Gandhi and his followers (among whom we should note were also Muslim devotees of nonviolence such as Abdul Ghaffar Khan).

7.1. The Pacifist Tradition

In the Western Christian world, the idea of just war developed out of a background commitment to pacifism. We find the idea of pacifism articulated in the Gospels. Jesus says in the Sermon on the Mount, "blessed are the pacifists" (Matthew 5.9). The typical English translation of this passage says "blessed are the peacemakers." But the term "peacemaker" can in fact be translated as "pacifist": the Greek term is *eirenopoios*, which is translated into Latin as *pacifici*, which is a cognate for the English word pacifism. The word in Latin (and in the Greek) means those who make peace. On this understanding, a pacifist is one who makes peace. And one way to make peace is to oppose war—to love your enemies and to turn the other cheek, as Jesus puts it in other places in the Sermon the Mount. There are rival interpretations of what Jesus had in mind with these sorts of claims. An obvious problem is the question of whether we should make peace through violent means or through nonviolent means; and whether we can love our enemies while also killing them. Thoroughgoing pacifists will maintain that peace should only be made through nonviolent means and that the idea of turning the other cheek must be taken seriously. Defenders of just war will emphasize other passages and interpret these passages differently.

The non-pacifist interpretation of these ideas appears to be a later development in Christianity. Early Christians seemed to be, for the most part, pacifist. They did not resist Roman domination with violence. And some refused to serve in the Roman military. Early Christians such as Tertullian (ca. 155–220) and Origen (ca. 184–253) argued against military service because it was a form of idolatry to serve in the Roman military. St. Maximilian of Tebessa (274–295) and St. Martin of Tours (316–397) both supposedly rejected military service by declaring "I am a soldier of Christ, I cannot fight." Maximilian was beheaded for refusing to serve, while Martin continued to serve in the military but, so the story goes, without killing. The history of early Christian pacifism prompts disputes. Christians who justify war offer divergent readings of this tradition. But historical peace churches—Mennonites, Quakers, etc.—and contemporary Christian pacifists often derive their pacifism by calling for a return to the original teachings of Jesus. This idea of a return to the original Jesus includes a critique of the development in Christian history of the idea of "just war," which arose as Christianity became the official religion of the Roman empire and Christians had to deal with the realities of political and military power. The contemporary Mennonite scholar John Howard Yoder called this a "Constantinian" shift in Christianity through which Christianity was transformed from being a minority religion without political power and became a church with political (and military) power (Yoder 1994, 2009).

To say that pacifism is a *tradition* is to point out that the critique of war and the general advocacy of peace and nonviolence involve a complex historical conversation that includes a broad continuum of ideas that can be considered as pacifist. There are disputes within this tradition that involve the interpretation of ancient religious texts/sources.

Key Figures in the Pacifist Tradition

Ancient Religious Sources	**Buddha** (ca. 500 BCE): founder of Buddhism, which focuses on *ahimsa* (non-harming or nonviolence)
	Mahavira (ca. 500 BCE): founder of Jainism, which focuses on *ahimsa* (non-harming or nonviolence)
	Jesus (ca. 4 BCE–30 CE): founder of Christianity, focused on turning the other cheek and not returning evil for evil
Classical and Medieval Christian Sources	**Tertullian** (155–220 CE), **Origen** (ca. 184–253 CE), **Maximilian of Tebessa** (274–295), **Martin of Tours** (316–397). These figures struggled to make sense of the Christian rejection of Roman military power.
	Augustine of Hippo (354–430) and **Thomas Aquinas** (1225–1274). Augustine and Aquinas are viewed as proponents of the just war tradition, who turn away from early Christian pacifism.
Modern and Contemporary Sources	**William Lloyd Garrison** (1805–1879) and **Adin Ballou** (1803–1890): American proponents of *nonresistance*, although Garrison did support the American Civil War because he was in favor of the abolition of slavery.
	Henry David Thoreau (1817–1862): American transcendentalist author who defended the use of *civil disobedience*
	Leo Tolstoy (1829–1920): Russian novelist who affirmed Christian pacifism and anarchism
	Jane Addams (1860–1935): American peace advocate (especially during World War I)— founded the Women's International League for Peace and Freedom
	William James (1842–1910): American pragmatist philosopher; called for the development of a "moral equivalent of war"
	Mohandas K. Gandhi (1869–1948): Indian activist and political leader who advocated for strategic nonviolence (*satyagraha*)
	Martin Luther King, Jr. (1929–1968): American civil rights icon who led a nonviolent protest movement based on Gandhian and Christian principles

As mentioned above, the Christian pacifist tradition developed in conversation with the just war tradition: the two inform each other. There are other pacifist traditions. We find pacifism in Jain, Hindu, and Buddhist traditions. And there are secular pacifists. In the past few centuries, these traditions have begun to overlap and inform each other. I have explored details of the pacifist tradition in other work (Fiala 2018b). Let's focus here on one important genealogy of contemporary concern: what we might call the Tolstoy-Gandhi-King tradition. This lineage of thinkers demonstrates the emergence of a global/cosmopolitan pacifist tradition. Mohandas K. Gandhi (1869–1948) is a well-known advocate of nonviolence, whose philosophy is grounded in his own South Asian heritage and his experience in South Africa. His work inspired the work of Martin Luther King, Jr. (1929–1968), whose thinking was informed by a critical reading of secular philosophy (including Hegel, Marx, and Nietzsche) and by his own American Protestant Christian tradition. A crucial source for Gandhi was the work of Leo Tolstoy (1829–1920), the 19th century Russian Orthodox thinker. Late in his life Tolstoy was in correspondence with people in India struggling for liberation from Britain. His "Letter to a Hindu" was eventually published by Gandhi in 1909. In that letter, Tolstoy explained that there is a universal ethic of love found in all the world's religions and that the idea of love is at odds with the use of violence by the world's political authorities. He condemned the world's religious powers for allowing the ethic of love to be subverted by political violence, calling this "the religious fraud justifying violence" (Tolstoy 1908, chap. 5, no page numbers). On a more positive note, Tolstoy outlined a model of nonviolent resistance that would be developed in more detail by Gandhi.

Tolstoy developed his rejection of violence and war from his reading of the Bible in conjunction with his study of, among others, American thinkers of the 19th century including William Lloyd Garrison (1805–1879) and Adin Ballou (1803–1890). Garrison and Ballou were advocates of Christian non-resistance, and were associated with American Transcendentalism, a movement that was (to complete the circle here) also interested in Hindu philosophy. As is well-known, Henry David Thoreau (1817–1862) is a crucial figure in this history. Thoreau's advocacy for civil disobedience in opposition to unjust political power also had a profound impact on the Tolstoy-Gandhi-King tradition. Behind this American tradition of the 19th century, we find

European traditions of non-resistance, including the Quakers, Mennonites, and other Christian denominations.

Tolstoy summarized and popularized all of this in his later work. He argued that war and violence had no place in Christianity, despite the fact that there was a long-standing tradition of justifying violence, war, and state power. At the beginning of his book, *The Kingdom of God Is Within You* (1894), Tolstoy quotes Garrison and Ballou extensively. Tolstoy had expressed his opposition to war and military service in *What I Believe* (from 1886), based upon his own discovery of the law of nonviolence in the heart of the Gospel's Sermon on the Mount. Tolstoy's Christian pacifism is also a cosmopolitan and anarchist position. He holds that Christians should reject allegiance to states out of a universal love of all human beings. It is allegiance to states that gives rise to war; and it is love that provides a solution to anger and enmity.

Tolstoy's cosmopolitan anarchism shows that pacifism and just war theory have different evaluations of nation-states and their armies. Not only do pacifists and just war theorists disagree about the justification of war—but they also disagree about the value and the function of the nation-state. Just war theory sees the nation-state and its border as something worth defending with violent force; and they understand the structures of political authority within the state as having a kind of legitimacy that includes the authority to declare war and force people to fight and die in war (and also to tax people to pay for it). Pacifism calls much of this into question. The cosmopolitan anarchism of Tolstoy and Ballou represents one option here, which develops out of a specific interpretation of Christianity. Ballou, for example, argued that Christian non-resistance demanded that one disaffiliate oneself from all religious, social, and political organizations that were founded upon violence (an idea that was put into practice by Thoreau in his symbolic act of tax resistance). While Ballou recognized that this sounded like lawless anarchism, he said that he was not opposed to states and religions per se—but only insofar as those organizations are "based on the assumption that it is right to resist injury with injury, evil with evil" (Ballou 1848, 16). Of course, the serious question here is whether there can in fact be a state that is not based upon violence or that does not utilize violence in its penal system and in its self-defense through war and military power. While Tolstoy and Ballou offer a fairly dogmatic and absolutist conclusion here, it is possible that a more moderate critique of state power and military force could be offered from a different perspective. But non-Christian (non-religious) and non-anarchist pacifists will have to mount other arguments and inter-pretations about the value of the nation-state, its structures of authority, its justifications of war, and the duties of citizens.

7.2. On the Unity of Means and Ends

Let's leave aside these issues in political philosophy. A further important point to emphasize here is that the pacifist tradition generally holds that peace is healthy, natural, normal, and what we pursue as an end in itself. Just war theory also sees peace as an end to be pursued. However, the crucial difference can be stated as follows.

> **The pacifist tradition** demands that the means used to pursue peace should not be violent. This tradition holds that there should be a unity of means and ends.

Pacifism and just war theory differ here. Just warriors maintain that war can be used as a means to bring about peace; pacifists reject this idea. But an important point of common ground can be found in the fact that both pacifists and just war theorists will reject the idea that "the end justifies the means," which is an idea typi-cally found in realism.

Gandhi's fundamental idea is that peace or nonviolence (*ahimsa*) is the highest good and the only proper means. He explained in 1945: "If we are careful about the means, the end will take care of itself. In other words, there is no difference between means and ends" (Gandhi 1999, vol. 89, p. 266). And also: "I believe means and ends to be intimately interconnected. That is, a good end can never be achieved through bad means" (Gandhi 1999, vol. 36, p. 29). Martin Luther King Jr. developed this idea, which can be found in an oft-quoted statement made by King:

> Returning hate for hate multiplies hate, adding deeper dark-ness to a night already devoid of stars. Darkness cannot drive out darkness; only light can do that. Hate cannot drive out

hate, only love can do that. Hate multiplies hate, violence multiplies violence, and toughness multiplies toughness in a descending spiral of destruction.

(King, Jr. 2012, 49)

King's philosophy weaves together Christian, Modern European, and Gandhian themes. We cannot unpack this all here. Instead, let's focus on the Western Christian tradition. Peace is a primary value in this tradition.

Let's begin with an ancient text, the 34th Psalm, which says "Depart from evil, and do good; seek peace, and pursue it." The word for peace here is *shalom*. This is a central concept in Abrahamic traditions, translated as *salaam* in Arabic and *pax* in Latin. Hebrew and Arabic traditions use these terms—shalom/salaam as greetings and blessings. In English we say, for example, "peace be with you," "peace unto you," and "go in peace." We have already mentioned the importance of peacemaking in the Gospels. Paul adds—in Romans 12—that we should not return evil for evil and that we should live peacefully with others. But—and here is a primary source for the just war tradition—in the next chapter (Romans 13) Paul says that the sovereign is the minister of God who uses the sword to execute justice upon wrongdoing. This passage is cited, for example, by the great medieval Christian author St. Thomas Aquinas (1225–1274) in his discussion of the idea of just war—and the notion of legitimate authority for war: Aquinas claims that Paul is saying that only the sovereign power can legitimately wage war and that individuals cannot wage war (Aquinas *Summa* II: II, Q. 40, art. 1). But Christian pacifists such as John Howard Yoder interpret this passage in a different way that connects it with the idea of nonresistance and love. Yoder (1994) suggests that this passage implies that Christians should simply submit to the Roman authorities in a spirit of love and acknowledge the power of sovereignty without actively participating in violence or in war.

This tension between pacifist and just war interpretations of biblical texts presents significant hermeneutical difficulties. The goal here is not, however, to resolve deep issues in biblical exegesis—nor to offer a specifically Christian defense of pacifism. Rather, the point is to consider some common ground between pacifism and just war theory. One point of common ground for Christian pacifists and Christian just war theorists is the Bible itself—a common text with rival interpretations. But beyond this sectarian commonality, a larger point is found in the idea of peace as the highest good. Augustine explained in *City of God* (Book 19, chap. 12) that all men desire to be at peace with others and within themselves—and that men make war in order to have peace. Aquinas quotes this with approval in *Summa Theologica* (*Summa* II: II, Q. 29, art. 2), adding "whoever desires anything desires peace, in so far as he who desires anything, desires to attain, with tranquility and without hindrance, to that which he desires." Aquinas's point is that peace is another name for the satisfaction of desire. Peace is a synonym for wholeness, harmony, integration, tranquility, serenity, and so on. Now Aquinas and Augustine are not pacifists. They thought that war could be used as a means toward the pursuit of peace. But in the thinking of more explicitly pacifist authors of the 20th century, we see the same idea of peace as a larger whole and the greatest good. The American peace activist Jane Addams (1860–1935) wrote, for example: "Peace has come to be a larger thing. It is no longer merely the absence of war, but the unfolding of life processes which are making for a common development" (Addams 2005, 1). The theologian and humanitarian physician Albert Schweitzer (1875–1965) said: "Good consists in maintaining, promoting, and enhancing life ... destroying, injuring, and limiting life are evil" (Schweitzer 1923/1987, 79).

The dispute between pacifists and just war theorists is not a dispute about the value of peace. Nor is it a dispute about the terrible horror of war. Neither pacifists nor just war theorists think that war is something that is intrinsically good; nor do just war theorists deny that peace is good. Rather this is a dispute about the permissible means for the pursuit of peace. Just war theory agrees with the pacifist tradition that war is not an end in itself, seeming to agree that peace is the end in itself that we pursue (although we should note that for the just war tradition peace must include *justice*—a point we will return to below). In this regard, just war theorists and pacifists find common ground. Just war theory also holds that nonviolent means ought ordinarily be employed in pursuit of social and political goods—which provides another source of agreement between the pacifist and the proponent of just war. Just war theory holds that war can only be used as a last resort, when sustained nonviolent efforts have failed. Pacifists agree about the importance of nonviolent methods; but they deny the resort to violence as a last resort. While just war theory holds that war is morally exceptional and in need of special justification, just war theory allows that this justification is possible—a conclusion that pacifism rejects.

This idea—the presumption of peace as a background condition of just war theory and the related presumption that war is wrong and in need of special justification—has been a matter of dispute in the literature.[5] But key sources in the tradition help to ground this claim. Aristotle said in *Nicomachean Ethics* (1177b), that we "make war in order to bring about peace." This implies that war is not an end in itself but only a means to the end of peace. Plato suggested, as well, in *Laws* that peace is superior to war. While he admitted that there are some values found in war, he said, "it is peace (*eirenen*) in which each of us should spend most of his life and spend it best" (803d). Peace allows for education and play and contemplation—all of which are requisites for a fully human life. The ancient non-Christian philosophers provide us with the basic idea that the goal of war should be to bring about peace. This idea is taken up by Christian philosophers in a way that combined it with the more explicit pacifism of Jesus and the early Christians. Augustine is again quoted by Aquinas in his discussion of basic principles of waging a just war. Aquinas explains in *Summa Theologica*, "Those who wage war justly aim at peace, and so they are not opposed to peace, except to the evil peace" (*Summa* II: II, Q. 40, art. 1). He then quotes Augustine:

> We do not seek peace in order to be at war, but we go to war that we may have peace. Be peaceful, therefore, in warring, so that you may vanquish those whom you war against, and bring them to the prosperity of peace.
>
> (*Summa* II: II, Q. 40, art. 1)

Augustine wrote those words in the year 418 in a letter to Boniface. It is helpful to read Augustine's words set in its context (and by way of a different translation):

> Peace should be the object of your desire; war should be waged only as a necessity, and waged only that God may by it deliver men from the necessity and preserve them in peace. For peace is not sought in order to the kindling of war, but war is waged in order that peace may be obtained. Therefore, even in waging war, cherish the spirit of a peacemaker, that, by conquering

those whom you attack, you may lead them back to the advantages of peace; for our Lord says: Blessed are the peace-makers; for they shall be called the children of God.

(Matthew 5:9) (Augustine 1887, #189, para. 6)

The last line quoted by Augustine—from Jesus's Sermon on the Mount—is, as noted above, an important source of Christian pacifism.

The history of the just war tradition rightfully looks to Augustine as a prominent figure. But let's consider the crucial idea found in the passage quote above (in Aquinas) where Augustine says, "Be peaceful, therefore, in warring." In the alternative translation, this says "even in waging war, cherish the spirit of a peacemaker" (the Latin original is *pacificus*, which can be translated as "pacifist"). The limitations imposed by just war theory can be understood as ways of being peaceful in warring, as Augustine puts it here. But critics of war will argue that there is a fundamental contradiction in the idea of fighting peacefully—since means and ends ought to be unified.

7.3. Peace and Justice

If this genealogy is correct then there is substantial overlap between pacifism and just war theory. The pacifist argument against war is based upon a fundamental and profound commitment to peace. But this is true, as well, for just war theory as conceived by Augustine and Aquinas. For the pacifist, peace is presumed as a primary good representing the healthy condition of social and political life. The just war tradition typically adds that peace depends upon justice, and emphasizes—as Augustine did—the idea of a just and lasting peace (what Augustine called *tranquilitas ordinis*—the tranquility of order). It is important to note here that if justice is presented as the highest good (or as a good that is as important as peace), a different sort of theory results. Just war theorists have generally argued that peace without justice is not good. We could, for example, imagine a kind of peace that is based upon slavery, domination, and submission. For some pacifists an unjust peace may be acceptable. Early Christians did submit themselves to martyrdom under the Roman empire. But in recent centuries the idea of nonviolent civil disobedience to injustice has come to the fore, indicating that injustice remains a problem—even if it is one that must be confronted only with nonviolent means. But for just war theorists, justice implies the possibility of using violence in defense of what is right or just. In the modern version of this idea, the basic idea of human rights is appealed to. Actions that violate human rights are wrong and can be resisted, with violence if necessary, according to just war theory. Indeed, the just war idea may not only permit violence in pursuit of justice; it may also stipulate a more positive duty or obligation to take necessary action (including morally limited violent action) in defense of human rights. In the background of this idea is the idea of a right of self- and other-defense (as discussed earlier). According to this idea, if someone is violating my right to life, I am justified in using lethal force to defend my right. This idea is extrapolated in the case of international aggression and oppressive states, appealing to the basic idea that nations have a right to defend themselves. A more positive duty emerges with the idea that we have obligations to protect those who are being oppressed and whose rights are being violated (for example in the idea of humanitarian intervention and the "responsibility to protect" also known as R2P).

While just warriors believe that violence can be permitted (and may be obligated) in pursuit of a just peace, pacifists think we ought to pursue peaceful ends only through peaceful means. This is a crucial distinction. Pacifists do not give up on justice. Indeed, a robust and lasting peace ought to include justice, since justice allows for respect and social harmony—and since just social conditions also help to prevent violence. When people are treated justly, they are more likely to cooperate and less likely to resort to violence. But pacifists worry that war ends up producing injustice. As I argued above in the section on deontological arguments against war, a significant problem is collateral damage and harm to noncombatants. Those noncombatants who are killed in war suffer an injustice: their right to life has been violated and they have not been given what they deserve. We could also add the further point (as mentioned in the discussion of autonomy above) that those who are forced to fight and kill are also treated unjustly.

While just war theory permits some injustices (such as those mentioned here) in pursuit of justice and peace, the pacifist tradition rejects this permission. There seems to be a contradiction in the idea of committing an injustice in order to bring about justice—just as there seems to be a contradiction in using war in order to bring about peace. Martin Luther King Jr. explains this well in a sermon he gave at Christmas in 1967. I quote at length here:

> If we are to have peace in the world, men and nations must embrace the nonviolent affirmation that ends and means must cohere. One of the great philosophical debates of history has been over the whole question of means and ends. And there have always been those who argued that the end justifies the means, that the means really aren't important. The important thing is to get to the end, you see. So, if you're seeking to develop a just society, they say, the important thing is to get there, and the means are really unimportant; any means will do so long as they get you there—they may be violent, they may be untruthful means; they may even be unjust means to a just end. There have been those who have argued this throughout history. But we will never have peace in the world until men everywhere recognize that ends are not cut off from means, because the means represent the ideal in the making, and the end in process, and ultimately you can't reach good ends through evil means, because the means represent the seed and the end represents the tree.
>
> (King, Jr. 1967, 70–71)

As King suggests, there is a problem in saying that the end justifies the means (as realists often say), which means that unjust means cannot be employed in pursuit of a just end and that violence cannot be used to create peace.

Summary

In this section, we considered common ground between pacifism and just war theory. We discussed a common background in a shared tradition that is connected to early Christian pacifism. We also indicated that there are non-Christian sources such as Gandhi, who were in conversation with Christian pacifists about the importance of nonviolence. The pacifist and just war traditions diverge, however, over the question of the unity of means and ends. Pacifists want means and ends to be unified. Just war theory allows for violent means to be used in pursuit of justice.

8. The Argument against Realism and Bellism

Let's return to our attempt to find common ground with just war theory. One key point is that from the standpoint of both just war theory and pacifism, war is not considered good in itself. Pacifists argue, obviously, that war is not good and cannot be justified. Just war theory sees war as a kind of lesser evil: a destructive action that can be justified in an effort to defend something valuable or avoid some worse outcome. But a lesser evil still remains evil. From the just war vantage point, it is immoral to reject war because war is a necessary means for defending and promoting things we value, including both peace and justice. But just war theory would prefer not to fight wars, demanding that nonviolence be used first and that war is only a proportional last resort. For just war theory, war is not an end in itself. In this regard, just war theory agrees with pacifism.

We should note, however, that there are theories that do not see war as an evil. One alternative theory—often called realism— maintains that moral judgment simply does not apply to war. We defined this already above. One version of realism holds that war is part of the normal background condition of social and political life, something like earthquakes and storms. This point of view considers war as something that happens as a necessary part of the life of political organizations. But as in the case of an earthquake or a storm, to condemn war as evil is to make a category mistake. Moral condemnation of war is absurd, according to realism, since there is nothing we can do to avoid or eliminate war and since war has a logic of its own that is not properly subject to moral evaluation. As in the case of an earthquake, the point is to survive. And to survive war, you must do whatever the logic of power requires. Realists typically invoke Thucydides, the ancient Greek historian who showed in his history of the Peloponnesian War that the strong do what the strong are able to do and the weak are subject to the power of the stronger party. From this point of view, the goal of war is to be strong—to emerge victorious and to avoid defeat.

The logic of realism is strategic and not moral. To the question of whether war can be justified, the realist responds by saying that the question is flawed and subject to a category mistake. War is not a matter where the discourse of moral justification applies. Wars will occur and you will have to fight. Moral justification is not on the table for realism. Rather the question for realism is about the necessity of fighting and the strategies for winning. This is where the idea that the end justifies the means comes in. If the goal is to win a war, then realism says that we ought to do whatever it takes to win. Often this is put in a way that makes it seem that this logic is a matter of rational common sense. The realist says, in the real world, moral limitations on means make it difficult or impossible for us to achieve our strategic goals. Furthermore, the realist will claim, pacifists and just war theorists are utopian dreamers if they think that moral limitations on violence (or complete nonviolence) will be effective.

The worldview of realism sees social and political life in general as a struggle for power that inevitably flares up into violent conflict. Something like this is suggested by Hobbes, who describes the state of nature as a state of war, and by the Prussian general Carl von Clausewitz (1780–1831), who says that war is politics by other means. Proponents of radical political violence such as Karl Marx (the theorist of Communist revolution), Frantz Fanon (a proponent of Black liberation), Ward Churchill (a Native American activist) and contemporary Leninists/Maoists, terrorists, and radicals also propose that violence is a potent social force that has the power to unify resistance and revolutionize society. From the realist point of view, it is not prudent to give up on war as the pacifist does—since war is ubiquitous and potential enemies are waiting to pounce. Radical revolutionaries will also point out that the power of the status quo includes varieties of structural and institutional violence (including the state's legal monopoly on the use of force) that can only be overturned with violence—often adding that pacifism is a position for a privileged few who are not interested in radical social change. Realists basically hold that the moral limitations of just war theory and the pacifist critique of war ignore the reality of the need for power to defend and extend itself. The realist will maintain that a pacifist critique of war in general will result in defeat. And the realist will also maintain that the limitations on warfare imposed by just war theory tie the hands of generals, soldiers, and statesmen, preventing them from doing whatever is necessary in order to obtain victory and consolidate power.

Some forms of realism point beyond mere strategy toward a moral argument. In this moral iteration, realists might argue that pacifism and just war theory are immoral. It would be morally wrong, from this point of view, not to do whatever it takes to win. This sort of argument is often made from within a one-sided kind of utilitarianism. This argument holds that the well-being of "our side" should not be sacrificed out of concern for those on the other side. A moral distinction is drawn here between us and them, often employing some kind of claim about "our" moral goodness as opposed to the enemy's depravity. A less moralistic kind of realism simply eliminates the enemy from a calculation of harms, costs, and benefits. On this view, we will kill as many of them as necessary to obtain victory and in order to preserve our own lives.

The general problem with realism is that by rejecting the moral evaluation of war (by saying that war is practically necessary and a matter of prudence that is outside of the realm of moral justification), discourses of justification no longer apply. This problem would be noted both by pacifists and by just war theorists. If realism is conceived as an a-moral theory of practical necessity, then it is not properly speaking a theory of moral justification. The realist does not say that war can be morally justified; rather, she asserts that war is simply necessary. And this leaves realism out of a conversation about the justification of war. The realist may view the question of our book—"can war be justified?"—as a category mistake.

But—and here is a problem for just war theory—many just war theorists seem to remain sympathetic with the realist assumption of the necessity of war and of the necessity of considering moral exceptions to the limitations imposed upon war by their own theory. When just war theory gives way to what has been called "supreme emergency" exceptions, for example, the logic of realism comes back into play. This idea has been discussed by Michael Walzer (2006), John Rawls (1999), and others (see Fiala 2008). The basic idea is that moral limitations on war ought to be respected—but only up to a limit. At some point, so the argument goes, when we encounter "back to the wall" situations, we can set aside moral limitations on war. When this occurs, it is possible to justify terror bombing, torture, and other strategies that would presumably violate the ordinary principles of just war theory's account of *jus in bello*. One solution to this problem might be simply to insist that just war theory be considered as a more deontological and absolute theory—one which admits of no exceptions. But for just war theorists who flirt with the issue of supreme emergency exceptions, the issue of winning comes back in. If the theory prevents you from doing what is necessary in order to win (or as in the case of the back-to-the-wall situation, which prevents you from doing what is necessary in order to survive), then the theory is set aside. This set of issues is connected to a subtle but important point about just war theory itself. Michael Walzer has explained that just war theory "made war possible in a world where war was, sometimes, necessary" (Walzer 2004, 3). Walzer's point is informed by realism: in the real world, war is sometimes necessary. But—and here is the problem—when we conform our ethical judgments to the real world in this way, they become less stringent and more flexible. And there is a slippage toward those kinds of rationalizations that permit us to do "whatever it takes" to respond to the necessities of the real world. Pacifism, of course, questions this slippage. And indeed, pacifists will suggest that a problem for just war theory is that in real world applications, it tends to give way to this slippage.

8.1. Realism, Moral Slippage, and the World War II Example

We can see this problem of the slippage from just war to realism in the World War II example. The sort of argument that has been made to defend the use of firebombs and atomic bombs in World War II shows us how realist logic comes into play in the real world. Rather than sacrificing American soldiers' lives in an assault against the home islands of Japan, for example, the realist holds that we ought to bomb the enemy into submission. There is no doubt that this strategy saved American lives, while killing large numbers of Japanese civilians. Just war theory would condemn this as a violation of the *jus in bello* principle of discrimination—since Japanese noncombatants were deliberately targeted. But—and here is another real-world difficulty—the American forces viewed themselves as the good guys in the battle, even though they adopted this immoral strategy. From the point of view of a one-sided realism, the bombing campaign against Japan was successful; and the use of atomic bombs to destroy Hiroshima and Nagasaki was "justified." Japan surrendered unconditionally. American lives were saved. President Harry Truman explained in a radio address to the American people after using the atomic bomb that the bomb was used "in order to shorten the agony of war, in order to save the lives of thousands and thousands of young Americans" (quoted in Malloy 2012, chap. 4, no page numbers). This kind of argument expresses a kind of narrowly focused realist justification: we will kill thousands of them in order to save thousands of our own. But in a later account of his decision, Truman revised the argument saying he had no qualms about using the bomb, "if millions of lives could be saved." He added, "I meant both American and Japanese lives" (Truman 2015, no page numbers).

These two different ways of putting things express a moral shift from a straightforward and narrowly realist justification toward a more complex justification that offers a more universal utilitarian calculation. In the first case, the point is to save our soldiers from harm by killing Japanese civilians in mass numbers so that American soldiers do not have to die in an invasion. In the second case, the point is that an invasion of Japan would have caused harm to both American soldiers and to the Japanese who would have been killed in an invasion. But both arguments ignore just war theory's moral distinction between combatants and noncombatants and the moral demand to avoid deliberately killing noncombatants. Both arguments also assume that the only option was for the United States to demand that Japan unconditionally surrender.

Pacifists will dig in here and suggest that when the logic of realism leads to the demand for unconditional surrender, we see the fundamental flaw of realism, which is that the logic of victory leads to obvious violations of morality. They will also point out that there is a tendency to set the details of just war theory aside in the middle of war, as the logic of realism is soon employed to override just war limitations. The dispute about Truman and the bomb has prompted a wide-ranging discussion among moral theorists. Elizabeth Anscombe, who is also a critic of pacifism, condemned the atomic bombing of Japan as a kind of crass and immoral consequentialism. Anscombe said this was murder: "For men to choose to kill the innocent as a means to their ends is always murder" (Anscombe 1981, 64; also see Rawls 1999 and Fiala 2010). This points toward one of the fundamental flaws of realism: it ignores the question of the morality of the means employed and focuses entirely on the end of power and victory. Just war theory imposes restrictions on the means employed (in the general category of jus in bello). And pacifists insist that nonviolent means are the only appropriate means. Here again we see some common ground between pacifism and just war theory: neither thinks that "anything goes" in war as realism often does; both maintain that there are moral restrictions on the means we can employ.

But—and here is the pacifist point—in real wars, just war theory seems ineffective at preventing the slippage toward realism. While this point is clear, I think, from the World War II example, we could add in other examples here: escalation in America's war in Vietnam, the use of torture in the war on terrorism, and more recently the assassination of Iranian General Qasem Soleimani. Each of these is controversial and would require a much deeper analysis. My point here is that, in the real world, military necessity and realist logic often leads military power to violate just war limitations.

Let's conclude our discussion of realism by making a further point, which is that realism—in reality—is typically one-sided. The ethnocentric or racist calculus of the sort proposed by those who maintain that the American bombing of Japan saved American lives is morally problematic. And in reality (in the real world!) realism is typically linked to some kind of partial view of morality. Crass realism tends to paint a dehumanizing picture of the enemy based upon an "us vs. them" dichotomy: we are the good guys and they are "the other." More sophisticated realism in foreign policy circles may avoid demonizing the enemy (and in fact may recognize that the enemy is engaged in the same game of rational calculation for power and advantage); but foreign policy realism remains one-sided since it is usually only concerned with national self-interest.

Just war theory may present a less unilateral evaluation of war. But just war theory is typically employed in one-sided ways: focused on the question of whether "we" are justified in going to war against "them." But here is where pacifism is different. Pacifists tend to emphasize the need for global justice and a universal moral point of view. Pacifists want to avoid demonizing and dehumanizing the enemy. Pacifists are not only concerned with whether "we" are justified in fighting. Rather, they focus on the harm of war for all parties involved. And pacifists are obviously not only concerned with the narrow focus on national power and self-interest.

8.2. Bellism

Let's now consider another point of view of war, related to realism, which sees war as having value in itself—as a way to obtain glory. I have called that point of view "bellism," which might be described as "the worship of war" (see Fiala 2004, 49). While realists see struggles for power as necessary and view violence as a necessary means to obtain power, bellists see *glory* as something more than mere power while also tending to think that the means employed in war have a kind of value in themselves and not only as a means.

Bellism holds that war and violence are a place to demonstrate courage, strength, and strategic cleverness.

There is a kind of pride that is found in outmatching, outfighting, and outsmarting your opponent. On this view, strength and power are not merely means, they are ends in themselves. Just war theory would seem to reject this idea. And pacifists certainly do: pacifists will argue that pacific virtues are different from the values celebrated in bellism.

A classic source for bellism is found in the warrior culture portrayed by Homer. In Homer's *Iliad*, Achilles is offered a choice between a long peaceful life and the glory of war. Achilles chooses glory and war. His pursuit of glory leads him to live a life of rage, resentment, and excessive violence. It is through excessive violence that Achilles earns glory. Achilles' comrade Odysseus also earns glory through his cleverness—and at the end of the *Odyssey* (in the slaughter that unfolds when Odysseus finally returns home) through the unrestrained spirit of vengeance. While Achilles' glory is connected to his physical prowess, Odysseus's glory is connected to his ability to lie and deceive his enemy. One of the Greek words for glory is *kudos*. *Kudos* is earned through victory. There is no other way to obtain the glory of war except by fighting and winning. In the *Iliad* and the *Odyssey* there is a sense that the gods themselves are involved in the fighting: glory is bestowed upon great warriors by the gods, who are watching the fight, cheering it on, and helping their champions. In the world of bellism, fighting is simply what men must do to earn glory in a world that is structured by violence, power, and war. If war is ubiquitous and we will die anyway, then we ought to fight and die well, earning glory along the way.

This idea—of war as a source of glory and struggle and fighting as ends-in-themselves—has a variety of modern iterations. The German philosopher Friedrich Nietzsche (1844–1900), for example, seemed to point in this direction, suggesting that we should not be embarrassed by the will-to-power and that life is best understood as a constant struggle. Another German philosopher, Georg Wilhelm Friedrich Hegel (1770–1831), provides a related theory in his claim that war strengthens nations, while peace creates stagnation and complacency. There is spiritual power in war, according to Hegel, insofar as it requires individuals to sacrifice and subordinate themselves to the state, which is, for Hegel, a spiritual entity that is larger and more substantial than any individual. Hegel also thought that war was used by the world-spirit to sort out clashes of ideas and conflicts between civilizations. War is something that is used by the world-spirit as it evolves new ideas and generates new spiritual entities (see Fiala 2010). The Hegelian view of war is connected to another idea about the glories of war that is found in the thinking of the American President Theodore Roosevelt. Roosevelt was an advocate of what he called "the strenuous life" and an advocate for rugged warrior virtues (Roosevelt 1901). He saw struggle and war as beneficial both for nations and for individuals. And he argued explicitly against peace and against pacifism. His advocacy for the strenuous life was an argument against "the timid man, the lazy man, the man who distrusts his country, the over-civilized man, who has lost the great fighting, masterful virtues." He continued, "these are the men who fear the strenuous life ... they believe in that cloistered life which saps the hardy virtues in a nation, as it saps them in the individual" (Roosevelt 1901, 7–8). Roosevelt went on to argue explicitly against pacifism during the run-up to World War I. He said,

> Only mischief has sprung from the activities of the professional peace prattlers, the ultrapacifists, who, with the shrill clamor of eunuchs, preach the gospel of the milk and water of virtue and scream that belief in the efficacy of diluted moral mush is essential to salvation.
>
> (Roosevelt 1915, 244)

The pacifist argument against bellism presents an alternative worldview. Pacifists might argue that there are other, less brutal, ways to earn glory than through war. This is in fact what American philosopher William James (1842–1910) seemed to suggest in his idea that we ought to find "a moral equivalent of war," a way to enjoy the virtues of a strenuous life without violence (James 1911). Pacifists will argue that bellism simply fails to account for the negative consequences of war, assuming as it does that glory is worth all of the blood, sweat, and tears of war. Pacifists may also argue that the worldview of the bellist seems hyper-masculine and can be subjected a critique that might be articulated from the vantage point of feminism and care ethics.

Now, just war theory will also be critical of bellism as an old-fashioned and mystical approach to war. Just war theory should not speak of the glory of war. But pacifists will point out that there is also a kind of slippage here in the real world (related to the slippage we discussed above with regard to realism). The problem is that our ordinary discourse about war is infused with bellism. We don't typically speak of soldiers as reluctant fighters who have done something dangerous and difficult in the name of justice—as just war theory might encourage us to do. Rather, we lionize our soldiers as heroes and usually ignore the moral complexity of the wars they fight. Thus our thinking about the question of whether war can be justified is skewed and corrupted by a whole mythological complex in which patriotism, bellism, and realism make it difficult to apply just war principles in an unbiased and self-critical way.

This leads me to conclude that war is not as easily justified as the just war tradition supposes. And in fact there are reasons to think that the pacifist argument against war is often ignored or rejected because of the cultural assumptions typical of realism and bellism, and because of the cultural abuse that is often directed against pacifism.

Summary

In this section, we considered the argument against realism and bellism. The realist tradition tends to hold that the end justifies the means. While just war theory and pacifism reject that view, pacifists worry that there is a significant problem of slippage "in the real world": just war theory may give way to realism and to bellism. And cultural presumptions in favor of war make it difficult for the anti-war argument to be taken seriously.

9. Might Does Not Make Right

As discussed above, realists tend to hold that the end justifies the means. This is closely linked to the idea that might makes right (see Fiala 2018c; Temam 2014). But as school children learn, it is not true that might makes right. Said in more sophisticated terms, victory in a contest of arms proves nothing in the contest of ideas and moral principles. Nor, according to pacifism, is violence or the threat of violence the proper means for bringing about social, political, ethical, and spiritual change. This point is familiar from basic lessons in critical thinking, where the fallacy known as *argumentum ad baculum* ("appeal to force") is frequently discussed. If I threaten you, for example, in order to get you to agree with me, this does not mean you actually agree with me. You may go along with me; but the agreement is merely external conformity. And indeed, it is a fallacy to say that the person with the biggest gun has the best argument. While there are prudential reasons for going along with someone who is more powerful than you, that prudential argument has nothing to do with the logic of the argument or the justice of the cause.

There are many examples we could consider here, connected to a variety of issues in thinking about ideology, force, persuasion, and conformity. The English philosopher John Locke (1632–1704) suggested, in his defense of religious toleration, that it is not appropriate to use force to try to convert someone, since external force should not be employed to change people's minds. He explained: "For the truth certainly would do well enough if she were left to shift for herself ... She is not taught by laws, nor has she any need of force to procure her entrance into the minds of men." And: "Anyone may employ as many exhortations and arguments as he please. But all force and compulsion are to be forborne" (Locke 1997, 310). Of course, force and compulsion have often been employed in the name of ideology. Later theorists simply embraced this fact and connected it to the justification of violence. When the Communist mastermind Karl Marx (1818–1883) suggested that the ruling ideas have always been the ideas of the ruling class, he suggested that power determines ideology. For Marx, this leads to the call for revolution: to change the power structure in order to change the dominant ideology. This idea was taken up by the Chinese dictator Mao Tse Tung (1893–1976), who famously quipped, "power grows out of the barrel of a gun." A related set of considerations can be found in Nietzsche's discussion of the genealogy of morals and the conflict between master morality and slave morality. For Nietzsche there is an ongoing struggle for power in morality and ideas, known as "the will to power." The French philosopher Michel Foucault (1926–1984) picked up on this idea, which has become influential in social philosophy, which is that social power constructs values and ideas. George Orwell hit upon something similar in *1984*, when the novel asks us to consider whether coercion may lead people to say (and believe) that "2 + 2 = 5."

The problem here is that might does not make right. Consider the Orwellian example. Coercion may be effective at getting us to repeat "2 + 2 = 5," when Big Brother asks us to. But affirming a false equation as a result of coercion does not make the false equation true. Nor does legitimate political power grow out of the barrel of a gun. Indeed, as pacifists argue (as we discussed above), there ought to be a unity of means and ends, which means that war should not be used to bring about peace and might is not the proper tool for making right.

We have jumped down a philosophical rabbit hole here in this discussion of power and ideology. But this point is crucial in thinking about the justification of war. Can war be justified, we ask? One typical response says, you are justified if you win. But what makes it right if you win and wrong if you lose? To suggest this is to accept the ideology-power matrix that is familiar from Marx, Mao, Nietzsche, and Foucault. But pacifists and the just war tradition both reject this kind of relativism. And yes, the idea that might makes right is really a kind of relativism. This point has been made by ethicist Lloyd Steffen, who connects this with the pacifist tradition: "Ethical relativism implicitly endorses a 'might makes right' ethic that eliminates the possibility that a dissident—a Jesus or a Thoreau, a Gandhi or a Martin Luther King, Jr.—could represent anything but social deviance against behavioral norms determined by a majority" (Steffen 2012, 34). It should come as no surprise that critics of war appeal to objective moral norms in articulating their critique. The just war tradition appeals to natural law, consequentialism, and other moral theories in order to ground its account in an objective theory of morality. Pacifism also appeals to similar objective moral ideas—as we've discussed throughout this chapter.

War opens up the question of moral objectivity and relativism: war is often fought because of ideological disputes. Even if you reject the conventionalist or non-objective account of ideology found in Marx and Nietzsche, the idea that "might makes right" is woven deeply into our thinking about war. In popular discussions of war, the idea that war is right if you win hovers in the background. We believe that we are the good guys, that we have the right to fight against the bad guys, and that this will be proven once we win. A different way of putting this is to say that we will use our might to make things right. This implies that the mighty have the right to rearrange things, punish enemies, and justly deal with the spoils of war. The problem is, however, that those who are on the losing end of a war will often believe that what is being done to them is unjust. They will describe the aftermath of war as so-called "victor's justice"—which is not really justice at all but only the will of the victor being imposed upon the vanquished.

Often the idea that might makes right gets switched around in a way that says "right makes might"—or more eloquently, "justice makes us powerful." Naïve patriots tend to think that there is some mysterious power in the universe guaranteeing the connection between justice and war. This is part of what I call "the just war myth." Two key ideas in this myth are (1) the idea that we are the good guys in war, and (2) the idea that we win the wars we fight because we are the good guys. Another way of putting it would be to say that since we are righteous, we will be mighty and prevail (i.e., "right makes might"). History shows that the first part of that myth is flawed: the United States is not an unambiguous "good guy" in history. In fact, there is no nation that is and always has been "the good guy" in war. The second part of that myth points toward a metaphysical or mystical view that seems to imply that the universe itself is on the side of justice, making it such that in the long run, good guys win. History again shows that this is not true. Bad guys have won wars and have ruled for long periods of time. Roman history provides one example. If we assume that the Jews and early Christians were the good guys, then history shows us that good guys lose in the short run: Roman power killed Jesus and his disciples, the Jewish temple in Jerusalem was destroyed, and Christians suffered long centuries of domination and persecution. Now someone may respond by saying that in the longer run, Christians came to power and the Roman empire fell. But we can see that at some point we move beyond historical analysis toward wishful thinking, eschatological hope, and mystical pronouncements about the course of history. In the short term and near at hand, there is no guarantee that good guys win. And this is so because victory at arms does not have much to do with the righteousness of one's ideas. A righteous cause is no guarantee of victory. Victory depends upon a variety of social, political, and other factors, including economics, discipline, geography, the weather, and luck. In other words, victory depends upon contingencies that have no necessary connection to justice.

A different way of making this point is to note that while external conformity (physical obedience, cooperative behavior, and so on) may be instituted by force, external conformity does not indicate justice, agreement, or peace. We mentioned above that some kinds of peace are the result of submission: a slave society may be at peace. But when force or the threat of force is essential to keeping the peace, there is something missing here and we would not say that this is a just or lasting peace. In political discussions, this is related to the question of legitimacy. A government may be instituted by force. But that government is not thus a legitimate government. A similar point holds with regard to criminal justice: good guys sometimes end up in jail or being executed, as happened to Socrates, Jesus, and Martin Luther King Jr.

Let's summarize here and point out that pacifists tend to reject both the claims we have considered here. Instead, pacifists tend to agree with the following:

Might does not make right: The more powerful party does not necessarily have justice on its side. Overpowering your opponent does not show that your ideas are better. And having the power to do something does not mean you have the right to do that thing.

Right does not make might: Those who have justice on their side do not always prevail. Sometimes unjust parties win. And those who have justice on their side are not thereby justified in doing whatever they want in pursuit of justice.

Let's push this analysis deeper toward a point that helps explain how this is linked to a critique of war. The pacifist is ultimately concerned about the fact that violence and war are fundamentally irrational—or perhaps better "a-rational." This does not mean that there is no logic or strategy to war, nor that people cannot make rational decisions about going to war or within war. The just war tradition attempts to apply rationality to war. Realists seek to rationally calculate power in war. This is true. But the pacifist's point pushes deeper, toward the idea that what occurs in war is sub-rational, inhuman, or animalistic. In war, there is a contest of bodies and physical force. Yes, in the background, there is technology, military intelligence, and strategic planning. But battle and wars are ultimately about killing bodies, imprisoning them, subduing them, and forcing them to submit. War is about occupying territory and controlling physical assets. War operates on the material body—not on the mind, spirit, or soul. Yes, there is propaganda, *esprit de corps*, and strategic resolve. But at the end of the day war is about dead bodies, living bodies, maimed bodies, and imprisoned bodies. And—most importantly—the carnal or corporeal result of war proves nothing in the realm of ideas.

Immanuel Kant (1724–1804), the German philosopher, points in this direction in his essay, *Perpetual Peace*, written in 1795. In that book he appeals to an idea borrowed from the French philosopher Jean-Jacques Rousseau (1712–1778). Rousseau said, "Force is a physical power, and I fail to see what moral effect it can have. To yield to force is an act of necessity, not of will—at the most, an act of prudence" (Rousseau 1923, Book 1, chap. 3, no page numbers). Kant connects this to a critique of just war theory. He sees a kind of practical uselessness in the just war theory of Grotius, Pufendorf, and Vatel—whom he cites. His point is connected to the problem of what I called "slippage" above, that is, that states rarely are prevented from fighting unjustly—from slipping beyond just war limitations toward realism and unjust warfighting. Kant says that "there is no instance of a state" ever restraining itself from going to war by just war theory (Kant 1991, 103). And this is because states seem to believe or at least act upon the basic idea that might makes right. As Kant puts it, the word "right" is used in the context of war in the sense that Rousseau suggests: "Nature has given to the strong the prerogative of making the weak obey them" (Kant 1991, 103). And Kant points out that this usage of the word "right" is employed here derisively and in jest. He continues to say: "rights cannot be decided by military victory, and a peace treaty may put an end to the current war, but not to the general warlike condition within which pretexts can always be found for a new war" (Kant 1991, 104). And: "reason, as the highest legislative moral power, absolutely condemns war as a test of rights" (ibid.). From this Kant concludes that peace is a duty and that a federation of peace must be set up that can resolve questions of international right so that war is no longer necessary.

We could add here a number of other voices who have claimed that war operates, as Rousseau put it, in a realm of necessity that has nothing to do with morality. The current Catholic Pope, Francis, put it this way in a homily commemorating the 100th anniversary of the outbreak of World War I. He said, "War ruins everything, even the bonds between brothers. War is irrational; its only plan is to bring destruction: it seeks to grow by destroying" (Francis 2014, no page numbers). John Steinbeck said, reflecting on World War II, "all war is a symptom of man's failure as a thinking animal" (Steinbeck 2007, 9). A number of critics of war—pacifists and just war theorists alike—have made this sort of point. And in the background of this critique is an idea that is as old as Socrates, who made this kind of argument against Callicles (in Plato's *Gorgias*) and against Thrasymachus (in Plato's *Republic*), saying that justice is not merely whatever the strong say it is and that, therefore, might does not make right.

If this is true, then the argument against war is further strengthened. War is wrong because its use of violence and force has no moral merit: it operates at the level of bodies and proves nothing in the realm of ideas. Even if victory is achieved, such a victory does not prove the truth of the ideas that are fought for. And indeed, the idea that might makes right operates in a world of physical power that is at odds with the image of human beings as possessing reason, spirit, and morality.

Summary

In this section, we have critically examined the idea that might makes right. This idea tends to be connected to discussion of the justification of war. But critics will point out that this is a kind of relativism and that there is a risk of "victor's justice," which is based on the idea that those who win are empowered to determine what counts as justice. Just war theorists reject this idea. But pacifists—who call for a unity of means and end—are especially critical of the idea that might makes right. Pacifists typically argue that physical and martial victory prove nothing in the realm of ideas. Victory is no sign of justice. And the use of violence and force is subhuman.

10. Pacifism as Transformative Critical Theory

As I conclude my contribution to this debate, let me bring in a few other important considerations for answering the question of whether war can be justified. Pacifists and critics of war have tended to adopt a much broader point of view when confronted with the question of justified violence. In other work I have defended a broader and more comprehensive theory of pacifism that I call "transformative pacifism." Such a critical pacifist theory digs deeply into psychological, social, cultural, economic, and political sources of violence, seeking to criticize violence in all aspects of life while hoping to transform the world so there is less war and more peace. So let's bring a critical and transformative theory to bear on the problem of war with regard to two problems that are typically not addressed by just war theory: (1) the problem of militarism and (2) the problems of moral injury and PTSD. As I argue here, these social and psychological problems give us further reason to be skeptical of war. After discussing these problems, we will conclude by briefly considering the promise of creative and active nonviolence.

10.1. Militarism

The pacifist critique of war also includes a critique of economic, cultural, and political systems that encourage and support war. This is what is often called militarism.

Militarism is a political, economic, and cultural system that is grounded on military power, including extensive defense and arms industries as well as a standing army.

Militarism is obviously related to bellism (as described above) and what philosopher Duane Cady has called "warism" (Cady 2010, 2018). Militarism can be woven very deeply into a culture and civilization, especially in connection to spending priorities and industrial infrastructure. The term "military-industrial complex" has been employed to describe this, at least since President Dwight Eisenhower used the phrase in his 1961 Farewell Address (see Fiala 2012; Gay 2018). In the United States, for example, military spending makes up the lion's share of the federal budget. There is a revolving door between defense industries, the military, and the government. This also includes the news and media landscape, which employs retired military brass as experts and which does not critically engage military and defense spending priorities. Beyond this, there is a general cultural focus on war and the military: in public monuments, in public holidays, and in symbols, flags, and rhetoric.

We could spend quite a bit more time describing militarism and the military-industrial complex. But let's move on and consider why this matters for thinking about the question of whether war can be justified—and what the task of transforming militaristic culture would look like. The first point to make is that there is very little room in public discourse in militaristic cultures for voices to be heard that are critical of military spending, military priorities, and the nation's warfighting efforts. In militaristic cultures, pacifists are marginalized and mocked. One example from American history was discussed above in connection with Theodore Roosevelt, who mocked pacifists as eunuchs. This point shows us how militaristic values are also related to ideas about gender and masculine assumptions about power and potency. If the background assumption is that pacifists are impotent and emasculated, then it is no wonder that the critique of war is not taken seriously. Furthermore, in a militaristic culture, support of war and the military is linked to patriotism and loyalty to the state. This point was also made by Roosevelt in 1917, when the United States was entering into World War I. He said, "In such a crisis the moral weakling is the enemy of the right; and the pacifist is as surely a traitor to his country and to humanity as is the most brutal wrongdoer" (Roosevelt 1919, 871). When pacifism is viewed as moral weakness and treason, there is no reason to take the critique of war seriously. But, as should be obvious, such an ad hominem and hyperbolic rejection of pacifism prevents critical thinking about war. This dismissal of pacifism is, as these examples show, typical of militarism of the sort associated with Roosevelt.

The transformative project associated with pacifism must thus engage a broad range of issues. It must confront gendered assumptions about morality and war. It must criticize a certain kind of patriotism. And it must seek to give voice to a kind of morality that does not simply assume that might makes right and that war is manly, necessary, and heroic. It must engage this critique at a variety of levels, including a criticism of dominant cultural models and prevalent political rhetoric. It must also seek to transform the economic and political system such that the critique of war could be taken seriously. Until we engage in this broad social and political critique it will be difficult to think critically about the question of whether war can be justified. Moreover, when militaristic ideologies are prevalent, it is likely that unjust wars will be waged—since there is very little incentive to resist war in a militaristic culture, where the critique of war is marginalized and mocked.

10.2. Moral Injury and PTSD

That such critical thinking about war is necessary can be seen when we consider a topic that is often overlooked in typical justifications of war—the problem of moral injury (see Fiala 2017). Moral injury can be defined as follows.

> **Moral injury** is a result of transgressive acts that one has committed or participated in and supported, which violate one's conscience or sense of self.

Moral injury is different from post-traumatic stress disorder (PTSD), although obviously related. PTSD results when one has suffered or witnessed trauma. There may be physiological roots of PTSD, which may in some cases be treated through organic bio-medical intervention. But moral injury is not about trauma in the physical sense and cannot be as readily reduced to physiological causes. Moral injury results when one has committed or participated in an action that is immoral. There is a complex etiology of these phenomena. Not every soldier suffers PTSD or moral injury. And some soldiers cope better than others. There are interventions that can be employed before battle and after the fact that can help. Most of the conversation at the level of etiology and treatment ignores the question of whether war can be justified. Of course, the problem of moral injury does force us to ask a question about the morality of war. But usually this conversation is located at the level of *jus in bello*: it is about moral transgressions that occur within war. Rarely does the conversation about moral injury rise to a consideration of *jus ad bellum* and the question of whether war in general can be justified.

Furthermore, from the standpoint of the typical concerns of just war theory, PTSD and moral injury are not a subject of much consideration.[6] This points toward a critical point that may be directed at just war theory, which is that the discussion of the justification of war often simply ignores the suffering of those who do the fighting. It has been pacifists and critics of war who typically focus on the problems of PTSD and moral injury, asking whether the trauma endured by soldiers is worth it. Surely the question of the justification of war must include the question of whether the long-term suffering, disability, and social dislocation that war creates for soldiers must be taken into account. But the issue of moral injury and PTSD pushes us far beyond the typical questions asked by just war theory. The problem of moral injury, in particular, is related to the question of whether the killing that soldiers do can be justified. The serious question, which is typically ignored in just war theory, is whether a soldier ought to feel guilty and suffer trauma and moral injury for participating in a war that is unjust. But if we took that question seriously—if we realized that war asks some human beings to kill others—we might find it more difficult to say that war can be justified.

As noted, my goal here is to show how the standpoint of pacifism as a critical theory pushes us to consider how we might transform our social, cultural, and political system. So, let's conclude this section by suggesting that the problems of PTSD and moral injury show us that society as a whole ought to be more careful in thinking about the justification of war. The soldiers who fight in wars eventually return home. They bring their injuries and traumas home with them. This includes physical, mental, emotional, and spiritual injuries and traumas. We know that veterans often struggle—and that there is a problem of veteran suicide, domestic violence, and drug and alcohol abuse. Those negative repercussions of war must be taken into account in thinking about the justification of war. We must also think about finding ways to support those suffering soldiers, their families, and others who are traumatized by war.

10.3. Creative and Active Nonviolence

Let's conclude by noting that pacifists usually do not merely advocate non-resistance. We noted at the outset that pacifism is not "passive-ism." Pacifists don't argue that we simply do nothing in the face of violence, evil, injustice, and atrocity. Tolstoy and some of the other members of the broad pacifist tradition did advocate non-resistance (although they often did not mean it to be simply doing nothing). But after Tolstoy—under the influence of Gandhi and then Martin Luther King Jr.—this tradition evolved to focus on active and creative nonviolence. Indeed, this evolution in the tradition has led some to argue that we should speak of nonviolentism instead of pacifism (Christenson 2010; Holmes 2013). Regardless of the terminology, the point of this tradition is that we should be active and creative in our usage of nonviolent techniques and strategies. Following upon the work of activists such as Gandhi and King, and academics such as Gene Sharp and Johan Galtung, empirical studies have been done and a whole field of study ("Peace and Conflict Studies") has emerged in an effort to understand the power of active nonviolence (see Galtung 1996; Sharp 2005; Sharp, Finkelstein, and Schelling 1973). There is much more to be said about these techniques and strategies. But there is a growing body of evidence that shows that nonviolence can be effective (see Chenoweth and Stephan 2011). It will not work every time or in every case. But this is also true for war: wars often fail to deliver peace and justice.

Now here is my point about the need for a critical and transformative pacifist approach: until we get smarter about nonviolence and until we are less sanguine about the efficacy of war, we will continue to think that war is easily justifiable. And so, to conclude, to answer the question of whether war can be justified, we must recognize that this question cannot be asked without also asking whether nonviolence can be efficacious, whether there are plausible nonviolent alternatives to war, and whether the nonviolent response has been given the same creative and intelligent energy as war. To return to our discussion about the military-industrial complex for a moment, we should note that we spend substantially more social, cultural, and economic capital on preparing for war than we do on creating peace. A transformative pacifist theory would insist that before we can answer the question of whether war can be justified, we should also demand that social and political reality be transformed in a way that is more supportive of nonviolence and peace.

Summary

In the preceding section, we considered some issues that are typically left off the table in thinking about the justification of war: militarism and the military-industrial complex, moral injury and PTSD, and the power of creative and active nonviolence. These important issues are often ignored by defenders of war.

Conclusion

As I conclude my contribution to our debate, I summarize and conclude my whole argument as follows. I believe that I have supported my initial three points:

(1) War produces bad consequences including death, destruction, and dislocation.
(2) War involves bad (evil or wicked) intentions and actions that are intrinsically evil.
(3) War solves nothing in the realm of ideas.

In each of the sections of this chapter, I fleshed out lots of details. This includes the following:

- The burden of proof for the justification of war is quite high, since war is a prima facie evil involving killing, harm, and, often, wicked/evil intentions.
- War is complex as are those pacifist theories that argue that war cannot be justified. It is important to keep those complexities in mind. But we can weave together a general critique of war that is non-dogmatic.
- There are several good moral arguments against war: consequentialist arguments, deontological arguments, and arguments based in an account of virtue and democratic values.
- There is a robust pacifist tradition that agrees to some extent with the just war tradition, especially in an argument against realism. But while the just war tradition allows that violent means can be employed in pursuit of peace and justice, the pacifist tradition insists on a unity of means and ends.
- The claim about the unity of means and ends leads pacifists to reject the idea that might makes right, which is often a background assumption in appeals to violence.
- The pacifist tradition is concerned to criticize the larger social, cultural, and political context in which the question of the justification of war is often asked.

> I made this argument by considering examples of war, including the supposed paradigm of World War II. I noted that there are historical contingencies that must be considered. But my conclusion is that the weight of these arguments and examples points toward a negative answer to the question of whether war can be justified.

Notes

1 For those who are interested in more detail, a chart outlining the varieties of pacifism can be found as an appendix to this chapter.
2 The general question of the theoretical background and structure of pacifism and just war theory has been called "the demarcation problem" (see Ryan 2018).
3 This is a complicated issue. Forms of the idea can be found in a number of places: Ballou 1848; Thoreau 2000; Tolstoy 1894. I discuss in Fiala 2013.
4 See Airwars.org, which monitors drone killings. They estimate as many as 52,000 civilians have been killed in various drone attacks. Their estimate is contrasted with on secrecy about drone killings under Obama and Trump see *New York Times* editorial, "The Secret Death Toll of American Drones" March 30, 2019 (https://www.nytimes.com/2019/03/30/opinion/drones-civilian-casualties-trump-obama.html).
5 For example, James Turner Johnson has argued that the Catholic just war tradition does not begin with a presumption against war and that recent Catholic teaching is wrong to understand just war theory in this way. See James Turner Johnson, "Just War: As It Is and as It Was" *First Things*, January 2005 (https://www.firstthings.com/article/2005/01/just-war-as-it-was-and-is). A source that Johnson considers is a 1983 pastoral letter by the American National Conference of Catholic Bishops, "The Challenge of Peace" (http://www.usccb.org/upload/challenge-peace-gods-promise-our-response-1983.pdf). The bishops write: "Catholic teaching begins in every case with a presumption against war and for peaceful settlement of disputes. In exceptional cases, determined by the moral principles of the just-war tradition, some uses of force are permitted." Johnson claims that this is wrong and based upon a flawed interpretation of the just war tradition.
6 There is no discussion of "moral injury" or PTSD in May, ed., *The Cambridge Handbook of the Just War* (2018). There is no discussion of either topic in Lazar and Frowe, eds., *The Oxford Handbook of the Ethics of War* (2018). There is a brief discussion of PTSD but no discussion of "moral injury" in Allhof et al., *The Routledge Handbook of Ethics and War* (2013).

Appendix: The Varieties of Pacifism

One difficulty in understanding the argument against war has to do with the question of whether pacifism is directed against *all* wars (*wars in general*) or against *particular* wars (*this* war or *this kind* of war). Another difficulty points to the question of who has an obligation to be a pacifist: is rejection of war a theory for everyone or only for a select few—say, for saints and priests. Here is an attempt to provide a brief overview of some of the kinds of pacifism.

Absolute Pacifism	War can never be justified. There is no imaginable case when war could be justified.
Contingent or Conditional Pacifism	This war (or war in these circumstances) cannot be justified. But it is possible that war could be justified in some cases, under some conditions.
Skeptical Pacifism	War may be justifiable. But we do not have enough information to determine that a given war (or type of war) is justified.
Just War Pacifism	The just war standards cannot be fulfilled (in the present war or in wars in general under present conditions). But the standards of just war theory provide a valuable guide for making this judgment.
Vocational Pacifism	Pacifism is not for everyone. It is only required of people in certain professions who take a vow of peace (e.g., priests).
Prima Facie Pacifism	There is a presumption against war and until that presumption is defeated, war is presumed to be wrong.

Chapter 2

War Can Be Justified

Jennifer Kling

Contents

Just war theorists generally hold that some wars can be morally justified. They also maintain that some warfighting strategies, tactics, and rules can be morally justified, and that there are some morally justified standards for how to end wars. The just war tradition is complex, and there are a variety of particular positions under this umbrella. But these positions are all unified by their commitment to the general claim that sometimes, war is morally justified.

Whether we realize it or not, many of us are already familiar with some of the central arguments in support of just war theory. Many countries trace their origins back to a revolution or war that they think was justified, to the hard-fought and seemingly worthwhile violent overthrow of internal or external oppressors. In addition, many countries have large and well-funded militaries, the ostensible purpose of which is to protect them from aggressive attacks by other states. Just war theory is entrenched in international law; the Geneva Conventions, which outline the laws of war, are the most widely ratified set of treaties and protocols in history. Importantly, the Geneva Conventions—and the Hague Conventions before them— do not outlaw all war; rather, they support defensive war as a last

DOI: 10.4324/9780367809850-3

resort, and set the standards for humanitarian treatment of war-fighters and civilians in war. As we will see, contemporary just war theory both undergirds, and draws support from, these international laws of war.

Furthermore, every cadet in the American military academies reads Michael Walzer's tour-de-force defense of just war theory, *Just and Unjust Wars*, and it is a key part of the officers' curriculum in many professional militaries around the world. *Just and Unjust Wars*, first published in 1977, draws extensively from history to make its case that some, but not all, wars can be justified. Walzer considers the battles between the Greek city states, the medieval wars between England and France, World Wars I and II, the wars surrounding Israel's founding, and the Irish Troubles, among others, to argue that war is subject to both moral critique and moral justification. Sometimes, we must *not* fight—but other times, we *may* fight for our lives and our compatriots, and when we are justified in taking up arms, we must fight fairly, so that a just peace is possible after the fighting is done. Walzer thus concludes that the international laws surrounding war are (mostly) appropriate.

A common critique of the just war tradition is that it, like much of international law, is deeply Eurocentric. We might think, why take moral advice about war from a small set of demonstrably hyper-militaristic cultures with proven histories of genocide and unjustified wars? The underlying thought here seems to be that non-European philosophies of war will tend to point toward pacifism, rather than just war. And it is certainly true that many important strands of pacifist thought originate in, and draw from, Indian and Buddhist philosophies, among others.

But while it is accurate to say that the Western just war tradition originated in medieval Europe with Catholic scholars such as Saint Augustine of Hippo and Saint Thomas Aquinas, and politician-scholars such as Hugo Grotius, who were concerned to justify both religious and political wars, it is not the case that a broader, more global approach to war would demonstrate the idiosyncrasy of the Western just war tradition. Rather, it demonstrates that many cultures across the world have strong just war traditions. This is not to make an argument from popularity—everyone thinks war is sometimes justified, so it must be true!—but rather to point out that there are a number of traditions to draw upon in our thinking about war, as well as peace. So, we needn't take up a Eurocentric view (either a derogatory or laudatory one) to do so. While a comparison between these and the European just war tradition is not the central focus of the chapter, throughout I use arguments and examples from the Chinese and Native American just war traditions to support the general claim that sometimes, war is justified.

This chapter has five areas of focus. First, I outline just war theory as it is understood today, along with some of the major debates and areas of contention. Second, I present several prominent arguments in support of justified war, including arguments from defense and emancipation, as well as humanitarian intervention. Third, I consider the practicality of just war traditions in our non-ideal world, along with the development of the concept of "force short of war" and corresponding advancements in military technology. Fourth, I examine the fundamentally coercive nature of war and the subsequent importance of developing jus post bellum principles and methodologies in greater depth and detail. Finally, I take up challenges to the just war tradition from feminism, philosophy of race, and philosophies of oppression more generally, and argue that while these critiques support a transformation of just war theory, they still leave space for the conclusion that war is sometimes justified.

I. Contemporary Just War Theory

Before discussing whether or not war can be justified, it is important to first say what war is.

> **War** is *large-scale, sustained, direct political violence between organized political groups.*

Some theorists have argued that war can only occur between states; that is, non-state actors (such as terrorist groups, cartels, tribes, or community groups) cannot engage in war. But this seems to put too much importance on the notion of the state, which is a somewhat Eurocentric notion. So, this definition focuses us on ordinary cases of war, including wars between states (e.g., India versus Pakistan, France versus Germany, the Axis powers versus the Allied powers), wars within states (e.g., the U.S. civil war, the Russian revolution), wars including non-state groups (e.g., ISIS versus the "West," indigenous Amazonians versus drug cartels), and various combinations thereof. It avoids other kinds of violent clashes that do not rise to the level of war, such as one-off violent protests, assassinations, and personal assault and murder. It also steers clear of labeling various kinds of indirect violence, such as institutional, economic, or structural violence, as war. At the same time, this definition recognizes that war is a group activity; no one individual can go to war. While we appropriately call Hitler a genocidal maniac, he did not engage in World War II and commit the Holocaust by himself—he couldn't have done. These events took an organized group of people acting more or less in concert. (They need not be *thinking* in concert, to be sure; but they must be so acting, for war and genocide to occur.) This definition of war, like any definition, is sure to be contentious; but it does capture the kinds of events with which just war theorists are usually concerned.

Just war theorists fall in the middle of the spectrum between anti-war pacifists, on one end (war is never morally justified) and political realists, on the other end (war is easily or always morally justified, or falls outside of moral constraints altogether).

> **Just War Position:** *War can be morally justified, when certain stringent, normative conditions are met.*

These conditions fall into three general categories:

> **Jus ad bellum:** *The justice of going to war* (when, if ever, may a group go to war?)
> **Jus in bello:** *Justice in war* (what may individuals fighting in a war do?)
> **Jus post bellum:** *Justice after war* (how should groups transition from war to peace?)

This classification scheme reflects general thinking about wars as discrete events that have a beginning, a middle, and an end. When you may start a war is a separate question from what you may do in a war, which is itself a separate question from when and how you should end a war. To what extent these are wholly separate categories is a matter of debate within just war theory; but most agree that this is a useful conceptual schema for thinking morally about war. If nothing else, it encourages us to view wars as events that *should* end, rather than going on perpetually! Let us consider the specific conditions of each category in turn.

1.1. Jus Ad Bellum

When we ask the general question of whether war can be justified, we might be asking the more specific question, is it ever right to go to war? The category of jus ad bellum focuses on this question and says that it is only right to go to war when the following conditions are met.

- **Just Cause:** *The war must be an attempt to block, stop, or mitigate/ameliorate unjustified aggression.*
- **Right Intention:** *The group going to war intends to achieve the just cause; it is not using it as an excuse to pursue some other unjustified end.*
- **Reasonable Prospect of Success:** *Going to war is sufficiently likely to achieve the just cause.*
- **Proportionality:** *The just cause that will be achieved by the war must be good enough, or important enough, to outweigh the inevitable bad effects that the war will also cause.*
- **Last Resort (Necessity):** *There must be no other less harmful way to achieve the just cause.*
- ***Legitimate Authority:** *The group going to war must have the authority to fight such wars.*

While just war theorists often argue about how to interpret these conditions (what counts as a "reasonable" chance of success? How should we weigh bad effects against good possibilities?), they mostly agree that these conditions are all necessary, in one form or another, for *jus ad bellum*. I place a star by legitimate authority, because of the *jus ad bellum* conditions, this is the one whose inclusion is most commonly questioned in the contemporary era (Coady 2004; Fabre 2008; Lazar 2016; Reitberger 2013). For many philosophers, it appears to be a throwback to the medieval European idea that wars can only be fought between states, and so if the head of state does not declare a war, then no war exists. This is clearly false—all we need to do is look at events such as the Vietnam War (which was famously never declared as such by the U.S. government) to see that. However, there may be something to legitimate authority, in the sense that war involves organized political groups, and not just any member of a group can commit the group to war. For the group to go to war, its authoritative decision-maker (whether that be an individual person or a subgroup of the group as a whole) must decide that the group will do so.

Jus ad bellum is traditionally conceived of as being separate from *jus in bello* because it involves different groups of actors and decision-makers. For instance, in the United States, Congress and the President commit the U.S. military to war. The members of the U.S. military have no say in the matter; they must do as they are commanded (or face severe penalty). Conversely, Congress and the President do not typically decide military strategy, tactics, and rules; that is mostly up to the military itself. In other words, the political authority of the group is responsible for jus ad bellum, for the decision to go to war; the military arm of the group is responsible for jus in bello, for the decisions about how to fight that war. So, we now turn to jus in bello.

1.2. Jus In Bello

When we ask the general question, can war be justified, we might be asking the more specific question, is it ever possible to fight justly? After all, the political authority of a group may decide to—and is historically likely to—commit their group to an unjust war. (Wholly pacifist societies, and wholly just societies, are historically and contemporaneously rare.) World War I leaps to mind here as a classic case of a war that was committed to unjustly on all sides. Alternatively, the political authority of a group may push its military to commit atrocities in the service of an initially just war. Consider the famous example of British Prime Minister Winston Churchill ordering the RAF (Royal Air Force) to bomb civilian centers in World War II. (Note that the then-commander of the RAF Bomber Command, Arthur Harris, could have legally and morally refused that order—although he did not—as it contravened the *jus in bello* laws and moral conditions of war. This further demonstrates the traditional distinction between jus ad bellum and jus in bello.)

Some just war theorists, often called **traditionalists,** claim that it is possible for warfighters to fight wars well, or justly—even wars that don't meet the standards of jus ad bellum—when certain moral constraints are obeyed (Lazar 2017). That is, warfighters fighting in an unjust war, or on the unjust side of a war, can still act morally correctly, so long as they meet the following conditions of jus in bello.

- **Discrimination (Noncombatant Immunity):** *Warfighters must always discriminate between military targets and civilian targets (both objects and people), and may intentionally attack only military targets. (In other words, noncombatants are morally immune from intentional attack.)*
- **Proportionality:** *The advantage achieved from any military action must be good enough, or important enough, to outweigh the foreseen but unintended bad effects caused by that same action.*
- **Necessity:** *The least harmful means possible to achieve any particular military goal must be used.*

One of the key ideas behind jus in bello is to create the possibility of a fair fight: an old definition of warfare is combat between combatants. "Combat between combatants" carries connotations of honor and equity, in the sense that outside, irrelevant factors should not be pulled in to create an unfair advantage or disadvantage on either side. For instance, kidnapping a warfighter's child to force them to stop fighting is, we might say, cheating—it takes what should be an irrelevant factor to a combatant's warfighting abilities (that they have a child) and makes it scarily relevant. Who wins the war should be determined by strength of arms and strategic intelligence, rather than by which side is most willing to engage in indiscriminate scorched earth, total war tactics and accept Pyrrhic victories.

Traditionalists argue that, so long as the warfighters on all sides adhere to jus in bello constraints, they are all acting morally correctly (despite the fact that they are trying to kill each other, and despite the fact that at least some of them must be fighting for the unjust, or wrong, side). This concept is referred to as the **moral equality of combatants** (Walzer 2006, 34–41). It is based on the recognition that, in contemporary war, it is mostly, if not purely, a matter of luck whether warfighters happen to be on the just or unjust side of the war, and so they ought not be regarded as responsible for the jus ad bellum decisions of their respective groups.

Consider Jim from Indiana and Hans from Berlin, both 18-year-olds fighting on the Western Front in World War II. (I take it as given that Germany was on the unjust side of World War II, while the United States was on the just side. While World War II is not a perfect example of a just war, it is often taken as a close-to-paradigm case by contemporary just war theorists.) Neither Jim nor Hans could have influenced their respective countries' broader political positions or decisions to go to war. Both have been heavily influenced by domestic political propaganda, and as a result, both believe that their side is fighting a just war. Neither are aware that their side is committing, or planning to commit, war crimes. (Germany hid the Holocaust from its frontline soldiers, while the United States hid the Manhattan Project.) Both face serious formal and informal socio-political-legal penalties if they refuse to fight or otherwise aid their countries' war efforts. Given these factors, which generalize to other contemporary wars as well, traditionalists claim that Jim and Hans are morally equal; Hans is not a criminal, or morally evil, for fighting on Germany's side. So long as both Jim and Hans fight according to jus in bello constraints (neither engages in terrorist activities), and obey international laws of war as outlined in the Hague (pre-World War II) and Geneva (post-World War II) Conventions, they are morally on a par. Neither is a criminal, or morally evil, simply for fighting in accordance with moral and legal wartime rules of force.

Revisionist just war theorists, by contrast, maintain that jus ad bellum and jus in bello are conceptually connected, such that warfighters on the unjust side of a war act wrongly when they fight, even if they follow jus in bello constraints (Lazar 2017). They argue that while Hans might be a good warfighter, in the sense that he is able to complete the military tasks to which he is set without breaking international laws or jus in bello constraints, we are confusing his fighting well with his being moral. By analogy, we can speak of committing a crime well; but we do not mean this in a moral sense.

Prohibition-era Chicago mobster Al Capone, while a good criminal, wasn't really *morally* good, because he was engaged in overall unjust activities. Similarly, revisionists argue that Hans is not acting morally correctly, because he is fighting for an unjust cause. Just because he does not know—and perhaps could not reasonably be expected to know—that he is engaged in an unjust, wrong pursuit, does not mean that he is not, in fact, acting wrongly.

Revisionists argue that we should distinguish between subjective and objective justification (McMahan 2009). Subjective justification comes from the reasons Hans himself has, while objective justification comes from the reasons that exist independently of Hans. Revisionists do not argue that we should *blame* Hans for fighting; blame is a function of not being subjectively justified, and it appears that Hans is subjectively justified in fighting for Germany. Nevertheless, they argue that Hans is not objectively justified, and so it is morally wrong for him to fight. He is *not*, contra the traditionalists, morally on a par with Jim, who is objectively justified in fighting for the United States.

Despite this ongoing debate between traditionalists and revisionists about the moral equality of combatants, both agree that the jus in bello conditions set out above are pragmatically important. If nothing else, they form part of the basis for the international laws of war, which function as legal constraints on warfare in the actual world. While international laws of war are not, and have never been, followed perfectly, they do have an actual impact on what many warfighters are willing and unwilling to do in combat (McMahan 2009). So, if either Jim or Hans break said laws or the moral conditions of jus in bello on which those laws are based, that is a different matter. Traditionalists and revisionists agree, if they do commit such crimes or atrocities during the course of fighting, then they are legally and morally guilty, and ought to be held accountable, either during or after the war. This leads to the question of how groups should end wars, and permissibly transition back to peace. So, we now turn to jus post bellum.

1.3. Jus Post Bellum

The question of how to permissibly transition from war to peace is a (very) contemporary addition to the Western just war tradition. However, it comprises a prominent part of the Chinese just war tradition; many classical Chinese theorists argue that serious investigation is needed to determine how the ruler should restore social and political harmony after war. Harmony, in the Chinese tradition, is a moralized notion; socio-political harmony does not refer merely to everyone more or less "getting along," but rather to a society organized in such a way that all of its members have access to the material, cultural, and spiritual resources necessary to live good lives and maintain their prosocial community (Twiss and Lo 2015). The cultivation and promotion of socio-political harmony is crucial to the classical Chinese theorists, because without such harmony, war will inevitably erupt again (Lewis and Kling 2022). So peace without harmony, or what the Western tradition might call justice, is no true peace at all.

There must be moral standards for moving from war to peace, so that the resulting socio-political situation is not seriously unjust and hence a prelude to future war. Philosopher Brian Orend (2000) proposes the following conditions for jus post bellum in the Western tradition.

- **Just Cause for Termination:** *A group may terminate a war when the just cause of the war has been reasonably satisfied, and when the aggressor is willing to negotiate terms of surrender that include rolling back any unjust gains from its aggression and submitting to reasonable principles of punishment (such as compensation, war crimes trials, and perhaps rehabilitation).*
- **Right Intention:** *The group terminating the war must intend to create a just and lasting peace by following only the conditions set out in the other jus post bellum principles. Revenge may not be intended. In addition, the group terminating the war must hold itself to equal investigation and prosecution of any war crimes committed by its, or its allies', armed forces.*
- **Public Declaration and Legitimate Authority:** *The terms of the peace must be publicly proclaimed and accepted by legitimate authorities of the groups at war.*
- **Discrimination:** *The victorious group must discriminate between the political and military leaders, the warfighters, and the civilians of the aggressor group when setting the terms of the peace. Punitive measures should be*

> *focused on those most responsible for the aggression and any war crimes, and undue and unfair hardship is not to be brought upon the civilian population in particular.*
>
> • **Proportionality:** *The terms of the peace must vindicate victims' rights without engaging in absolutist crusades against, or draconian punishments for, aggression. The defeated group must be permitted to participate in the world community.*

In addition, a war should be terminated if a group can no longer adhere to the conditions of jus ad bellum and jus in bello. For instance, if it becomes impossible for a group to fight without using excessive or indiscriminate force, then that group should withdraw from the war in question. But as the pacifist tradition notes, this does not mean that the group must give up on their political goals (assuming those goals are just); they need not become passive. Rather, they must instead use other, non-war methods to achieve their objectives.

Jus post bellum, because of its relative newness, is currently somewhat under-theorized in the Western tradition. Happily, we can here return to the Chinese just war tradition for a robust debate about the importance of harmony versus what is sometimes referred to as order (Li 2006). Order involves instituting a rule-based socio-political system where it is possible for everyone in the society to follow the rules, and it is likely that they will do so (either because they view those rules as authoritative, or because they are sufficiently afraid of the penalties that come with breaking the rules, or because they are unwilling to cause social and political upset). However, while having an ordered society is necessary, it is not sufficient for having a harmonious society; for that to occur, the socio-political rules must be conducive to individual and group flourishing. Flourishing involves not only forward-looking considerations, such as access to resources, but also, when a war has occurred, backward-looking considerations, such as reparations to victims for material, cultural, and spiritual harms. So, ending a war well essentially involves aiming at the ideal of social and political harmony, while also instituting and promoting socio-political order (Sawyer 2007). Jus post bellum thus seeks, at its core, to prevent future wars.

A key pacifist critique of just war theory is that war, in actual fact, is endlessly cyclical. War begets war, which begets yet more war, and so on and so forth. History, admittedly, supports this view. We need only look at the Wars of the Roses, or the 100 Years' War, or World Wars I and II, to see that. The only way to end the cycle of mass violence, carnage, and death, an anti-war pacifist might reasonably say, is to never start it. There is a fundamental disagreement here about the moral justification for starting wars; the anti-war pacifist argues that it is never morally justified to start a war, while the just war theorist argues that it is sometimes morally justified to start a war. But aside from that disagreement, the just war theorist can also respond to the pacifist concerned about the cyclical nature of war by agreeing with the worry, and then citing the importance of jus post bellum. Jus post bellum deserves more attention than it has so far received in the contemporary era, precisely because it is an attempt to break the recognized cycle of warfare and bring about a just and lasting peace.

1.4. The Goal of JWT

The entire goal of jus ad bellum, jus in bello, and jus post bellum is to restrict warfare to only those wars that are necessary and proportionate (Kling 2019a). War is truly horrific; it involves mass destruction and death, most commonly of those who are caught in the conflict through no fault of their own. From these facts, just war theorists, like pacifists, arrive at the claim that war is normally unjustified. In the usual course of events, groups may not go to war with each other. Instead, they must seek to resolve their conflicts nonviolently, via the multiplicity of non-war methods that are available. It is only when extraordinary action is needed in response to the threat or fact of unjust aggression that war becomes possibly justified. And even then, it must be a last resort (Lazar 2020). As the Chinese just war tradition insists, the military should be used only when there is no alternative. To quote briefly, "The Sage King does not take any pleasure in using the army ... he takes it seriously that his action will hurt people, other living beings and property. Weapons are ominous instruments, and the Dao of Heaven abhors them. However, when you have no choice but to use them, it accords with the Dao of Heaven" (Lo 2012, 410). This focus on necessity across the board emphasizes that just war theory, despite its numerous internal debates, is closer to contingent pacifism than political realism.

Consider Harvard law professor Roger Fisher's unorthodox suggestion for preventing nuclear war (1981): He proposes implanting the nuclear launch codes in a volunteer, in a little capsule next to their heart. The volunteer would carry a butcher knife with them as they accompanied the President daily. If the President ever decided to use nuclear weapons, the only way to actually do so would be for the President to take the butcher knife and lethally eviscerate the volunteer. Fisher argues that this scenario brings home the horror of war in a way that death statistics often fail to do. Broadly, war asks, and often demands, that people kill other people, which in everyday life, is a grave moral wrong. So the question is, under what conditions may we permissibly make such an ask? The anti-war pacifist's answer is that we may never do so. The just war theorist's answer is that we may do so only in extraordinary circumstances, when all other avenues are exhausted, and even in such extreme situations, we must require that proportionality be observed.

This sets just war theory apart from political **realism**, which states that war is easily or always morally justified, or that war is outside of the moral realm altogether. In response to the first branch of realism, it is difficult to reconcile the awful carnage of war with blasé claims that war is not really so bad, or that states may always do whatever is in their best interests to do, including go to war. First, war is clearly very bad; we need only look at the death tolls of the 20th century's World Wars to see that. Second, it is patently false that states may always do whatever is in their best interests; as human constructions, they are constrained by human morality, and egoism is not, I would venture to say, a serious moral philosophy (Walzer 2006). In response to the second branch of realism, war is a human activity. Although it is often metaphorically compared to natural disasters, it is in fact created, perpetuated, regulated, and shaped by human beings, acting in concert (Kling 2019c). And as a collective human activity, war is subject to morality. It may be extraordinary, but it is not actually a tsunami or hurricane that we are all passively subject to, whether we will or no. The just war theorist and the pacifist are in agreement here, against the realist: war is a series of difficult, but essentially moral, choices.

1.5. Moral Underpinnings of JWT

War requires very strong reasons to be morally justified. In the contemporary era, these usually take the form of rights-based, deontological reasons or, less commonly, consequentialist or utilitarian reasons. I set out the basics of each moral framework in this subsection, to complete my outline of contemporary just war theory. When seen through a rights-based lens, justification for war often takes the form of permission rather than obligation. A group *may* go to war—that is, it may engage its right of defense—if the jus ad bellum conditions are met, but it does not *have* to do so. The right to do something is not a requirement to do it. To take a domestic example, my right to free speech gives me permission to criticize the U.S. President's policies and actions; but it does not require me to do so. I am within my rights to stay silent. Arguably, the same holds for war. When the jus ad bellum conditions are met, a group is permitted to go to war, but it need not do so. It is within its rights to do nothing, to surrender, to call for international aid, to resist nonviolently, or to resist violently through force short of war (more on this concept later).

Few theorists in the just war tradition argue that a group is obliged to engage its right of self-defense when the jus ad bellum conditions are met. To say that a state *must* go to war when it is threatened or attacked comes uncomfortably close to realism or, even more radically, a kind of militarism. One theorist that comes close to this view, however, is Walzer, who is sometimes called the "dean of just war theory." He argues that a state, or group, going to war in self-defense, when the jus ad bellum conditions are met, while not strictly speaking obligatory, is praiseworthy. There is something good, he writes, about a people or a group being willing to stand up for themselves and fight back when they are the targets of unjust aggression (Walzer 2006, 70–71). This idea lines up with parts of the Native American just war tradition, wherein going to war is never required, but can be a worthy assertion of a group's dignity, humanity, and way of life in the face of those who would deny, denigrate, or destroy them. War can thus be admirable, when it is a fight against what Black Hawk of the Sauk (1767–1838) refers to as environmental, social, and political "poison" (Black Hawk 1832).

Consider the case of Finland in World War II. Finland declared war against the Soviet Union, in what is referred to by historians as the "Winter War" (Edwards 2006). The Finnish declaration of war was in response to the Red Army invading 70 miles of Finland in order to block the eastern German offensive against Leningrad. Despite assurances from Moscow that the Red Army would retreat after Germany was defeated, Finland refused to cede the border territory to the Soviet Union, and after negotiations failed, declared war in late 1939. After massive military and civilian casualties on both sides, Finland agreed to cede both the contested territory and additional territory to the Soviet Union, and the Moscow Peace Treaty between Finland and the Soviet Union was signed in March of 1940.

With the benefit of hindsight, we might say that all things considered, Finland should not have gone to war against the Soviet Union. This is especially true given that the Winter War took both Soviet and Finnish attention away from the eastern German offensive, which arguably enabled the German offensive to maintain complete control over Poland, Latvia, Lithuania, and Estonia. Needless to say, this was very bad: over 3 million of the 6 million Jewish victims killed in the Holocaust were Polish (Berenbaum 2006, 104). An anti-war pacifist might rightly point to the Winter War, especially in light of this information, as an example of the deep futility and harmfulness of war. Defending against unjust aggression, they might say, is simply not worth the inevitable aftermath. But Finland could not have known this in advance; so the question from the rights-based just war point of view becomes, was their decision to engage in defensive war admirable or praiseworthy, as well as permissible?

By contrast, we might read contemporary just war theory through a consequentialist or utilitarian lens. Consequentialism, as a moral framework, focuses on consequences as the determining factor in whether some action is right or wrong, good or bad. Importantly, consequentialism weighs short- and long-term consequences for everyone equally; so, you should do what you have good reason to believe will lead to the best state of affairs for everyone overall, rather than doing what is likely to have good short-term effects for you, but bad long-term effects for everyone else. Although just war theorists rarely take up a purely consequentialist framework (they are more likely to combine deontological and consequentialist considerations), it is possible to view just war theory as a kind of rule consequentialism. Rule consequentialism claims that determining what action, or set of actions, is likely to have the best consequences in any particular case is very difficult, if not impossible. So instead, we should follow rules of thumb which have been developed over time as moral rules for action, or codes of conduct, that are most likely to lead to the best results. Within this moral framework, the conditions of jus ad bellum, jus in bello, and jus post bellum are such rules of thumb; we should follow them when reasoning about war, because they have been developed over time to bring about the best possible results.

The difficulty with viewing contemporary just war theory through a purely rule consequentialist lens is that such rules of thumb always have thresholds beyond which they do not hold. For instance, consider the jus in bello condition of discrimination, which states that only military targets may be intentionally attacked. On a rights-based understanding of just war theory, this is because non-combatant targets have the right not to be attacked; they have not lost their security rights by engaging in warfare. As such, they are immune from attack, regardless of the consequences. But on a rule consequentialist understanding of just war theory, discrimination is a requirement because generally speaking, war goes better, overall and in the long run, when noncombatants are not attacked.

Now, surely there are exceptions to this rule; what if attacking civilians is the only way to prevent a fascist victory? It was precisely this reasoning that led Winston Churchill to order the RAF to bomb German civilian centers in World War II. (Notably, it was a variant of this reasoning that led U.S. President Harry Truman to authorize dropping atomic bombs on Hiroshima and Nagasaki during that same war.) The concern with a rule consequentialist approach to just war theory, then, is that it erases the absoluteness of the stringent moral conditions found in jus ad bellum, jus in bello, and jus post bellum. These conditions seek to make the bar for justifying war extremely high; if we soften them in this way, war becomes worryingly easier, although still difficult, to justify.

Summary

In this section, we set out contemporary just war theory, along with some of its major debates, points of contention, and areas in need of development. We considered a series of definitional and conceptual questions about war and peace, and introduced some historical case studies and thought experiments to aid our thought processes. Finally, we noted the importance of engaging with moral frameworks when discussing whether war can be justified.

2. Three Standard Arguments for Just War

Having outlined contemporary just war theory, let us now turn to some of the most prominent arguments in support of justified war, all of which revolve around the right to respond to unjustified aggression. While historically religious or resource wars were regarded as justified, in today's world, war is regarded as possibly justified only when it is defensive in nature. Such defense can take three forms: self-defense against an external unjustified threat or aggressive action, self-defense against an internal unjustified threat or aggressive action, or other-defense (against either an external or internal unjustified threat or aggressive action). I consider each argument in turn.

2.1. Self-Defense against External Unjustified Threats or Aggressive Actions: Repelling or Blocking Outside Invasion or Attack

It is relatively non-controversial that individuals have rights to autonomy and bodily integrity. If someone violates those rights—either by trying to make you do something you don't want to do, or by trying to injure your body without your consent—you have the right to defend yourself. This right of self-defense is sometimes called a corollary right; it follows from your rights to autonomy and bodily integrity. Without a corollary right to self-defense, your rights to autonomy and bodily integrity wouldn't be worth very much, practically speaking. Of course, to what degree you can defend yourself depends on a variety of factors, including the seriousness of the threat or injury, the broader context in which the threat or injury is occurring, and what options for action you have in the moment. But the baseline claim, that you may defend your autonomy and bodily integrity when they are unjustly attacked, still stands.

States, and other organized political non-state groups, being made up of individuals, have rights analogous to autonomy and bodily integrity. Just as individuals may defend themselves then they are unjustly attacked, so too may states and polities defend themselves. This comparison between individuals and polities is sometimes called the **domestic analogy**, and it is common in just war theory. However, it is important to note that the domestic analogy is only an analogy; it provides a helpful analogue for thinking about defensive war, but is not by itself an argument for states' or polities' rights (Kling 2015). For such an argument, we must turn briefly to domestic political philosophy. In the liberal social contract tradition, states or polities have rights because individuals consent to transfer some of their individual rights to the state or polity, which then wields those rights for the good of all. States or polities maintain their rights so long as they retain the consent of their people and act for the common good (Locke 2004).[1] For our purposes, the two state or polity rights that matter are political sovereignty and territorial integrity.

2.1.1. Political Sovereignty

The state or polity right analogous to individual autonomy is political sovereignty.

> **Political Sovereignty:** *The right of a state or polity to make and implement its own laws, policies, and procedures, and more broadly, to run itself, free from undue outside or external interference.*

Political sovereignty is worth defending with war, if need be, because of its direct links to the values of human dignity and autonomy. One way of respecting individuals' dignity and autonomy is to allow them to make their own choices about (1) what political system they want to live under, and (2) the overall shape and particular structure of that political system. Even when we think people are making bad political choices for themselves, the principle of respect demands that we let them do so. (This is, however, limited by considerations of other people's dignity and autonomy. If people's bad choices seriously impact other's rights without their consent, then we can curtail or block those choices.) Broadly, states' political sovereignty is an instantiation of their members' dignity and autonomy, and so political sovereignty is worth defending to the extent that individual dignity and autonomy are worth defending.

Like any other right, political sovereignty is not absolute or unbounded. There are limits to a state's or polity's sovereign powers, in much the same way that there are limits to an individual's autonomy. Your autonomy does not give you the right to punch another person in the face, or threaten to do so, unprovoked; similarly, political sovereignty does not give a state the right to invade and take over, or threaten to invade and take over, other states or polities unprovoked. To do so would be an act of unjust aggression. When political sovereignty is unjustly threatened or attacked in such a way, a state's corollary right of self-defense kicks in, and they may defend themselves from such aggression. Such defense, as we discussed earlier, should be nonviolent if possible, violent only if necessary.

2.1.2. Territorial Integrity

The state or polity right analogous to individual bodily integrity is territorial integrity.

Territorial Integrity: *The right of a state or polity to maintain its recognized territory and territorial boundaries.*

Territorial integrity is worth defending with war, if necessary, because it is a recognition of the fact that people have bodies, and so must have a place to live and create community. Despite analytic Western philosophy's historical focus on the mind as the essential element of humanity, humans are not simply "brains on sticks." We are minds and bodies, together, and so need space to stand and build physical communities in concert with others. In addition, we need that physical space to be somewhat secure and dependable over time, so that we can make and fulfill both personal and social life plans. Without secure territory, it is very difficult to live a flourishing life. So, states' territorial integrity is worth defending to the extent that its people's lives and essential communal spaces are worth defending.

Unlike our own bodies, the right to territorial integrity is complicated by the fact that historically, all territory has changed hands multiple times, often—if not always—unjustifiably. Current territorial boundaries are the product of genocide, land grabs, unjustified war, artificial encroachment, and a whole host of other straightforward moral and political wrongs. Existing states and polities would do well to recognize these facts, and work to repair their territorial wrongdoings. But even in light of the moral arbitrariness of current territorial boundaries, it is still true that we have to draw boundaries somewhere. There must be a line where one polity stops and another begins; otherwise, we lose the concept of separate states or polities altogether. (Perhaps the world would be better off without territorially bounded states or polities, or indeed, without any states or polities at all. I address this critique in Section 5.) So, when territories and territorial boundaries are under unjustified threat or attack, to the extent that such aggression threatens political sovereignty and individual autonomy, states' corollary right of self-defense kicks in, and they may defend themselves.

Underlying the importance of both political sovereignty and territorial integrity is the basic idea that part of protecting life is protecting people's chosen ways of life (so long as those ways of life don't essentially involve wronging others). A state or polity's primary job, we might think, is to protect its members and enable them to live their versions of full and flourishing lives (Aristotle 2017; Locke 2004). To be left literally alive, but without the material, cultural, political, or spiritual resources that people need to map out and fulfill their life plans and projects, is a kind of death. To be sure, it is not death proper, but it is devastating in a way that Chief Joseph of the Nez Percé (1840–1904) describes poignantly:

> You might as well expect all rivers to run backward as that any man who was born a free man should be contented penned up and denied liberty to go where he pleases. If you tie a horse to a stake, do you expect he will grow fat? If you pen an Indian up on a small spot of earth and compel him to stay there, he will not be contented nor will he grow and prosper. I have asked some of the Great White Chiefs where they get their authority to say to the Indian that he shall stay in one place, while he sees white men going where they please. They cannot tell me.
> (Fee 1936, 282)

The just war tradition claims that these unjust losses may be protected against, with nonviolent methods if possible, with war if necessary. It is morally permissible to die on your feet, fighting or resisting outside unjust invasion and attack, rather than live on your knees.

2.1.3. Defensive and Pre-Emptive War

When states or polities are subject to unjust outside aggression, fighting, nonviolently resisting, or submitting are the choices with which they are faced. Such unjust aggression can take the form of threats or action. When groups fight to repel outside invasion or attack, that is **defensive war**. When groups fight to block or prevent threatened outside invasion or attack, that is **preemptive war**. Defensive war is the most straightforwardly justifiable type of war. Although states or polities are different from individuals, in that a blow that would be lethal for an individual is often survivable by a state, roughly the same rights-based principles of defense hold. If someone unjustly hits me in the head with a baseball bat in a dark alley and I (1) survive and (2) can't do anything else to defend myself (there is no time to call the police, I can't run because it's a dead-end alleyway, no one answers my yell for help, etc.), then I am allowed to defend myself by hitting back. Similarly, if Japan unjustly attacks the United States by bombing one of its naval bases, and the United States can't do anything else to defend itself (diplomatic efforts stall out, allies are unresponsive/unable to provide aid, further disastrous attacks are immanent, etc.), then the United States is allowed to defend itself by hitting back.

Throughout these exchanges, necessity and proportionality must, morally speaking, be obeyed. Just as I may not respond to an attack with violence when I could easily run away toward help and safety, so too states may not respond with war when diplomacy or other nonviolent methods, such as sanctions, would suffice to stop further unjust aggression. And just as I may not respond to a trespasser by shooting them, so too states may not respond to minor strikes with all-out war. (I will note that, in the United States, "Trespassers Will Be Shot" signs are common. But these are patently morally ridiculous, as it is wildly disproportionate to value the pristineness of one's property over another person's life.) The difference between minor strikes and major attacks is difficult, but it has to do with whether political sovereignty or territorial integrity are being seriously infringed upon or violated. When serious infringements or violations are occurring, only then may war be proportionate.

To be clear, necessity and proportionality constraints on self-defense are not always observed, either by individuals or by military and political decision-makers. But to recognize that such moral conditions are not always followed is different than saying that they should not be moral conditions at all. The fact that people commit murder does not lead us to conclude that we should not have laws against murder; similarly, the fact that people, states, and polities do not always conform to the constraints built into the right of self-defense should not lead us to conclude that self-defense either does not, or should not, include such constraints. Rather, it should lead us to investigate how we might better motivate individuals, and military and political decision-makers, to take seriously and obey the moral dictates of necessity and proportionality.

Importantly, we can meet these standards of self-defense without having to wait until the blow actually falls to strike back. If I see the aggressor coming at me with the bat, I do not have to wait until he attacks to defend myself. Recognizing a serious imminent threat, I may engage in pro-active defense of my autonomy and bodily integrity. Similarly, states or polities may engage in preemptive war, or preemptive strikes, when the threat of unjust aggression is serious and imminent (Walzer 2006). For a threat to be serious, it must be both materially present, and have the capacity to do great harm. So, threatening me with the pool noodle you're holding, though materially present, is not serious, because it does not have the capacity to greatly harm me. Meanwhile, threatening me with sharks with laser beams is also not a serious threat, because while such an attack would greatly harm me, I have no reason to think such laser sharks are materially present (or even exist). Similarly, the global community mostly ignored North Korea's threats of nuclear annihilation before 2006, when it received evidence that North Korea has a working nuclear program (U.S. Defense Department 2015). Subsequently, such a threat has been, and still is, regarded as serious by the international community.

Whether such a threat is imminent, however, is a separate question. Imminent threats are those where the attack is highly likely to occur at any moment. The North Korean threat is serious, but not imminent, given North Korea's long history of threatening warfare without subsequent action, and its ongoing diplomatic engagement with China. A public condition of Chinese support for North Korea is that North Korea restrain itself from engaging in aggressive aerial bombardment of its enemies. So long as China-North Korea relations are ongoing, then, the likelihood of a North Korean attack is relatively low (U.S. Defense Department 2015). Not impossible, certainly, but low enough that there is time to attempt to de-escalate the threatening situation in other ways, via nonviolent political pressures and incentives. When there is such time, the imminence condition is not met, and so preemptive attacks or wars are not morally permitted. In other words, while you do not have to wait for the bat to hit your head, you do have to see that it's coming toward you before preemptively attacking. Otherwise, you're the one engaging in unjust aggression. In the world of war, preventative offense is not morally acceptable defense. Only pre-emptive and reactive defense, in response to threatened or actual serious rights violations, are possibly morally justified.

2.2. Self-Defense against Internal Unjustified Threats or Aggressive Actions: Emancipatory or Liberatory Revolutionary Struggle

When we ask the question, can war be morally justified, we might have in mind the wars between states—France versus Great Britain, Japan versus China, the United States versus Germany. But alter-natively, we might have in mind the wars that often occur within states, such as the American Revolutionary War, the Spanish Civil War, and the Russian Revolution. Traditionally, just war theory has focused on external unjust aggression, that is, wars between states or polities. Non-international conflicts—wars internal to a state or polity—are relatively undertheorized in the Western just war tradition (Meisels 2014). But in recent years, it has started to turn its attention to internal unjust aggression. Much like instances of international unjust aggression, the question of when, if ever, revolution or civil war is justified comes down to what people may do in defense of their fundamental individual or group rights.

> **Revolution** is *rejection of the current regime's authority and an attempt to replace it.*

It is difficult to distinguish between revolution and civil war. It might have to do with the size of each side. Revolutions are sometimes characterized as small bands of revolutionaries against large government forces, while civil wars are sometimes thought of as groups of roughly equal size fighting each other. Or, it might have to do with how things turn out historically. Revolutions are those internal conflicts that succeed or fail fairly rapidly, while civil wars are those internal conflicts that continue on for years and do not have a satisfactory, or just, resolution. Both of these ways of conceiving of the difference are arbitrary and don't capture important historical cases; revolutions can involve large numbers of people and can take several years, while civil wars can be lopsided and fast. And both can lead to justice more equally enjoyed by all, or to more severe, widespread oppression and human rights abuses.

Following classical Chinese theorists, I think it is best to regard the revolution/civil war distinction as merely a naming convention that does not actually point to any important differences (Tiwald 2008). The focus is on war within a state or polity; whether we refer to that conflict as a revolution or a civil war does not matter. What matters is whether those who instigate the conflict have the right to rebel, that is, whether it is permissible for them to reject their existing government's authority and attempt to replace it. So, I will refer to such internal conflict as "revolution" throughout, and this term, as I understand it, covers civil war as well.

The right to rebel, understood politically as a group right, is closely linked to the right of political sovereignty. Theoretically speaking, it is a corollary right that follows from understanding political sovereignty as a group instantiation of people's individual rights to dignity and autonomy. Because people, organized into political groups, have the right to decide for themselves about the nature and structure of their political systems, they also have the right to rebel against those systems when such systems no longer fulfill their function of protecting their members and their rights (Locke 2004; Walzer 2006). Of course, this right to rebel is not absolute or unlimited; like all rights, it has boundaries, which I discuss in more depth throughout this sub-section.

Famously, Enlightenment philosopher Immanuel Kant argues that revolution is never justified, not even in response to the most oppressive and genocidal of governments. This is because the state is the source of political authority, and so an attack on the state is an attack on political authority itself, which is, according to Kant's political philosophy, an attack on the very foundations of freedom (Hill 2012). Kant's point here is complicated; the idea is that the destruction of political authority is always wrong, because it inevitably leads to lawlessness, which is the opposite of freedom. Political power vacuums are undoubtedly dangerous—we need only look to the Somali Civil War, ongoing since a series of violent rebellions in 2009, to see this. With over seven political factions at war, and no stable government, the Somali civilian population has been subjected to indiscriminate attacks and killings, forced displacement, sexual violence and other violent threats, extortion, violation of their civil and human rights, and the forced recruitment of their children to become child soldiers, among other horrors (Human Rights Watch 2020). Clearly, Somali civilians are not free in any meaningful sense of the term. Faced with this, you might conclude, with Kant, that any government is better than no government.

But it seems clear that not every attack on the dominant political authority must be anarchic in nature; many revolutionary movements are not attempts to institute anarchism, but rather are attempts to wrest political authority away from the current government and put it in the hands of those less likely to engage in severe, widespread political oppression and human rights abuses. Such liberatory struggles are not about destroying political authority full stop. The goal is, instead, to transfer it to those who will use it better and more justly. To be sure, not every revolution is justified, because not every such struggle is in response to severe, widespread political oppression and human rights abuses. But when they are, they may be morally justified (Finlay 2017).

Certainly, revolution is never *legal*; it would be paradoxical for governments to legally allow for their own overthrow (Hill 2012). But the question here is not one of legality, but of morality. This is where the Geneva Conventions and other domestic laws of war and contemporary just war theory diverge. Because the just war tradition is concerned with moral justifications for war and moral constraints on warfare, it ultimately views the law as informative but not decisive. So, the fact that revolution is illegal is not a sufficient reason to refrain from engaging in it. Sometimes, the greatest harms and wrongs to people come from their own political leaders, and as just war theory is concerned with how we ought morally to respond to serious and direct large-scale political violence, it must pay attention to this fact.

Consider the Haitian Revolution. Between 1791 and 1804, enslaved locally-born black people and newly-enslaved Africans, as well as other captives and free persons of color, revolted against French colonial rule and white slaveholders, eventually successfully forming the sovereign state of Haiti, wherein slavery was abolished and all on the island were legally equal (Knight 2000). The uprising was in response to long-standing, widespread brutality by slaveholders and their employees against the enslaved, including mass rape, systemic whippings, castrations, and burnings, and an astronomical death toll (over 50% of newly arrived Africans died within a year of arriving in

Haiti) (Dubois 2004). King Louis XIV of France passed the infamous Code Noir in 1685 in an attempt to lessen and regulate such violence, but slaveholders openly and consistently ignored the law, and successfully passed local legislation to reverse key parts of it throughout the 1700s (Dubois 2004). In addition to such vicious cruelty across generations, a rigid class hierarchy developed on the island, wherein non-aristocratic whites' legal, civic, and economic rights were severely limited, as were those of free persons of color. As French historian Paul Fregosi puts it, "Everyone—quite rightly—lived in terror of everyone else. ... Haiti was hell" (Fregosi 1989; as cited in Perry 2005, 61–62).

The revolution was marked by extreme violence throughout its duration, on both sides; the rules of jus in bello were frequently broken, as were many of the conditions of jus post bellum in 1804, at the conclusion of the war. However, it seems difficult to say that the hundreds of thousands of brutalized and terrorized enslaved, captive, and oppressed peoples acted wrongly when they banded together and revolted in 1791. They were defending their lives, their basic human rights, and their fundamental well-being, in the only way left to them.

Contemporary just war theorist Christopher Finlay argues that revolution is morally justified when systematic subjugation and oppression of a particular social group (or groups) within the society is rampant and severe, and there is no clear hope for political change via democratic, civil mechanisms (either because those mechanisms do not exist, or because they have been subverted and undermined) (Finlay 2017, 19–52). In other words, people have a right to attempt revolution if their government or political authority is systematically and severely violating their human rights to dignity, autonomy, and bodily integrity, among others (Smith 2008, 436). So, when a government is enslaving, beating, killing, and otherwise seriously subjugating its own people, as was occurring in French colonial Haiti, said people are morally permitted to engage in collective self-defense against that government. Nonviolent, non-war defense if possible, revolutionary war if need be.

The justification for revolution that I am putting forward here is thus a continuation of the justification for war outlined in the previous section. Both have to do with defending and protecting fundamental human rights, although in different guises. The main difference between the two categories is that in revolution, the unjust aggression is internal to the state or polity, while in defensive and preemptive war it has an external source.

This contemporary account of justified revolution echoes the early Confucian account: rebellion, although it must be a last resort, may be the morally appropriate course of action when faced with tyranny (Lewis and Kling 2022). The Confucian branch of the Chinese just war tradition, though, is not rights-based, and so does not understand tyranny in terms of widespread, severe human rights abuses and political oppression. Instead, revolution becomes justified when the ruler "betrays benevolence [and] righteousness," that is, when they maliciously fail to fulfill their role of maintaining and supporting the socio-political harmony that is necessary for human and natural flourishing (Lewis and Kling 2022). Such a person, as Warring States-era Confucian philosopher Mengzi says, is an "oppressor," and may rightfully be deposed, provided that certain other conditions are met (*Mengzi 5A5*, ICS 9.5/48/7–31). These conditions include that the people regard the rebellion as beneficial to their well-being, and that there is a virtuous person ready and able to lead the rebellion and subsequent new regime in a morally appropriate way, such that both are conducive to harmony as well as order (Lewis and Kling 2022). This reflects the Chinese emphasis on jus post bellum as well as a concern for jus in bello.

It is important here to point out that revolution is not *necessarily* violent; to contend that it is misunderstands the nature of revolution, which is about the rejection of the current regime's authority and its subsequent replacement, not about the particular methods used to achieve such a transition. Again, the importance of necessity becomes apparent here. All war is seriously harmful and damaging—as the Confucian tradition says, it is chaos—and so if the just cause of ending widespread, severe human rights abuses and political oppression within a society can be achieved without engaging in revolutionary war, it should be. And there is some evidence that nonviolent revolution is more likely to be successful than violent revolution; in their landmark study of resistance movements in the 20th century, Erica Chenoweth and Maria J. Stephan argue that nonviolent resistance is more than twice as likely to achieve its goals as violent resistance (2011). So, should all revolutionaries be antiwar pacifists, and use only nonviolent methods?

The moral necessity of using only nonviolence to effect revolutionary change is espoused by Gandhi, King, and (later) Mandela, among others. Violence begets violence, they contend, and the only way to achieve a just and lasting peace is to ensure that the means used match the desired end (King, Jr. 1964). This is an attractive and compelling view. The worry with it is that it depends strongly on the ability of nonviolence to cause a change in the oppressors' hearts and minds, such that they either (1) come to see their brutal, terroristic actions as wrong, or (2) come to see that their oppression is pragmatically untenable because it is too costly, and so conclude that their oppressive political systems are in dire need of repair and change. If such a moral or pragmatic change does not occur (as sometimes it does not), those committed to and engaging in non-violent action will be as lambs to the slaughter. Public abolitionist speeches and pamphlets, work strikes, and boycotts did not end, or even ameliorate, slavery in French colonial Haiti; they simply led to more mass brutalization and executions of enslaved people (Dubois 2004). While nonviolence is certainly admirable, I cannot conclude that it is required; that is to demand too much of people, that they accept violence, brutality, and even death—from the political systems that are ostensibly tasked with protecting them!—without fighting back. So, I maintain that defensive revolutionary war is morally permitted, when it is necessary and proportionate.

2.3. Other-Defense (against External or Internal Unjustified Threats or Aggressive Actions): Humanitarian Intervention

Genocide, ethnic cleansing, and other mass atrocities occur with alarming regularity in the modern world. An urgent question for just war theorists is whether other states or polities should, or at the least are morally permitted to, interfere when such atrocities either occur or are on the brink of occurring. In the 1994 Rwandan genocide, roughly 800,000 people were slaughtered in 100 days. That is about 8,000 people per day, cut down with machetes or riddled with bullets and left to die where they fell (Harsch 1998). The international community watched the genocide happen; it was well-publicized and death counts were reported almost daily. The United Nations (UN) actually had peacekeeping troops in Rwanda at the start of the genocide, but withdrew them citing safety concerns, despite some troop members' protestations and general international outcry. The genocide ended with the arrival in Rwanda of the Rwandan Patriotic Front army and the subsequent normalization of political relations (Kling 2018). After the Rwandan Patriotic Front took control, an estimated two million Rwandans were displaced and became refugees, many in neighboring Zaire, where they were subject to further violence and political oppression. In response to the global community's non-action in the face of the Rwandan genocide, Kofi Annan, then leader of the UN, called for a new global doctrine to be added to international law, called the Responsibility to Protect (R2P). The R2P was endorsed by all UN member states at the 2005 World Summit. While it is not, strictly speaking, formal international law, it is an international "norm," in the sense that it has gained widespread acceptance in the global community.

The **Responsibility to Protect (R2P)** is *a global political commitment based on three broad pillars of action:*

- **Pillar 1:** *Every state has the responsibility to protect its populations from the four mass atrocity crimes (genocide, ethnic cleansing, war crimes, and crimes against humanity).*
- **Pillar 2:** *The wider international community has the responsibility to encourage and assist individual states in meeting that responsibility.*
- **Pillar 3:** *If a state is manifestly failing to protect its populations, the international community must be prepared to take appropriate collective action in a timely and decisive manner and in accordance with the UN Charter* (United Nations 2005).

Remembering the rights of political sovereignty and territorial integrity, we might think, contra R2P, that non-interference ought to be the standard position in regard to occurrences in other states or polities. As Kant argues,

> No state shall forcibly interfere in the constitution and government of another ... the interference of external powers would be a violation of the rights of an independent people which is merely struggling with its internal ills. Such interference would be an active offense and would make the autonomy of all other states insecure.
>
> (Kant 1991, 96)

Generally speaking, this seems right: states and polities should stay out of each other's domestic political affairs, in order to respect each group's right to make its own social and political decisions about how to live together. International political interference, considered broadly, smacks of colonialism and imperialism, not to mention systemic racism and oppression (Kling 2018). If some other group wants a monarchy, or a theocracy, or a socialist republic, who are we to tell them otherwise?

However, R2P reflects a general moral intuition that, when it is imminently possible to literally save hundreds of thousands of people, states and polities have a moral responsibility to do so if they can, regardless of national boundaries and political sovereignty. When the Tutsis of Rwanda were being brutalized and killed in 1994, when the killing fields of Cambodia were red with the blood of thousands in the 1970s, those groups with the resources to do so should have intervened to stop the slaughter. (Eventually, Vietnam invaded Cambodia for other reasons, ending the Cambodian genocide, but only after over 1.5 million Cambodians, conservatively, were killed by the Khmer Rouge (Locard 2005).) To fail to take swift, decisive, preventative action to protect people from their murderous governments, according to R2P, is morally unacceptable; it represents a dereliction of global duties that states and polities have as members of the international community.

Notice that R2P goes further than the arguments we've examined so far, which claim that war is sometimes morally *permissible* in response to external or internal unjust aggression, but not that it is morally *required*. R2P claims, by contrast, that humanitarian intervention is a moral duty. Bluntly, a regime's right to make its own political decisions stops where its attempt to engage in mass atrocity begins. When mass atrocity starts, the international community is obliged to intervene—nonviolently if possible, with war if necessary. To return to the domestic analogy for a second, the idea basically is as follows: you can choose whether or not to defend yourself; that's up to you. But when someone else is being attacked, and you can help defend them, you ought to do so, in whatever ways are available to you. This is sometimes called the moral obligation of other-defense.

This closely matches parts of the Native American just war tradition, especially the position taken up by Chief Tecumseh of the Shawnee (1768–1813) in his quest to create a Native American confederacy to resist white invasion, violence, and settlement. As he puts it, speaking to the Choctaw and Chickasaw tribes, "listen to the voice of duty, of honor, of nature ... assist in the just cause of liberating our neighbors [other tribes] from the grasp of their faithless invaders and heartless oppressors" (Tecumseh 2000, 50–53). Tecumseh is arguing here not merely that such assistance would be permissible, but that it is an obligation based in nature, honor, and duty. He goes on to claim that if the Choctaw and Chickasaw do not come to the aid of other tribes now, they themselves will soon be wiped out, as white encroachment and violence had already begun against them. So, we can see here not only an argument in support of collective other-defense, that is, humanitarian intervention, in the Native American just war tradition, but also support for preemptive war.

But while humanitarian intervention, according to both R2P and parts of the Native American just war tradition, is a moral duty, it is controversial. Essentially, it prioritizes individual human rights over state or polity rights to political sovereignty and territorial integrity, and so concludes that we ought to protect people everywhere from mass atrocity. First, this is a blow to state sovereignty, on which the current international political system is based, and which was initially established by the 1648 Peace of Westphalia in order to stop internecine, endless wars (Kling 2018). I must confess I do not find this very worrying as I regard state sovereignty as valuable only insofar as it undergirds and supports individual dignity, autonomy, and other fundamental human rights. Humanitarian intervention is a defense of these rights; so, it works in concert with the moral ideals on which state sovereignty is based, if not its common practice.

However, there is a concern that R2P commits members of the international community to too much. Do we really have to go to the defense of people on the other side of the world? If we take the fundamental premise of the Universal Declaration of Human Rights (UDHR) seriously, that all people deserve equal consideration and care, the answer to this question is simply, yes. The obligation of other-defense requires that we put forth at least some effort, and accept some level of risk, in order to protect victims of unjust aggression. Sometimes, we must try to save people, even when doing so is somewhat costly to us, just because they need the help (Singer 1972; Walzer 2006). The counterbalance to this point, though, is that we need not kill ourselves to provide that aid; there is some level of hardship beyond which we are not required to go. What precisely that level is, is difficult to say. But it is enough to conclude that states and polities are required to intervene to stop or lessen mass atrocities, even when doing so is inconvenient or somewhat costly, so long as such other-defense does not decimate the intervening groups in turn.

This provides support for encouraging nonviolent humanitarian intervention rather than military intervention. When military intervention occurs, combatants on the intervening side will inevitably die, and that, we might think, is too high a cost. Nonviolent humanitarian intervention, by contrast, is less likely to lead to members of the intervening group dying. Furthermore, nonviolent humanitarian intervention can be extremely active, creative, and effective; it can include not only economic sanctions and slowdowns, but also cross-border rescues, so-called "safe passage" or "safe haven" border openings, technological interventions, and educational interventions (Kling 2018). These options appropriately give the lie to the caricature of the pacifist as passive. As philosopher Larry May writes, "Being generally opposed to the recourse to war does not mean that one favors inaction in the face of tyrants or humanitarian crises ... The pacifist can be just as much an activist ... as those who support war in such cases" (May 2015, 62).

Ultimately, though, if nonviolent humanitarian intervention fails, I contend that states and polities must be willing to step in with military force. Otherwise, they abandon the victims of mass atrocity to their fate, and fail to stand up for the moral ideals, including fundamental human rights and flourishing, that form the bedrock of human society as we understand it.

Summary

In this section, we considered three standard arguments for justified war, all of which flow out of the right to respond militarily to unjust aggression, when such a response is necessary and proportionate. Defensive and preemptive international wars are possibly justified when they are responses to external unjust attacks on political sovereignty and territorial integrity. Revolutionary wars are possibly justified when they are responses to internal unjust attacks on autonomy, dignity, and bodily integrity. Military humanitarian interventions are possibly justified when they are responses to mass atrocity crimes. Throughout, we examined alternative approaches to these arguments, as well as historical case studies.

3. The Real World, and Force Short of War

In this section, we turn to a serious worry with just war theory, sometimes called the problem of "moral slippage." The just war tradition is full of fancy ideals, rules, and conditions: but we must ask ourselves, in the real world, how often are they carefully and rigorously followed? Isn't it more likely that political and military decision-makers will simply use just war theory as a mask for self-interested military pursuits, or manipulate the tenets of the theory so that it seems to confirm whatever military actions they wish to take? Or, less cynically, isn't it possible that well-meaning decision-makers will engage in rationalizations, using just war theory, to convince both themselves and others that some immoral military pursuits really are morally justified? Better, perhaps, to outlaw war altogether, so that no one can take advantage of the just war tradition to either deliberately prosecute or inadvertently rationalize unjust wars and military actions.

The anti-war pacifist is certainly right to be worried about the moral slippage that can come with applying just war theory to the real world. I am deeply sympathetic to this concern; I too worry that just war theory can provide cover, so to speak, for deeply immoral and harmful military pursuits. War is always catastrophic, and we should not try to justify it in any circumstances that do not warrant it. Nevertheless, we live in a world where large-scale, sustained, direct political violence is often used. Instead of dismissing all of it as equally immoral, I maintain that it is better to put moral constraints on war, which differentiate between different situations, contexts, and actions. This does allow for the possibility of moral slippage; but it is worth it for two reasons.

First, this reflects the reality of the world. Some wars are better and worse than others, and some military actions within war are better and worse than others. To ignore this is to fail, in a way, to recognize the moral nuance inherent in the world. Would it be better if there were no wars altogether? Yes. But that would require that the world as a whole be radically different than it is. Given the widespread, severe injustices and human rights abuses that permeate our world, defense against them is justified. And sometimes, if and when non-violent resistance against such injustices and abuses fails, war is all that is left to do besides submit. In such dire circumstances, we must recognize that war is permissible—tragic, but permissible—as the last mode of defense. Otherwise, we collapse into a black-and-white view of the world that misses the moral import of the myriad of circumstances in which people and groups can find themselves through no fault of their own. The world is a morally complex place; just war theory appropriately acknowledges and appreciates this fact.

Second, putting moral constraints on war, rather than dismissing all war as equally immoral and wrong, is a pragmatic move. While people are likely to ignore blanket condemnations that do not align with their intuitions, they are perhaps more likely to pay attention to moral constraints that take into account a variety of real-world factors, and that respect the fact that war happens, and it is not going away anytime soon. Think about the following analogy: if you tell your friend everything he does is wrong, he is likely to start ignoring any further suggestions and comments you make. But by contrast, if you tell him that he is doing the right thing, but in the wrong way, or that he should perhaps try something else first, to ensure that he acts as well as possible given his circumstances, he is much more likely to take into account your further recommendations. Just war theory is here acting as a kind of palliative—given that we know war happens, we do better to work with its existence, and so make it as least bad as possible. It is horrific to have to count the numbers of the dead; but insofar as we have to do so, it is better when there are fewer of them, and when fewer of them are noncombatants.

Just war theory, as currently conceived, is not a radical theory—it does not seek to fundamentally transform our moral understanding of the world and our place in it. What it does seek to do is provide us a moral framework for making sense of the world as we find it, and for making sound moral judgments within this world. In this way, just war theory is a deeply practical area of philosophy. It attempts to "sit at the table" with the people and institutions who are the actual political and military decision-makers in our global and regional communities, and urges them to take all people's rights into account when making military decisions, through the method of meeting the standards of jus ad bellum, jus in bello, and jus post bellum. For instance, during the run-up to the Persian Gulf War in 1990, the United Nations (UN) consciously worked to adhere to the rules of jus ad bellum. The UN first attempted to diplomatically negotiate Iraq's withdrawal from Kuwait. When that failed, the UN instituted economic sanctions with an accompanying naval blockade. Saddam Hussein still refused to withdraw, at which point the UN Security Council authorized the use of "all necessary means" to force Iraq out of Kuwait (Resolution 678). At this point, member states of the UN created a coalition military force, led by U.K. and U.S. forces. Throughout the diplomatic processes that led to the coalition, the highest emphasis was put on formulating a strategy to expel Iraq from Kuwait while adhering to jus in bello constraints (Freedman and Karsh 1993). Subsequent military operations Desert Shield (the build-up phase of the war) and Desert Storm (the combat phase of the war) were successful in expelling Iraq from Kuwait. Although it was not a "perfect" just war (and I am not a historian, to be able to make such a case definitively!), we can conclude that, in many respects, the Persian Gulf War reflects the influence of just war theory on real-world international politics.

Bluntly, political and military decision-makers have the power of life and death over millions; better that they have some concrete moral conditions to meet when considering war—which they will inevitably do—than that they view war as a kind of moral black hole, wherein everything is forbidden, so why not do whatever they wish. In the end, the likelihood of some moral slippage is a cost worth paying to maintain just war theory's influence in the real world. Better to have decision-makers calculate proportionality imperfectly, than to not care about it at all.

3.1. The "Optimism" of JWT

A common response to just war theory's claim of practicality, outlined above, is that it is overly optimistic. This takes the just war theorist's answer to moral slippage and turns it on its head, suggesting that just war theorists are deluding themselves if they think they have any chance of influencing the world's decision-makers, who are unlikely to listen to philosophers and other moral theoreticians. Just war theory, this response states, is an ideal theory in a non-ideal world and, as such, is doomed to fail its stated goals. But this charge of optimism is mistaken in two ways: first, it does not take account of legal and political history and contemporary military cultures, and second, it misunderstands the relationship between just war theory and the reality of war.

To see the influence of just war theory, we need only look to historical and contemporary international law. As I mentioned in the introduction, the Geneva Conventions, and the Hague Conventions before them, are the most widely ratified set of treaties and protocols in history. Furthermore, the Geneva Conventions have legal teeth, in the form of criminal investigations, trials, and convictions overseen by the International Criminal Court (ICC), economic sanctions enforced by the International Monetary Fund (IMF) and World Bank, and other social and political sanctions enforced by the United Nations. Signing on to the Geneva Conventions is not an empty promise, but one with real consequences. Also, it is worth bearing in mind that many states and polities have domestic laws and policies surrounding war that closely match, if not copy, international law. So while states and polities do not always hold to their sworn word (of course), the fact that they have agreed to abide by the laws of war, which largely reflect traditional just war theory as I have set it out, shows that their public values are influenced, to some degree, by the just war traditions. This strongly suggests, if not outright determines, that just war theory has had, and continues to have, an impact on the global community. What the law is, both domestically and internationally, *matters*; otherwise, individuals, states, and polities would not spend so much time and effort trying to change it!

Additionally, just war theory forms the moral backbone of many professional militaries around the world. Far from simply following orders, there are several cases of warfighters and commanders refusing to fight when doing so would contravene jus ad bellum and jus in bello. To take just one example, consider the Vietnam War. Once the moral circumstances surrounding the war became widely known, several American warfighters and draftees refused to go to war, despite threats of death, court-martialing, deportation, imprisonment, and massive fines. At some points, whole units of the U.S. Army in Vietnam refused to fight, attempted surrender, and even attacked and killed (fragged) their commanding officers, allegedly in response to those officers either committing or ordering the commitment of war crimes (Kling 2019a, 110). Although these warfighters' actions were doubtless morally imperfect, they reflect an awareness of, and commitment to, military ethics broadly construed, even under highly stressful and difficult circumstances.

More generally, complex ethical thinking and decision-making is very much a part of the contemporary warfighting experience, as evidenced by the numerous professional organizations within militaries devoted to providing training in the application of moral principles, ethical leadership, and the prevention of moral injury (Emonet 2018). These organizations often pull directly from both the laws of war and just war theory proper to develop their curriculums. To be clear, I am not saying that every warfighter acts ethically, or has just war theory in the forefront of their mind at all times; but I am saying that just war theory plays an influential role in the actual training and development of military professionals, including on-the-ground warfighters, officers, and commanders. So, it is not optimistic to claim that just war theory impacts actual political (given international and domestic laws) and military (given widespread ethical training) decision-making; rather, it is an acknowledgement of the way the world currently is.

Far from being an ideal theory, then, just war theory is, in many ways, a non-ideal theory that takes the world as it is, and recommends ways that it might be made more just. The relationship between just war theory and the reality of war is not one of complete disconnection—a.k.a. who cares about the practice? I'm doing theory!—or general moral disparagement—a.k.a. all war is, and always has been, deeply immoral and wrong. It is, instead, a relationship that generates a kind of moral friction—theorists seek to understand and take account of wars and military pursuits happening in the world and decision-makers' actions and reactions to those events, and try to revise and sharpen their moral feedback and practical recommendations in response without giving up on the fundamental moral principles that underlie the theory. Simultaneously, political and military decision-makers study the laws and stated ethical rules of war and (sometimes) attempt to act in accordance with either their letter or their spirit. The result is a complicated feedback loop that both recognizes that war takes place in our non-ideal world and nevertheless calls on people, imperfect though we are, to work within set moral constraints and to try to meet high moral standards.

Of course, there is a sense in which just war theory is optimistic: no war has ever perfectly met all the standards of jus ad bellum, jus in bello, and jus post bellum, and it is highly unlikely that such a war will ever occur. But the hope is that, by remaining in conversation with decision-makers and warfighters, just war theorists can encourage incremental moral improvements that will eventually lead to a more just, and more peaceful, world. Such small shifts and changes are frustrating, to be sure, but it may be the most pragmatic way to achieve the end goal of a world without war. And to be clear, a just and lasting peace is certainly the ultimate goal: the just war theorist shares this vision with the anti-war pacifist. Unfortunately, the just war theorist maintains, in our non-ideal world, we sometimes cannot get there without war.

3.2. The Means-Ends Problem, and Force Short of War

On its face, to say that sometimes the only way to achieve a just and lasting peace is via war seems paradoxical. Many wrongs, as we tell our children, don't make a right. As Martin Luther King, Jr. argues,

> We will never have peace in the world until men everywhere recognize that ends are not cut off from means ... We must pursue peaceful ends through peaceful means ... means and ends must cohere because the end is pre-existent in the means, and ultimately destructive means cannot bring about constructive ends.
>
> (King, Jr. 1967, 71)

In the same sermon, he concludes, "we must either learn to live together as brothers or we are all going to perish together as fools" (68). Taken together, King's point here is twofold; not only is he saying that violence is *likely* to beget more violence and destruction, but also that violence, because of its nature, *cannot help but* beget more violence. You cannot put out a fire by throwing more wood on it; that only makes it flame higher. What you need is water, which has a nature suitable to your end. Similarly, to achieve peace, we need nonviolence, not war.

Just war theorists are sympathetic to this argument—sometimes called the **means-ends problem**—and they do agree that in many cases, what is needed is nonviolence, not war. Just war theory maintains that war is an extraordinary response, and so should be contemplated only in the most terrible, unjust circumstances. But at the same time, just war theory concedes that sometimes, when water has failed, wood can be used to smother an existing fire. As Chief Sitting Bull of the Sioux (1831–1890) argues in a series of speeches in the late 1800s, white American invasion and settlement must be resisted with force, for white Americans have broken every treaty made with Native American tribes, and any nonviolent resistance is met with white violence and massacres of Native Americans. So, he concludes, "What would you do if your home was attacked endlessly ... and your peaceable efforts failed time and again? You would stand up ... and defend it [with force]" (Sitting Bull 2000, 169–170). Ideally, the means used should match the ends sought; but sometimes, as parts of the Native American just war tradition suggest, that is simply not a workable solution in the real world.

Still, it is better to avoid war whenever possible, both because of the means-ends problem and because of serious worries about moral slippage. In recognition of these concerns, and in light of emerging technologies that make it possible to engage in more limited uses of force, just war theory has recently developed an intermediate step between nonviolent resistance and war called force short of war, or *jus ad vim* (Galliott 2019b).

> **Force short of war (jus ad vim)** is *the selective, limited use of military force to achieve particular, pre-determined political objectives.*

The advantages of force short of war are numerous: not only does it help prevent moral slippage, but also, as Walzer points out, it avoids the "unpredictable and often catastrophic consequences" of a "full-scale attack" (Walzer 2006, xv–xvi). Emerging technologies, such as drones, lethal autonomous weapons systems, and digital/cyber weaponry, allow for pinpoint/precision missile strikes, the imposition of no-fly zones, special-forces raids, targeted killing/assassination, and "low intensity, limited duration" bombing campaigns. All of these options, because they avoid conventional ground invasions and large-scale bombing campaigns, make the use of force more predictable than it used to be, in terms of both discrimination and widespread destructive consequences. Hence, some just war theorists argue that jus ad vim "should serve as an *alternative set of options* to the large quantum of force associated with war," rather than as an intermediate step between nonviolent resistance and war (Brunstetter and Braun 2013, 97, emphasis in original).

The theory of force short of war is still being developed; however, many theorists agree that a number of moral conditions must be met before a state or polity may permissibly engage in such political violence. These moral conditions include, perhaps unsurprisingly, that the use of force short of war is only permissible in response to a just cause; that it must be used with right intention; that it must be a last resort; that it must be proportional; that it must discriminate; and that it must have a reasonable chance of success (Galliott 2019a). More controversial is the legitimate authority requirement, and a newly proposed standard that, to be possibly justified, the use of force short of war must have a low probability of escalation (Brunstetter and Braun 2013). The idea here is that the benefit of force short of war is that it avoids war—so, to avoid nullifying this advantage, for force short of war to be justified, it must be unlikely to lead to the elevation of hostilities to the level of war. But other theorists argue that this is already included in the reasonable chance of success criterion, and so is not a conceptually distinct requirement (Kaplan 2019).

Regardless of the particular moral requirements of jus ad vim, it is clear that force short of war, in addition to its other benefits, avoids the wholesale societal mobilization often involved in war. Thus, it can help prevent what we might call a "wartime orientation" of social and political systems, wherein legal and economic resources are re-directed toward the military, and social and political resources are co-opted to begin or continue "Othering" enemy states, polities, groups, and individuals in problematic and oppressive ways. Just think of the ways Japanese Americans were treated during World War II, and the contemporary lack of public funding for primary education and poverty eradication in the United States, which has been paying for wars in Afghanistan and Iraq for over 20 years. A wartime orientation can be, and often is, materially damaging to the pursuit of other important domestic justice issues, as well as socially and psychologically damaging both to members of the societies going to war, and to people across the world (McPherson 2018). Pacifists thus rightly worry about the movement of societies to a wartime footing; the use of force short of war, to my mind, helps to prevent, or at least ameliorate, some of these issues.

3.3. Emerging Military Technologies and the Nature of War

As I mentioned in the previous sub-section, the development of new military technologies is what makes force short of war possible. We are now capable of engaging in targeted strikes and limited, precision kinetic attacks, in a way that was not possible prior to the development of radar, digital, and cyber technologies. Lethal autonomous weapons systems (LAWs) are gaining traction, as are cybernetic enhancements that will enable human warfighters to operate successfully in enemy battlespaces without large amounts of ground and aerial support (Masakowski 2020). Space—truly, the final frontier—is opening up as a potential arena of war. What this means is that the character, or nature, of war is changing; it is becoming less about the number of people a state or polity can put in the field, or the number of the dead, and more about technological resources and political suasion. We might say that the capacity to engage in force short of war brings the contemporary world ever closer to Prussian general and military theorist Carl von Clausewitz's old 19th century definition of war as "the continuation of politics by other means" (Walzer 2006, 79). While traditional war is wildly different from everyday politics, it is not clear that force short of war is so different, especially when we consider that most politics, speaking globally, involve certain amounts of more-or-less intense domestic political violence.

To be sure, force short of war is not ideal. It still fails to solve the means-ends problem inherent in using violence to achieve peace. But it is better than the land wars of the past, in that it holds out the possibility of avoiding the death tolls in the millions, and the catastrophic infrastructure damage, that were the hallmarks of 20th century warfare. Force short of war, therefore, meets some of the standards of specifically anti-war pacifists. It is a double-edged sword, though. The worry with force short of war is that, because it allows political and military decision-makers to use military force without creating numerous (military and civilian) casualties and large amounts of collateral damage, it will lead to more, rather than less, political violence overall (Galliott 2019b). So, it is essential that a robust theory of jus ad vim continues to be developed, to take account of, and put moral constraints on, the changing nature of war.

Ultimately, technological change provides states and polities with new methods for warlike interactions in our non-ideal world that do not involve mass killing and death. The development of **non-lethal weapons (NLW)** is a key part of this shift (Kaurin 2010). NLW such as rubber bullets, stun guns and tasers, kinetic nets, chemical agents, water cannons, and directed energy weapons are certainly violent; however, they do avoid the lethality that worries many varieties of pacifist. In addition, NLW may enable warfighters to better follow the discrimination requirement (in the sense of avoiding civilian casualties and unnecessary suffering), even when fighting in highly populated areas. At the limit, NLW may allow for the possibility of waging war largely without killing anyone (Kaurin 2010). In which case, we must ask ourselves, is the resulting struggle war at all?

I suspect that it is. But this is because, regardless of whether conventional lethal weapons or NLW are used, the situation is still aptly described as one in which states or polities are using large-scale, sustained, direct political violence in order to secure their political goals. You might think, straightforwardly, that not killing people is better than killing them, and I would agree with you. But surely the anti-war pacifist would not be satisfied by the replacement of all lethal weapons of war with NLW. As a number of classic Chinese theorists point out, "all weapons are brutal implements. Conflict is a contrary virtue" (Lo 2012, 409). The emphasis here is on the badness of violent conflict that is propagated by weapons, regardless of the outcome of that conflict. Laozi, founder of the Daoist school of thought, goes further when he argues that all military weapons are unnatural—because they disrupt the course of nature, the *dao*—and so true rulers do not use them except in extremis. When weapons must be used, it is an occasion for grief, not celebration (Zhang 2012). So, in a sense, the introduction of NLW does not change the fundamental debate. At the end of the day, it is still a question of whether groups may permissibly take up arms in their own and others' defense.

Summary

In this section, we considered two common critiques of just war theory, that it allows for moral slippage in the real world, and that it is altogether too optimistic. We also introduced the means-ends problem. In response to these concerns, we discussed the practicality of just war theory, as well as the recent development of force short of war (also known as *jus ad vim*). Force short of war is made possible by the advancement of military technologies, and so we concluded with a discussion of the extent to which such emerging technologies change the nature of war.

4. Those Who Would Have Peace, Must Prepare for War (and Its Aftermath)

War is fundamentally coercive. It does not persuade by giving good (intellectually respectable) reasons, but rather via violence and threatened violence. It is not *reasonable*, in the classic liberal sense of the term. Just war theory fully admits this—war goes directly against the idea, articulated by Saint Anselm of Canterbury in the 11th century, that only non-coercive arguments can cause us to rationally assent to beliefs (Anselm 1998). Coercion can cause us to act *as though* we believe something, but it cannot make us actually change our minds about that thing. For example, holding a sword to someone's throat and commanding them to assent to Christianity (as happened during the Crusades) is a good way to get someone to act as though they have converted to Christianity; but it cannot really convince them to accept—in their hearts and minds—Christian beliefs.

Faced with this challenge, just war theorists respond that yes, war is unreasonable. But unfortunately, many people in the world are not susceptible to reasonable argumentation about any number of particular topics. (To be fair, it is rare to find someone who is *wholly* unreasonable, in all ways and about all topics.) When faced with such unreasonable people, organized into powerful groups, who would bring unjust aggression to bear against you and yours, what should you do? You can take the so-called high road and try to non-coercively reason with them. Without a doubt, this should be the first line of defense. And in the ideal case, such reasoned argumentation would work; as liberal philosopher John Stuart Mill (1806–1873) argues, if ideas, like seeds, are given the opportunity to grow in the sunlight of free expression and thought, then eventually, the court of public opinion will land on the truth (Heldke 1991). But this is only true if we assume that all people will judge between ideas fairly, dispassionately, and without bias. As contemporary philosopher Barrett Emerick argues, such an assumption strikes him as "hopelessly naïve"; people are unreasonable in a variety of ways, and about a variety of topics, and so the Millian line of defense does not always work (Emerick 2021, 135).

Given that people and groups are sometimes unreasonable, we must be prepared to use unreasonable means, such as violence and war, against them. This is not ideal, of course; but it reflects the fact that humans are not wholly rational, reasonable beings, no matter how much we might like to think otherwise. To take an old example from Aristotle, it is sometimes impossible to persuade people, and the groups of which they are a part, simply through the use of logos (logic) and ethos (ethical reasoning) (Brady and Fricker 2016). This is when pathos (emotion) comes into play; it is sometimes possible to persuade people, and their groups, by appealing to their emotions, when appeals to reason have no effect. Emotional appeals are neither rational nor reasonable—but they do work, on occasion, where reason and logic fail. By analogy, reasoned argumentation is what political and military decision-makers ought to try first, before war. But if and when such appeals fail, it is permissible for them to turn to war as an alternative that is admittedly unreasonable, and yet might work to stop the unjust aggression. Against unreasonableness, they must be prepared to be unreasonable in turn.

Importantly, I am not here making the claim that humans are "naturally violent," or anything like that. This is not an echo of English philosopher Thomas Hobbes' (1588–1679) famous conclusion that individuals, left to their own devices, will inevitably descend into a war of all against all (Hobbes 1991, chap. xiii). Rather, my point is simply that humans can be unreasonable, and that is a fact that we must consider. In our world, much unjust aggression comes from people's unreasonable beliefs, ideologies, and worldviews. Those in a position to do so should try to change aggressors' hearts and minds, without a doubt; but if and when that fails, it might suffice to hold a sword to their throat to coerce them to change their aggressive behavior. Think here about the Rwandan genocide. Ideally, the Hutus would have been persuaded by rational, reasonable, non-coercive argumentation to not slaughter the Tutsis. But failing that, it would have been enough to have gotten them to *stop* committing mass atrocity crimes.

In this sense, sometimes war works. To take a classic example, World War II stopped state-sponsored Nazism and fascist aggression (at least for a time. We will see what the remainder of the 21st century holds). Of course, in the process of stopping state-sponsored Nazism and fascist aggression, many civilians were injured and killed, and a great deal of physical, economic, and psychological damage was done. It is essential not to discount the horror of war, or the crimes that were committed by the "good guys" in World War II. Still, it would have been, as Walzer puts it, an "immeasurable evil" had Nazism prevailed; it was "an ideology and a practice of domination so murderous, so degrading even to those who might survive, that the consequences of its final victory were literally beyond calculation, immeasurably awful" (Walzer 2006, 253). World War II stopped that moral apocalypse from occurring. So, at a pragmatic level, to say that violence never succeeds is simply not reflective of the world; sometimes, it can cause people to change their actions, so that they stop violating fundamental rights. This is an important first step in the process of protecting those rights.

Furthermore, sometimes the threat of war works. Consider the Civil Rights Movement in the United States. Although now celebrated as a paragon of a nonviolent protest movement, the reality is more complicated. As philosopher and political theorist Candice Delmas puts it, most movements commonly classified as nonviolent, including the U.S. Civil Rights Movement, "often in fact include violent flanks" (Delmas 2018, 58). Many Black activists in the late 1950s and early 1960s were prepared to, and did, engage in armed conflicts with the KKK and other white terrorist organizations, and Malcolm X famously called for war if Black Americans were not afforded their civil rights. Arguably, such violent threats were part of what led the U.S. government to negotiate with the nonviolent wing of the Civil Rights Movement in the mid-1960s (Kling and Mitchell 2019, 226–228). The U.S. government was not responding solely to reasonable, non-coercive argumentation when it passed the Civil Rights Act and the Voting Rights Act, among other laws; rather, it was changing its laws, policies, and procedures (a.k.a. its behavior)—to better respect individuals' fundamental rights—at least partially in response to threatened revolution.

Now, war is no guarantor of justice. Sometimes, it doesn't work. And moreover, it can be used to propagate injustice and oppression as easily as it can be used in the service of justice. These are key reasons why war must be a last resort, when all else has failed (and must meet the other moral conditions of jus ad bellum, as well). But sometimes, when it is so used, war, and the threat of war, can cause unreasonable people, and the groups of which they are a part, to act as though they accept and respect fundamental rights (whether in the guise of political sovereignty and territorial integrity, or in the guise of individual dignity, autonomy, and bodily integrity). Such "acting as though," while it does not meet Millian standards, is not nothing, and so should not be wholly discounted when working toward a just and lasting peace. After all, justice—considered as a political value—does not particularly have to do with hearts and minds. It has to do with the outcomes produced by the laws, policies, and procedures of social and political institutions, organizations, and systems. Bluntly, if a white supremacist President passes robust civil rights legislation, not because they are rationally convinced that civil rights are right, but because they are afraid of revolution, that legislation still brings about a more just society.

4.1. War Is a Stopgap

So far, I have been arguing that war can sometimes work to change unreasonable people's and group's unjust aggressive actions, where and when reasonable, non-coercive argumentation fails (and the other moral conditions of jus ad bellum are met). However, it is crucial to note that war is only a stopgap solution for unjust aggression. Because war is unreasonable, it can only suppress beliefs and action on the basis of those beliefs, not cause people to actually change their minds about things. We are seeing this at the beginning of the 21st century: it turns out that some people never stopped believing in white supremacy and fascism after the upheavals of the mid-20th century, they just learned to be quiet about it (for a time) (Bray 2017).

In other words, war is merely a way of *bringing* groups to the negotiating table; it cannot settle the ideological conflicts that led to war in the first place. It is awful that war must be engaged in to get states and polities to that table. The anti-war pacifist and the just war theorist are in full agreement that it would be better to simply start at the negotiating table, as that is where all parties to the conflict will inevitably end up. (Despite popular political slogans, there are no actual endless wars, nor is endless war permissible. Recall the moral conditions of jus post bellum: when continuing to fight is too costly, groups are morally required to end the war.) But sometimes, people, and the groups of which they are a part, are stubborn in addition to being unreasonable, and only the violence and destruction of war is able to convince them to seek peace. Then, once all groups are at the negotiating table, reasonable, non-coercive argumentation can resume.

This work of non-coercively encouraging people to rationally assent to different beliefs must begin and continue after the initial forceful stopping of their behavior that is war (and, in our modern era, force short of war). So, *jus post bellum* must be explored in much more depth than it has been so far in the Western just war tradition. Far from being a victor's peace, there must be truth, reconciliation, and restitution after war, re-integration programs that facilitate the emergence of trust between former enemies, and honest, ongoing political discussions domestically, regionally, and internationally about how to move toward justice more equally enjoyed by all (Fabre 2016). While such proposed moral structures for the transition from war to peace cannot guarantee that people will change their beliefs, ideologies, and worldviews, they at least put the conditions in place for such rational, reasonable change to occur. To return briefly to Anselm, he concedes that no one can convince an unreasonable person to change their mind; but what you must do is provide them with good (intellectually respectable) reasons and the freedom to change if they so choose. Only then is it possible that they will come to accept different beliefs (Anselm 1998).

These moral imperatives surrounding what we must do after war are in line with the Chinese just war tradition, which (as I discuss in Section 1.3) contains several focused analyses of jus post bellum. From the Daoist perspective, the transition from war to peace must include funereal and honoring commemorative practices, social methods that work to transmute natural desires for revenge into other, more prosocial attitudes, and political transformation to virtuous, harmonious rule (Zhang 2012). From the Confucian perspective, war is chaos and destruction: a return to peace must be marked by the restoration of proper social and political orders, humanitarian treatment of the enemy—in particular, there should be no requirement of unconditional surrender, as such a requirement is anti-social in the extreme—and benevolence toward all who were caught up in the fighting through no fault of their own (Lo 2012). While the Daoist and Confucian traditions occasionally conflict, they have in common a recognition of both the need for what we might call "closure" and the importance of resuming prosocial, non-coercive, reasonable social and political discourse among all belligerent parties after war.

In this vein, I suggest that *jus post bellum* is where many of the ideas and concepts from pacifism, broadly construed, can be usefully applied. Preventing future wars, after all, is undoubtedly a much better idea than having to continually deal with war's destructive aftermath. Concrete social, political, and psychological transformations along pacifist lines should all be a part of the long, difficult, but ultimately morally essential transition from war (and warism) to peace (Fiala 2018c). To give three quick examples, societies should acknowledge and reckon with the role of institutional violence in many organized religions today, and should rethink common interpretations of religious texts that seem to, but may not actually, justify violence and war (Fitz-Gibbon 2019). Political institutions should build in policies and procedures that respect the human and civil rights of all, including previously ostracized minorities. Social safety nets should be structured so as to recognize people's dignity, autonomy, and fundamental connectedness. If such pacifist transformations were to occur after war, there might never be the need for another war. And that should be, I maintain, the ultimate goal of every just war theorist.

Importantly, to say that jus post bellum should include creating the conditions for social, political, and psychological transformation of societies is not to support or endorse nation-building.

> **Nation-building** is *the creation, from the outside, of self-sustaining political, social, and economic institutions that will permit competent governance, social stability, and economic growth.*

Morally, nation-building smacks of colonialism and imperialism, not to mention systemic racism and political paternalism. (Intentional or not, efforts to nation-build often have the ring of, "You clearly can't do it yourself; here, we'll set up your institutions for you." This is obviously distasteful for a variety of reasons.) Practically, experiments in nation-building in the Middle East have been spectacularly unsuccessful, leading to a series of political and social morasses with no clear solutions or endpoints. As military theorist Rebecca Johnson points out, when one group imposes particular political, social, and economic institutions on a populace, that populace is unlikely to accept them. She argues that the terms of peace should instead include commitments from all the warring groups, as well as the surrounding regional and international communities, to help build a state's or polity's *capacity* to govern well and justly, in political, social, economic, and military terms (Johnson 2008). This is a subtle, but crucial, difference. For instance, instead of handing the defeated state or polity a new constitution, which they must obey on pain of renewed war (as the

United States did to Japan at the conclusion of World War II), the terms of peace could include setting up and helping manage something like a constitutional convention, wherein all constituents within the defeated group are represented. This may not lead to the particular type of political institutions that the victorious group(s) would prefer, but it will help to prevent future war, and may enable future pacifist transformations as well.

Ultimately, when we understand jus post bellum to be about preventing future war, rather than the victorious group getting everything it wants, we begin to make needed progress toward a just and lasting peace. If there is a way to avoid war, without sacrificing fundamental rights, it should be done. War is hell. But unfortunately, sometimes other groups unreasonably bring hell to you, or to those you care about, or to those who deserve protection in virtue of their common humanity. Sometimes, when this happens (to borrow a sentiment from Winston Churchill) the only way to get through hell is to keep going. Afterwards, the critical process of working to change hearts and minds can, and from a just war perspective should, begin.

Summary

In this section we considered what war can and cannot do in response to unjust aggression. In particular, it can coercively stop the violation of fundamental rights, and can force groups to the negotiating table. But it cannot change people's or group's beliefs, ideologies, or worldviews. Thus, war is a stopgap solution to the problem of unjust aggression. We concluded that what is needed after war is a moral transition from war to a just and lasting peace. This will include creating the background conditions necessary to enable people and groups to freely change their beliefs, ideologies, and worldviews.

5. The Transformation of Just War Theory

You might worry that just war theory is too old-school for our new-school world. Philosophies of oppression, in particular feminism, philosophy of race, and radical political philosophy have drawn attention to issues and problems traditionally ignored or brushed aside by just war theory. For instance: military culture reproduces toxic masculinity on a grand scale. *Jus in bello* discussions of the discrimination requirement focus primarily on intentional attacks, and so brush aside the millions who are accidentally harmed and killed in war as collateral damage. Just war theory is a defense of the international status quo; but the status quo ignores long histories of colonialism, imperialism, ecological destruction, and other forms of oppression. Given these critiques, perhaps an entirely new approach to global politics is needed.

These critiques of just war theory are valid, and important. However, they should not cause us to reject just war theory in its entirety. Instead, I argue that just war theory can and should take these critiques on board. Doing so transforms it from an old-school dogma into a nuanced, contemporary way of thinking through domestic and international conflicts. So much of our lives are global now; a transformed just war theory has the resources to help us understand what that means, and how we ought to handle it going forward. It can push us to think critically about how we ought to live politically in the world.

5.1. Bellism, Toxic Masculinity, and Just War Theory

War is often viewed as a man's arena: it is a place for him to test his mettle, vanquish his opponents, and find glory. This view of war as both a site of masculinity (war is where we see masculinity in action) and as a proving ground for masculinity (war is where people prove they are "real" men), has often led to war's valorization as a worthwhile, honorable pursuit. This view of war is sometimes called bellism (Fiala 2004, 47–50).

Bellism: *War is valuable for its own sake, as a way to demonstrate courage, cleverness, and martial skill, and to obtain honor and glory.*

Bellism has a long history, which I will not recite here, and still occupies a central place in many contemporary cultures. Despite knowing that warfighters are often coerced into militaries (either physically or via severe economic and socio-political pressures), we nevertheless often treat them like the mythical knights of medieval Europe, who—in the stories we tell—freely and bravely chose to go to war for gold, God, and glory. (An exception here is the treatment of U.S. troops returning from Vietnam, who were often demonized and outcast by their local communities as the visible faces of an unpopular war. Perhaps unsurprisingly, such treatment coincided with the rise of critical feminisms in the West.) We see bellism throughout our classic and popular literary texts, music, and movies—mature heroes are praised for their martial skills and virtues, as evidenced by their success in war, and wanna-be heroes often long for war and violence as a chance to prove themselves and earn honor and glory.

The valorization of warfighters and the military is dangerous, though, because it can lead political and military decision-makers, as well as warfighters, to love war for its own sake, rather than regard it as a necessary evil that should be entered into reluctantly, and only as a last resort. In addition, once we recognize that war is a traditionally masculine space, we can see that bellism and toxic masculinity are intertwined (Andrew 1994). Briefly, **toxic masculinity** refers to those traits traditionally associated with men and masculinity—such as violence, anger, aggression, the will to power and dominance, martial skill, and an obsession with social and political hierarchical status—which are harmful to men, women, and society overall. Bellism encourages and reinforces these traits in warfighters as well as political and military decision-makers (who are, of course, traditionally all men), and more generally reproduces the culturally constructed gender roles of men as strong warriors and leaders and women as weak and passive peacemakers (Peach 1994). Bellism feeds toxic masculinity, and toxic masculinity feeds bellism.

Now, just war theorists are not bellists; hopefully that much is clear from what I have said so far. Still, just war theory must grapple with this critique, which argues that in our world, war and military culture reinforce deeply problematic and harmful gender norms, roles, and hierarchies. To give just one example, studies show that violent domestic abuse (both husband-to-wife spousal abuse and child abuse) is twice as prevalent in the U.S. military as in comparable civilian populations (Kling 2019b). This is horrible; but in a world where war and military culture—like so many other things—derive support from and encourage toxic masculinity, it is perhaps not surprising.

Broadly, this intertwining of toxic masculinity and bellism should worry just war theorists, as it makes it less likely that political and military decision-makers, as well as warfighters, will be able to apply jus ad bellum, jus in bello, and jus post bellum principles in an unbiased, critical, equitable manner in the real world. However, there is no reason to think that war and military culture *must* reproduce toxic masculinity and associated bellism. To say this would be to fall into the trap of **essentialism,** which states that particular groups of people all have inherent or essential traits. But not all warfighters are violent, aggressive dominators; not all women are nonviolent peacemakers. So, it is open to just war theorists to take this feminist critique on board and use it to jump-start a critical interrogation of contemporary military training and culture.

Following philosopher and international relations theorist Yvonne Chiu, we might argue that warfighters don't need all the traditional masculine traits, but rather need a mix of traditionally masculine and feminine traits to be successful in modern warfare. Specifically, she cites modern warfighters' need for cooperation, teamwork, empathy, and an ability to recognize and acknowledge context (all traditionally feminine traits) in order to successfully prosecute wars, which are often now fought in urban areas and across multiple modalities, such as land and cyber (Chiu 2019). Just war theory is deeply embedded in contemporary culture more broadly, and specifically in the military academies and training centers. So, just war theorists are in the perfect position to investigate, and call for changes to, those aspects of military training and culture that reinforce toxic masculinity at the expense of making war less rare, and less measured, than it morally should be.

Tackling toxic masculinity in war and military culture will also help with the problem of bellism. Assuming my analysis above is correct, part of the reason people love war is because it makes them feel like "real" men. If just war theorists can recommend ways of de-coupling war from toxic masculinity, presumably people will come to love it less. Importantly, this does not entail that just war theorists must give up on the importance of self- and other-defense. Instead, just war theorists should insist on right intention: don't defend people with war because it makes you feel masculine, defend them with war because it is the only way (when this is true) to defend their fundamental rights from unjust aggression. This will not erase bellism, of course; but by embracing the analysis of war through a gendered lens, just war theorists can make some concrete progress against it.

5.2. Collateral Damage

Throughout this chapter, we have been discussing organized groups, political and military decision-makers, and warfighters. This is unsurprising, as the Western, Chinese, and Native American just war traditions all focus on these agents. However, this leaves out all of the people who are unintentionally killed or otherwise deeply harmed by war. As of the time of writing, there are 70.8 *million* refugees and refugee-like persons in the world, over ½ of whom are children (UNHCR 2019).

A **refugee** is *a person who has been forced to flee their country of origin due to either:*

(1) *Well-founded fears of persecution on the basis of their social identity (international law)*
(2) *Forcible displacement by war or violent conflict (international norm)*

Refugee-like persons are those who have been forcibly displaced due to persecution, violence, conflict, or human rights violations, but who have not crossed an internationally recognized border or otherwise met the UN Refugee Agency (UNHCR) standard for being a refugee. While there is some debate about who counts as a refugee, the account I provide here matches the most common moral and political definitions (Kling 2019c).

Traditionally, unless war refugees have been deliberately targeted or intentionally attacked, the harms done to them, and their subsequent suffering, are viewed by just war theory as **collateral damage**. Collateral damage is the regrettable and unintended consequence of doing what is right in war, that is, of committing necessary and proportionate wartime actions. The creation of collateral damage is morally allowed by two factors, one pragmatic, the other philosophical. The pragmatic factor is that, if collateral damage were not morally allowed in war, war would be absolutely morally prohibited. It is impossible to fight a war without collateral damage, be it human, civil, economic, ecological, or what have you. The philosophical factor is the doctrine of double effect (Walzer 2006).

Doctrine of Double Effect (DDE): *Well-intended actions with harmful side effects are permissible, so long as: (1) the action itself is good, (2) the good done by the action outweighs the harm done, (3) the harm isn't the means to the good end, and (4) the harm isn't intended as an end in itself.*

The DDE, first developed in the Western tradition by medieval philosopher Thomas Aquinas, has spawned something of a cottage industry in analytic philosophy. There are serious disagreements about how the doctrine should be interpreted, and whether it is even a valid moral principle. For our purposes, however, it is enough to say that it is widely accepted in just war theory, and provides the philosophical backing for the moral permissibility of engaging in military pursuits—such as aerial bombing—that we foresee will cause collateral damage.

According to the DDE, so long as its conditions are met, war refugees are simply an unintentional by-product of legitimate military actions. As such, nothing is owed to war refugees as a matter of retributive justice. States, polities, or individuals might help them as a matter of benevolence or in obedience to international law, which says that refugees cannot be returned to their country of origin if doing so will place them in renewed danger (in the law, this is called the **principle of non-refoulement**). But war refugees may not demand retribution from the parties to the war—unless they were the targets of deliberate attack—because, according to traditional just war theory, no one has wronged them. The actions that severely harmed them were permissible.

This strikes many contemporary just war theorists, myself included, as the wrong conclusion to reach about war refugees. Care ethicists and racial oppression theorists, in particular, worry about the abstract dismissal—as mere collateral damage—of those who the world does not deem "important" (Peach 1994). In other work, I respond to this worry by arguing that war refugees have been both harmed and wronged, and so deserve recompense (Kling 2019c). Briefly, refugees have security rights that are infringed upon by even legitimate military actions; due to this infringement, and their status as innocent bystanders, refugees have rights of recompense against those who (permissibly) infringed on their rights. In addition, given the ways in which they are treated by our domestic and international social, political, and legal systems, refugees constitute an oppressed group. So, they are owed restitution and aid across the board.

Whether my particular arguments succeed or fail is beyond the scope of our discussion here: what is important, however, is that I bring to bear principles and arguments from within just war theory itself, and rights theory more generally, to argue against the traditional view of war refugees as collateral damage. Furthermore, I am not alone in this endeavor; other contemporary just war theorists agree that much more can and should be said about war refugees than exists in the classic just war texts (Davidovic 2016; Parekh 2017). The theoretical focus of just war, in other words, is slowly shifting. Although just war theory in the past has mostly ignored those impacted by war in favor of those making and enacting the decisions of war, this is no longer true. A robust, contemporary just war theory has just as much to say about the victims of war as about the dogs of war.

5.3. Oppression and Global Politics

As I discuss in Section 3, just war theory is not radical; it does not seek to overthrow the current state-based international political system, but to sit in conversation with the political and military leaders of that system. This, you might think, is precisely the wrong move. Why sit in conversation with those invested in upholding a manifestly unjust status quo? As noted anarchist Emma Goldman (1869–1940) argues, states are the source of our problems; so, we cannot turn to them for solutions (Goldman 2012). And even if states could theoretically bring about a just and lasting peace, the states we currently have are unlikely to be able to do so, steeped as they are in long histories of oppression, including colonialism, imperialism, racism, and ecological destruction (Mills 1997). Famously, out of the past five wars that the United States has been majorly involved in (Iraq, Afghanistan, Persian Gulf War, Vietnam,

Korea), four of them have failed to meet the criteria of jus ad bellum. (And this does not even mention the United States' numerous force short of war engagements of the past 50 years, many of which are morally questionable, if not downright morally wrong.) Given all this, what are the odds that any existing state will fight on the side of the angels?

It is undoubtedly true that many states' historical and current operations on the world stage are morally indefensible. However, it is important to avoid the trap of concluding that an oppressive history determines an oppressive future. As Irish poet and playwright Oscar Wilde writes, "every saint has a past, and every sinner has a future" (1921). Just war theory has traditionally been used to defend the unjust status quo; but as I have argued throughout this chapter, it need not continue to be used this way. Just war theory, with its emphasis on fundamental rights and dignity, self- and other-defense, and the need for a just transition from war to peace, has the theoretical resources necessary to mount a radical critique of states as they currently operate. It can also provide, as we have seen, support for justified revolution and emancipatory action. To bring just war theory to bear in the service of anti-oppression movements follows in the footsteps of abolitionist and statesman Frederick Douglass, who famously argues, explicitly using jus ad bellum principles, in support of civil war to end American slavery (Sundstrom 2017).

This demonstrates that there is nothing in the theory that demands that the just war position be a conservative one. It can, and should, hold all states and polities equally to account. Such a transformed just war theory provides a way of thinking about global politics that transcends the usual self-interested squabbles within domestic and international arenas. It asks us to consider seriously what we owe to those whose fundamental rights are being unjustly and severely violated, and insists that we ensure that all people have the resources necessary to live a flourishing life with dignity. Only then can there be a just and lasting peace.

The cumulative point of all this is that the question is not simply whether war can be justified or not. It is also a question about what war is and what it could be, and whether a transformation of war in certain respects is possible. War in all of its moral and practical complexity is difficult to describe abstractly; it always has a particular "look," based on its particular context. So, when we consider whether war is ever morally justified, we cannot do that purely abstractly either. We must consider each war in all of its particularity. No war, and no specific warfighting strategy, should ever be easily morally justified. But this is not the same as saying that no war, or that no specific warfighting strategy, can ever be morally justified. To say that paints a difficult, morally intricate subject—which can look wildly different in different places and times—with too broad a brush. War is sometimes morally justified; but how, and when, and to what degree, depends crucially on the details.

Summary

In this section, we discussed a number of critiques of just war theory from contemporary philosophies of oppression, including feminism, philosophy of race, and radical political philosophy. Throughout, I contended that contemporary just war theory can, and should, integrate these important critiques. Such integration will lead to a transformed just war theory that is able to provide important ways of understanding, critiquing, and responding to our globalized world. A transformed just war theory thus has the capacity to significantly inform the way we should live politically.

Conclusion

To conclude my contribution to our debate, I summarize my whole argument as follows:

(1) Just war theory is complex, and deeply moral. It contains a series of moral conditions and injunctions, about which there is serious philosophical debate.

(2) There are a number of good arguments in support of the claim that war is sometimes justified, when it is a necessary and proportionate response to unjust aggression.

(3) Just war theory is eminently practical. It responds to the world as it is, and suggests ways that it could be. In this vein, the advancement of military technologies has enabled the development of force short of war, which may be an alternative option to war itself.

(4) War is fundamentally unreasonable and coercive, and so is only a stopgap solution to unjust aggression. But what it can do is force people to the negotiating table, where the work of creating a moral transition from war to a just and lasting peace can begin.

(5) Just war theory can take on board many of the critiques leveled at it from philosophies of oppression. It need not remain mired in a medieval view of the world, but can transform itself to provide a model for thinking about fundamental rights, self- and other-defense, and global politics outside of the existence of states.

My conclusion, based on the weight of these arguments, is that war is sometimes justified.

Note

1 There is much debate about how to understand the domestic analogy, its structure as an argument, and the group rights that it purports to justify. Some argue that "states' rights" is shorthand for the rights held collectively by the members of a state or polity, while others argue that states or polities have rights over and above, or at least different, than the rights of their individual members. For more on this discussion, see Walzer (2004, 2006), McMahan (2009), and especially Rodin (2002).

Part II

Round of Replies

Chapter 3

Response to Kling

Andrew Fiala

Contents

In this chapter, Fiala responds to Kling's arguments as she articulated them in Chapter 2. Fiala addresses a number of concerns: the overlap between pacifism and just war theory, the question of "fighting back," the logic of pacifism, empirical/historical questions, issues regarding ideology and propaganda, the difference between individual and political pacifism, larger questions about social and political philosophy, the difficulty of defining violence/war, and the importance of preventative nonviolence. Kling responds throughout to Fiala's comments.

Professor Kling's explanation and defense of the just war idea is restrained, careful, and insightful. Our dialogue shows, I think, how fruitful it is to have conversations between pacifists and just

DOI: 10.4324/9780367809850-5

war theorists. Disagreements remain, of course. But this conversation has evolved in productive ways over the past hundred years or so—both in theory and in practice. What Kling describes as "revisionist" just war theory is subtle and circumspect. It is worth highlighting that Kling notes convergences and connections between revisionist just war theory and pacifism. She concludes, at one point, "just war theory, despite its numerous internal debates, is closer to contingent pacifism than political realism." She concludes that war is difficult—but not impossible—to justify. Indeed, war *ought* to be difficult to justify, since it risks serious physical, psychological, and moral harm. This cautious approach to the justification of war allows for significant overlap with the moral concerns of pacifism.

In other work, I have explained this convergence in more detail (Fiala 2018c). But let me borrow a graphic from that other work to make my point.

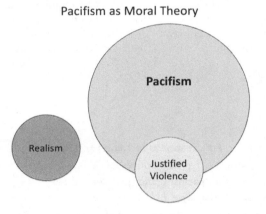

Pacifism as Moral Theory

What I call "pacifism" here is concerned with a large variety of issues, including domestic political arrangements, our treatment of animals, economic structures, family relations, and so on. The pacifist's goal on this construal is to transform social and political life in a way that produces peace. It might be that some kinds of violence could (reluctantly) be justified in pursuit of peace. But for the pacifist, the considerations of justified violence are not the primary concern—and the goal is to shrink the circle of justified violence down toward a vanishing point. Just war theory, however, is only focused on the narrow question of how and when war can be justified. In a sense it is a narrow and episodic theory, while pacifism is much larger, deeper, and more sustained. But there is overlap between just war and pacifism, while realism operates in a different space entirely. Realism is a-moral or even immoral, suggesting typically that the primary concern is power and that the end justifies the means. Both pacifists and just war theorists reject this idea.

This area of convergence—and the evolving dialogue between just war theory and pacifism—has led to theoretical developments that have had an influence on the practice of war and the practice of peace. Just war ideas have had an obvious influence on international law, in military training regimens, and in the general public's understanding of the morality of war. Pacifism and nonviolence have also been influential in shifting our understanding of violence and war in the real world. Racist violence, sexist violence, and old-fashioned nationalistic militarism are no longer taken for granted. And we have a growing awareness of how and why nonviolence works, as well as the ways in which nonviolence is linked to democratic social and political movements (see Fiala 2020).

In what follows here, I offer a few responses to Kling's argument, with the goal of helping the reader to imagine counter-arguments and further points of contention. This is not intended as a line-by-line response to Kling's chapter. Rather, I have focused on issues and ideas that I believe warrant further discussion.

I. On Fighting Back

Kling notes that nonviolence is an "attractive and compelling" idea. But she argues that it does not always work—even in domestic affairs. Kling also suggests that the advocates of nonviolence demand too much if they suggest that those who are suffering under oppression "accept violence, brutality, and even death … without fighting back." This point cuts to the heart of the debate. And indeed, this worry has been a focal point of the debate for a long time. To cite one famous example, consider Martin Buber's outrage at Gandhi's suggestion that the Jews of Nazi Germany should engage in satyagraha (I discuss in Fiala 2018c). Martin Buber (1878–1965) was a German-speaking Jew who left Germany for Jerusalem prior to the World War II. From Buber's perspective, Gandhi's suggestion is naïve and insulting. I don't intend to defend Gandhi's discussion of Hitler and the Jews here. Indeed, if the pacifist were to say that a victim should simply sit back and allow themselves to be brutalized, this would be callous and wrong. It would also be wrong for the pacifist to sit on the sidelines and assign blame to the victims of injustice. The spirit of pacifism should not lead one to engage in critical kibitzing. The goal of the pacifist is not to make the victims of history feel guilty when they are swept up in political violence and the struggles of history. Rather, the goal is to change the world so that there is less violence, war, bloodshed—and guilt.

The question of what should be done in the face of "violence, brutality, and death" is not about a choice between "fighting back" and doing nothing. With Gandhi's model in mind, it is clear that the contemporary advocates of nonviolence are not calling for "non-resistance." Rather, the question is about the nature of "fighting back." The advocates of nonviolence encourage active struggles that are coordinated and strategic but which are non-violent. In other words, one could "fight back" nonviolently. As I will argue subsequently, there is a continuum of tactics and strategies here that shades over into a further point of convergence between pacifism and just war.

Advocates of just war, such as Kling, would also seemingly prefer nonviolent struggle. They would likely agree that if and when violence appears to be justified this represents a failure. War represents a failure of reason, a failure of diplomacy, and frankly, a failure of humanity. Kling admits as much. She writes, "War is fundamentally unreasonable and coercive." On this view, war is not a heroic and glorious thing. Rather, it is a reluctant last resort, something like surgery. But as the pacifists argue, it would be better to prevent the disease in advance in order to make it less likely that we'll need surgery later.

Reply
Jennifer Kling

I agree with much of what Professor Fiala says here! And, if we have to do surgery, it's better to be prepared than not prepared. Contemporary just war theory is preparation, should the worst occur, and we are forced—by others' unrelenting aggression—into defending ourselves or others with war. The just war theorist maintains that it is important to have moral constraints in place ahead of time, so that if we must enter the arena of war, no one has any reason to claim that they didn't know the rules. Better to never need those rules, of course, but until we arrive at the transformed world for which pacifism strives, it strikes me as prudent to have the rules of war well-articulated and understood, so that there is no room for states and other political groups to claim ignorance. Nonviolent resistance is best; but if violent resistance becomes necessary, then we need to know how to do it as well, morally speaking, as possible. This articulation and dissemination is a large part of the purpose of contemporary just war theory.

2. The Logic of Pacifism's Rejection of Just War

One important divergence between the pacifist and the just war theorist can be found in the logic that explains their difference. Kling describes just war theory in modest terms, saying that the theory holds that "some wars" can be justified. Her conclusion is that war is "sometimes justified." This qualification—using the words *some* and *sometimes*—creates a structural challenge for properly understanding pacifism, depending upon how we understand the pacifist's negation of the just war claim. On the one hand, pacifism might be understood as arguing:

(1) War is *sometimes not* justified.

On the other, pacifism might be understood as arguing:

(2) War is *not sometimes* justified.

In the first case, we would have a moderate kind of pacifism, which might find itself in agreement with much of just war theory. The first claim may only claim that in this or that case, war is not justified. In this regard, one could be a "pacifist" with regard to a given war, even if one is not a pacifist about all wars—this is one way that "contingent pacifism" can be understood (Fiala 2014). In the second case, we have a version of absolute pacifism, which rejects war. The second claim might also be understood as "It's not true that war is sometimes justified" or more simply as "War is always wrong."

As discussed in my primary contribution above, there are varieties of pacifism. This structural or logical analysis helps to clarify some of the differences among types of pacifism. The absolute pacifist will refuse to admit that war can ever be justified. In a sense, absolute pacifism is easy to understand, even if it seems more difficult to fit within a non-ideal world. Kling explains that just war theory is "a non-ideal theory that takes the world as it is, and recommends ways that it might be made more just." Absolute pacifism may in fact be understood as an ideal theory, which is not willing to traffic in the messiness of the non-ideal world. Some will see that as a virtue of the theory, by the way. Absolute pacifists may worry that we are often too willing to compromise our ideals in the name of a pragmatic accommodation to the world as it is. If we are not careful, the absolutist warns, compromise becomes complicity.

But let's leave aside the moral purity of absolute pacifism and consider a less absolute type of pacifism that might be willing to admit, in agreement with Kling and the just war theorists, that sometimes war can be justified. The question for non-absolute pacifism is what that might mean—and why it still makes sense to describe this as a type of pacifism. One way of digging into this question is to raise the issue of how much and how often. This is a way of unpacking the meaning of vague terms such as "some" and "sometimes" in the claims that "some wars are wrong" or "war is sometimes not justified." The word "some" can mean that there are *only a few cases* of wars that are wrong or unjustified. In logic, "some" can mean "at least one." But the pacifist critic of war typically makes a much stronger claim than this. The pacifist argues that "*most* wars are wrong" or that "war is *usually* not justified." Or to state this negatively, the pacifist argues that "war is rarely justified" or "war is hardly ever just." These qualifying terms—most, usually, rarely, and hardly ever—indicate the difference between pacifism and just war. A non-absolutist can still be understood as a pacifist, if he or she holds that war is generally, mostly, and usually wrong. And even if a defender of war were to say that war is sometimes justifiable (in one or a few cases), the non-absolute pacifist could still maintain that the general rule holds, which is that war is usually not justifiable.

Reply
Jennifer Kling

It is true that the words "some," "sometimes," "usually," and "rarely" are vague and allow for there to be many intermediate positions between absolute pacifism and just war theory. Where you fall on the spectrum depends, as Professor Fiala points out in a variety of places, on where you think the burden of proof lies. Is war usually, or mostly, unjustified, such that just war theorists always bear the burden of demonstrating that any particular war, and any particular action in war, is justified? Or is war sometimes justified, such that pacifists always bear the burden of demonstrating that any particular war, and any particular action in war, is unjust? In popular culture, the burden of proof lies on the pacifist. However, within the contemporary debate that takes place among theoreticians and practitioners of war, the burden of proof is shifting, *as it should*, to lie on the just war theorist. War is horrendous: we should always start with the belief that it is unjustified, and then work backwards to see if the circumstances are such that it happens to be justified in that specific situation. So, contemporary just war theory is really, at its heart, the claim that a just war is possible. Possibility has to do with what *can happen* in the world (regardless of likelihood), and so is less vague than the usual qualifying terms that theorists and practitioners on all sides tend to use.

3. Empirical and Historical Questions

While absolute pacifists simply deny that war is justifiable by stipulating this as a moral first principle, less absolute forms of pacifism grow out of an analysis of the non-ideal world. It is important to emphasize this because pacifism is often caricatured as being an other-worldly ideal theory. In fact, non-absolute pacifism can be firmly rooted in the non-ideal world. And as I argue here, pacifists can argue that in fact it is the just war theorist who is wedded to an ideal theory.

Following our logical analysis above, non-absolute pacifists can admit that on very rare occasions war might be justified but that most of the time war is not justified. This generalization about the wrongness of war must be grounded in historical and empirical detail. We must admit that interpretations of history are difficult and that reasonable people will disagree about these interpretations. Nonetheless, a skeptical interpretation of the moral history of war is reasonable.

Indeed, Kling herself acknowledges that history presents a poor track record with regard to the justification of war. Kling states, "out of the past 5 wars that the U.S. has been majorly involved in (Iraq, Afghanistan, Persian Gulf War, Vietnam, Korea), 4 of them have failed to meet the criteria of jus ad bellum." We might bring in considerations of jus in bello and argue that each of these five wars violated moral principles. And to make the empirical point even more strongly, we might also argue that the paradigmatic "good war"—the U.S. and Allied fight in the World War II— failed to live up to the standards of just war theory. Just war theorists often use the World War II as a paradigm. Kling assumes that the U.S. involvement in the World War II was justified. She states in a parenthesis: "I take it as given that Germany was on the unjust side of WWII, while the U.S. was on the just side." Likely the justification of the U.S. fight against Germany is understood in relation to jus ad bellum consideration of just cause, with Germany viewed as an aggressor who invaded sovereign territory and as a genocidal power who was slaughtering innocent Jews, Gypsies, and others.

There are several difficulties for any clear-cut moral analysis of the justification of the U.S. involvement in the World War II. First, the U.S. was involved in wartime activities that violated principles of jus in bello. American bombers deliberately killed civilians, firebombing cities in Germany and Japan while finally using atomic bombs against civilian targets at Hiroshima and Nagasaki. American soldiers and civilians were fueled by racism and committed atrocities (as I discussed in my first chapter—see also Dower 1986). The U.S. also locked Japanese-American citizens up in concentration camps during the war. Both strategies—the bombing campaigns and the domestic civil liberty violations—were fueled by racism, by a desire for total victory, and by a frankly realist way of thinking about war. Second, the idea that the U.S. was a good guy who was provoked into war by a sneak attack at Pearl Harbor can be subjected to critical scrutiny. In Asia and the Pacific, the U.S. was engaged in imperial expansion for decades and a rivalry with

Japan that included the use of American naval power to "open" Japan, the American occupation of the Philippines during the Spanish-American war, the colonization of Hawaii, and the U.S. oil embargo against Japan prior to the Pearl Harbor attack. A different version of history makes the U.S. the aggressor in Asia and the Pacific. A similar revisionist history can be told with regard to affairs in Europe, that would also involve a discussion of American anti-Semitism, pro-Hitler sentiment before the war—and American interests in establishing itself as a global power through the war effort.

None of this is offered as the definitive moral history of the war. I am not suggesting that Japan was justified in attacking Pearl Harbor or that Hitler was justified in genocide. My point is to only show how difficult it is to claim that even this paradigm is in fact actually a just war. It is difficult to disentangle the causes of war from a long complex history in order to conclude that one side is the good guy. It is difficult to say that any war has been fought within the constraints of jus in bello. These difficulties of moral judgment hold also after the World War II with regard to how jus post bellum could be applied in this case. It is not clear that the World War II resulted in a good balance of benefit over harm. Not only were massive numbers of civilians and soldiers killed during the war, but also the aftermath of the war was a world divided by the Iron Curtain, a nuclear arms race, rampant militarism in the U.S., and other less than optimal outcomes. This brief discussion of the World War II shows that it is not obvious that any war has lived up to the standards of just war theory, even the paradigm case of the World War II.

I submit that the pacifist's claim that war is usually not justified (or is rarely justified) thus has a firm basis in historical reality. History teaches us that war has rarely (if ever) been just. This means that a very strong burden of proof rests upon the proponent of war who must show that *this war* (the war he proposes as an exception to the rule of unjustified war) will indeed be exceptional and different from the general historical rule that war is unjust. And in fact, the just war theorist who suggests that war is sometimes justifiable bases this claim on an idealistic and overly simplistic interpretation of history. In short, the pacifist can turn the tables on the just war theorist and claim that pacifism is actually more in tune with the non-ideal world (based upon a realistic interpretation of history), while just war theory is divorced from historical reality and views war in idealist terms.

Reply
Jennifer Kling

People can and do have different takes on history. How we interpret the historical record is, as Professor Fiala writes, subject to all kinds of ideological biases. In addition, it is also subject to the limitations of our records. For example, our common vision of early Viking warfare is that it was a predominantly male activity. The written and archeological records to which we had access for a long time supported this belief. However, these records are constantly changing as new discoveries are made. We now know that roughly one-third of Viking warriors were female, suggesting a vastly different military division of gendered labor than was previously accepted.

My point here is not that we can't learn anything from history: we clearly can, and history clearly matters. What I am saying is that interpretations of history change not only as ideologies and conceptual schemas change, but also as we gain more data. So, we should be wary of ever claiming to know the definitive history of an event, be it a war or something more peaceful. Consequently, given the long, complicated, at least partially shrouded history of warfare, we should avoid drawing any strong normative moral conclusions from it. Both pacifism and just war theory are to some extent guilty of doing this (it is difficult to write good applied political philosophy without using any real-world examples!), but I think the lesson to take from the discussion between Professor Fiala and myself here is that we should be cautious of treating historical examples as though they prove our positions, rather than merely illuminating certain aspects of them that we wish to draw out.

4. The Problem of Ideology and Propaganda

If what I argue here is plausibly true—that wars are usually not justifiable and that wars tend not to live up to the standards of just war theory—then why is pacifism often viewed as a marginal and far-fetched idea? One reason for this may be that many people (including especially military and political leadership) are basically realists about war. The realists don't think that moral categories apply in war; and they are only interested in winning wars for their own side. A related reason is connected to the problem of what Kling refers to as "moral slippage." Kling notes that military and political leadership can use just war language to mask self-interest and the pursuit of power—and that well-meaning leaders may engage in a process of "rationalization" that leads them to justify the unjustifiable. This is in fact the problem of underlying realism getting dressed up in the moral language of just war. There is a serious real-world problem here that is exacerbated by ideology and propaganda.

I discussed this in my original contribution in relation to what I call "the just war myth"—which is the mythological employment of just war theory in political discourse. But let me focus this issue here back upon the logical structure with which we began. The pacifist critic says that war is rarely (or never) justifiable; he supports this claim by offering the kind of history lesson provided above. So why is it, then, that the defender of just war suggests that war is sometimes justifiable and that there have in fact been just wars? Obviously one reason may be that the pacifist interpretation of history might be wrong. But the pacifist will also suggest that the reason the just war theorist thinks that war is sometimes justifiable is either because their theory is in fact an ideal theory (as mentioned above) or because the just warrior has imbibed an ideologically biased view of history, in which the interpretation of the historical record has been warped by pro-war and militaristic propaganda.

A number of authors other than myself have made this point. Bertrand Russell (1872–1970) is one of the most influential philosophers of the 20th century. He was a pacifist who was jailed during the World War I. Along with his pacifist friends, Russell noted the problem of propaganda and ideology during the World War I. Russell said, during the World War II, "very few wars are worth fighting ... the evils of war are almost always greater than they seem to excited populations at the moment when war breaks out" (Russell 1943, 8). But let's cite a more contemporary author: Nel Noddings—the influential proponent of what is called "care ethics." Noddings links her critique of just war theory to a critique of patriotism, patriarchal gender norms, and militaristic ideology— all of which are taught to children in the standard school curriculum. Noddings shares the conclusion that just wars are rare. She says, "we would be hard put to find a historical example of war conducted justly" (Noddings 2010, 112). She links our uncritical support of war to propaganda and ideology: "Heroic stories, parades, uniforms, flags, and holiday celebrations all support patriotism and, unfortunately, war" (121). She also connects this to a certain version of masculinity: "The persistent social admiration of masculinity itself supports war" (122).

Noddings is not an absolute pacifist. In fact, she suggests that care ethics and feminism ought to include a place for women who are willing to fight to defend those they care for. But the issue of mothers who fight to defend their children and women who fight to defend themselves against abusive husbands is qualitatively different from the issue of war. With war, we have a political, social, and cultural movement that involves a complex division of labor and a variety of problems linked to ideology, propaganda, and political interest. We need not offer up a radical Marxist account of how ideology blinds us to reality to admit that at some level moral judgment about war is warped by an ideology. And once we begin to think critically about this, it becomes difficult to find real wars that live up to the standards of just war theory.

Reply
Jennifer Kling

It is undoubtedly the case that propaganda and ideology can blind warmakers, warfighters, and civilians to the truth of whether or not their wars and wartime actions are justified. However, this does not preclude the need to engage in moral discussion about war, nor does it mean that all wars are inevitably unjust. Rather, it reminds us that we should keep our critical standards high, and be careful not to be swayed by pro-militancy narratives. In particular, we should avoid accepting the trope that masculinity, aggression, and heroism are inherently tied together, such that being a (male) hero means being a warfighter. Heroes come in all shapes and sizes, and they need not always use weapons to defend themselves and others. That being said, moving away from toxic masculinity, and being careful to question the patriotic narratives and positive media depictions of war, still leaves open the possibility that war is sometimes justified when it is in defense of people, their communities, and the moral character of the world in which we wish to live. As J.R.R. Tolkien writes, "War must be, while we defend our lives against a destroyer who would devour all; but I do not love the bright sword for its sharpness, nor the arrow for its swiftness, nor the warrior for his glory. I love only that which they defend" (Tolkien 1973, part 2).

5. Individual and Political Pacifism

If we admit that empirical reality presents us with a reason to be skeptical of the justification of war, we are then presented with a problem of individual judgment. If one follows the argument this far, difficult questions arise with regard to individual agency, personal responsibility, and the practical import of pacifism. Kling's discussion of revisionist just war theory also presents the problem of individual judgment—in her discussion of Jim, the American, and Hans, the German. While Kling raises this issue briefly and then sets it aside, her discussion helps us consider the question of what it means to be anti-war.

On the one hand, the conversation about pacifism and just war is like any other philosophical and moral conversation: it is about reaching a moral conclusion by way of reasonable argument. But on the other hand, this topic seems to demand that theory be connected to practice—especially in the life of soldiers, as well as in the lives of citizens and statesmen. This is part of the challenge of pacifism. Like moral vegetarianism and a variety of other moral commitments, pacifism seems to demand action—and that action puts you at odds with the mainstream. Pacifists are maligned as traitors and cowards, especially during wartime, when the war-spirit seems to demand that citizens rally round the flag and support the troops. For the pacifist, the idea of supporting the troops means that they don't want the troops to kill and die. But during wartime, this humane idea is viewed with suspicion.

One relevant question for both just warriors and pacifists is how much they are willing to "put their money where their mouths are," as the saying goes. It is reasonable to ask whether if a person believes that a given war is justifiable, they would be willing to fight in it—or at least, whether they would be willing to send their children or grandchildren to fight. Likewise, it seems reasonable to ask a person who is opposed to war whether they are willing to stop paying their taxes (as Thoreau did) or whether they are willing to go to jail in protest (as Thoreau also did).

Now of course, very few people are moral saints. So, we should admit that inconsistency, weakness of will, and self-deception are a normal part of our moral psychology. And we should be cautious about those kinds of pseudo-refutations that are typical of ad hominem arguments. But Kling's discussion of Hans, the German, and Jim, the American, seems to demand that we think concretely about how moral judgment factors into the way we live and what we do.

This comes to a head in discussions of conscientious refusal and civil disobedience. Revisionist just war theory appears to say that those who are asked to fight in unjust wars ought to refuse. This is an important idea that has often been embraced by pacifists. One of the obvious ways to stop war is for people to stop fighting. In the 1960s this became a kind of bumper-sticker slogan, as a question that asked, "What if they gave a war and nobody came?" This way of looking at things puts the burden of judgment on the individual's choice to fight or not to fight, to support the war or to refuse.

But none of this is easy. There are a number of difficult issues to consider here. One is the epistemological problem. How would Hans or Jim know whether the war he is fighting is just or unjust? Indeed, how would any of us know? Just war is a complex theory; and war is a complex historical phenomenon. The details of just war theory and its application in a given war require information and expertise that the average 18-year-old lacks. Indeed, even educated adults lack security clearances, geo-political knowledge, and the expertise to make informed judgments. A related question is about responsibility. What can Hans or Jim do about it, if he finds out that the war is unjust? Again, the average 18-year-old typically finds himself (or herself) in a position of subordination and dependence that would make it difficult to act in such a circumstance. And even for an ordinary citizen, there are questions about how much of a difference one's efforts will make. Thoreau went to jail for refusing to pay his taxes. But the war unfolded despite his protestations.

For these reasons and a number of others, it makes sense to distinguish between the pacifism of individuals and a more general kind of political pacifism. When we understand war as a political act, we see pacifism as a claim about politics. Yes, individuals have choices within political life—about war and about peace. But those choices are delimited by the historical and political situation. And this is why pacifism is not merely a question of an individual choosing to serve in the military or not. From a political vantage point, pacifism is about policy choices, who one votes for, the overall structure of society, and the way that economic and military power is deployed. Furthermore, it is not only about this or that war—it is also a tendency and a commitment toward creating systems that are less likely to be militant and more likely to engage in nonviolent conflict resolution.

Kling and revisionist theorists offer an important idea, when they discuss the difference between a subjective sense of justification and the objective reality of justification. An 18-year-old soldier may feel that a given war is justified, while in fact it is not (and vice versa). As mentioned above, the problem of ideology and propaganda makes it difficult for any of us to judge well in such circumstances. And since we were once 18 ourselves—and have children and students who are 18—we should rightly be reluctant to condemn the 18-year-old soldier for fighting in an objectively unjust war. This is why pacifists and anti-war activists should avoid maligning the soldiers who fight. Indeed, there may be soldiers who have decided that the war they are fighting in is unjust but who find it difficult to act on this judgment. Some militaries allow soldiers to declare themselves conscientious refusers, even in some cases allowing for selective conscientious objection that is not linked to a full-blown conversion to pacifism. But this is a difficult process, fraught with danger.

And at any rate, Jim and Hans did not declare the war. Nor did they determine how it would be fought. War is a political and social event. In constitutional democracies such as the U.S., this is grounded in "we, the people." Thus, those who should be blamed for unjust wars are not the soldiers but the military and political leadership—and ultimately the voters. This brings us back to the question of what it means to be anti-war. For the average citizen, an anti-war standpoint should have an impact on voting. It might lead to activism. And in some heroic cases it might lead to active war resistance of the sort associated with Thoreau, Dorothy Day, and others who are willing to be jailed in protest against unjust war.

Reply
Jennifer Kling

Professor Fiala brings up an important distinction between individual and collective action. While it is true, as one feminist slogan says, that the personal is political, it is also true that wars cannot be blocked, started, or stopped by one person, or even by a small group of people. Part of the definition of war is that it is a large-scale, collective event (or series of events, depending on the perspective that you take up). It can only exist when states or other large political groups decide to engage in it, and this means that individual activism can only go so far. What is actually needed is collective political action, and that requires communication and organization, of the sort that is neither glamorous nor individualistic, but community-oriented, local, and slow. Thoreau is an icon, certainly, but his actions weren't particularly effective. More effective was political organizer Stacey Abrams, who worked at the collective level to bring about Georgia's election of U.S. President Joe Biden in 2020. Such collective action could be in support of political pacifism, as Professor Fiala suggests, or it could be in support of contemporary just war theory, which enjoins states and other political groups to act morally on the world stage, rather than playing power politics or acting purely pragmatically. Of course, the pacifist and the just war theorist sometimes disagree about morality, but even getting states to a place where they are debating about the morality of war, rather than the expediency of war, would be a huge win for political activists and organizations.

To give a specific case, one policy change that activist organizations should fight for on moral grounds is changing the age of military enlistment. As Professor Fiala notes, it is unreasonable to condemn 18-year-olds, who are dealing with the fog of war, for fighting on the unjust side (assuming that the war is such that there is a just side). Given what we now know about psychological and cognitive development, we should not allow 18-year-olds to enlist. Now, this raises a whole series of problems about who should fill the military ranks, but these are good problems to work through. Contemporary just war theory should embrace the idea that warfighters should be only those who choose to fight in the full knowledge of the consequences of their choice—their frontal lobe must be fully formed, and they must have access to as much information as possible. It is important that just war theorists and practitioners do our best to ensure that warfighters maintain their autonomy and freedom of choice, and so avoid some aspects of moral injury, to the greatest extent possible.

6. Legitimacy, Autonomy, Cosmopolitanism, and Positive Peace

Let's now consider some other ways that pacifism differs from just war theory. One important issue is institutional and political questions. Just war theory is politically agnostic. It does not take sides with regard to the question of political legitimacy. Nor does it offer guidance for domestic politics. Kling and other contemporary just war theorists do consider the issue of jus post bellum, where the question of stability and prevention of future war can be connected to the political question. That is certainly an important area of concern. But it is not a primary concern of the justification of war. Ultimately just war theory is a narrowly focused theory that is primarily concerned with the justification of war in exceptional circumstances. It cannot offer guidance for the non-exceptional world of ordinary politics and the mundane prevention of violence. Kling acknowledges this when she suggests that war is only a "stopgap solution."

Pacifism offers a deeper and more comprehensive theory that is focused on a variety of issues in both domestic and international affairs. Again, there is overlap between pacifism and just war in this regard. Both approaches would support treaties and organizations that seek to prevent war and to minimize violence—including, for example, regulations that prohibit (and punish) war crimes. But typically, the theory of the justification of violence does not focus our attention on those preventative measures. I'll return to the issue of prevention again in a moment.

Let's focus here on a theoretical problem for political agnosticism. If just war theory is agnostic about domestic political arrangements, then this means that "outlaw states" and "rogue states" could justifiably go to war (see Rawls 1999). If the primary consideration of just cause is aggression, then this may mean that if an authoritarian regime's border were transgressed by a liberal regime that was seeking, for example, to defend the rights of an oppressed minority, then the authoritarian regime would be justified in fighting to defend its border. Of course, just war theorists have offered ways of working around this problem. One possibility is that the question of "legitimate authority" can be brought to the table. Another suggestion might be to give increased weight to considerations of humanitarian intervention and the "R2P" doctrine. Kling discusses this in her chapter. Just war theory has expanded to take in a broader purview. So maybe the theory is not as agnostic as I am making it out to be. But this agnosticism might reappear if one outlaw state's borders were transgressed by another outlaw state. Would an outlaw state have a just cause for responding to aggression by another outlaw state?

At any rate, as just war theory expands to consider issues regarding political legitimacy and human rights protection, there is more of a convergence with the general concerns of pacifism. Pacifism is often a broadly transformative theory that is interested in transforming domestic and international affairs in such a way as to make war less likely. The primary tool that just war theory has for preventing war is to build up a credible deterrent threat. Pacifists have other tools, including the development of cosmopolitan institutions and strengthening international laws and organizations.

In this regard there is substantial overlap between pacifism and some form of cosmopolitanism. There are complexities in the theory of cosmopolitanism that we cannot delve into here (see Fiala 2016). But important points of consideration for cosmopolitanism include a transformed understanding of the nation-state, universal concern for human rights, and a primary focus on nonviolent conflict resolution in global affairs. The history of cosmopolitanism includes proposals from Bentham, Rousseau, Kant, and others, which have had an influence on the development of pacifism and on international law. It is well-known that Kant's idea of a peace federation provided an inspiration for the league of nations. A lesser-known author in this tradition is Goldsworthy Lowes Dickinson, a British pacifist philosopher and colleague of Bertrand Russell's, whose writings on peace during and after the World War I had a direct impact on the formation of the League of Nations. Dickinson argued in philosophical terms that connected opposition to war to larger concerns including liberty and human flourishing.

Dickinson explained, "The object of war is to eliminate the foe, the object of peace is to grow strong by him" (Dickinson 1917, 59). He continued, arguing that peace is "the condition of all that is positive. For it is the space that gives the soul room to grow" (ibid).

This positive vision has been fleshed out by cosmopolitans in a variety of ways, with attention being directed toward respect for human rights, economic development, environmental sustainability, equality for women, religious liberty, toleration, and so on. In the literature of peace studies, these ideas have been gathered under the rubric of "positive peace." The terminology of positive peace has developed in the past 50 years in the work of Johan Galtung and those who follow his lead (Galtung 1969; Boersema 2018). Advocates of positive peace do not merely assert that peace is good (and war is bad). They also focus on the kinds of goods that ought to be found in a condition of positive peace, which includes justice, love, equality, liberty, and other related values.

I am not suggesting here that just war theorists are not interested in these goods. But the question of when war can be justified is narrowly focused. Given the fact that war is a broad social and political occurrence—an event of historical proportions that transforms societies, that can destroy political entities, and that can end or begin historical epochs—it seems that the narrow focus of just war theory is, to put it bluntly, short-sighted.

One way to make this clear is to consider the problem with the "domestic analogy," which is typical of just war theory. Just war theory often appeals to an analogy with personal self-defense. But war is simply not a form of self-defense: it is a political act that involves taking territory and putting other people to work killing and being killed. Kling recognizes the problem of the domestic analogy—and astutely points out that this is merely an analogy. She recognizes that there are other significant questions on the table when it comes to war: issues about sovereignty and territorial integrity. In this regard, Kling's cautious reinterpretation of the domestic analogy has something in common with the worries of pacifists and cosmopolitans. But Kling's analysis falls short of the critical point that is made by the pacifists and cosmopolitans.

The fundamental problem is found in the conceptual apparatus of just war theory. The problem is in the political morality and social ontology assumed by just war theory. The idea of the nation-state is problematic, for example, as is the notion of territoriality and the borders that have been established to divvy up the globe (often by war). Cosmopolitanism asks us to reconsider the importance we place upon political sovereignty—and how notions of sovereignty are imposed upon individuals and "peoples."

Another obvious problem is the fact that in war, the sovereign authority claims to have the power to require some people to kill other people. This leads to a claim about the duty that some have to die (and to kill) on behalf of others. This presents a deep moral problem, which Robert Holmes has criticized under the name of "existential pacifism." Holmes explains that this form of pacifism is based upon a fundamental commitment to the autonomy of the person. He says:

> One need only reject the idea that a free and open society is compatible with a coercive system which empowers some people to command others to kill, and requires those others, on pain of severe punishment for refusal, to obey those commands … It is grounded in faith in the institutions of a free and open society. Democratic processes are the antithesis of violent processes. At its best, democracy is a system of nonviolent conflict resolution.
> (Holmes 2017, 321)

Another problem has to do with territoriality and borders. We know, for example, that national borders often divide people in ways that go against the will of the people. In the Middle East, for example, Palestinians live without a nation in camps and settlements scattered through different countries. A similar story can be told about other stateless people or people who straddle borders— the Armenians, the Kurds, the Rohingya, the Tibetans, and so on. And modern nation-states may also include different sovereign entities within their borders: for example, First Nations and Native American tribes in the U.S. and Canada. There are also individuals who reside across borders: both the cosmopolitan elites and the wandering immigrant labor force, both of which often include family units with members who are citizens of different lands.

One of the difficulties of just war theory is that it takes sovereignty, borders, territoriality, and political identity for granted as a given. But when the problematization of these ideas that is offered by cosmopolitanism is taken seriously, it becomes more difficult to understand exactly how the just war categories ought to be applied. Would it make sense for Native American tribes to declare war against the U.S. government as a complaint against prior violations of sovereignty? Can the Palestinian people unite in war against Israel? How would we make sense of a war that forced members of cosmopolitan families to choose sides? And what ought we say about wars that are declared by the fiat of the executive branch of government without oversight by the legislative branch?

Real-world problems of this sort are significant—and typically overlooked by those who justify war. The justification of war usually simply draws a line in the historical sand while assuming that the current political structure, current borders, and the imposed identities of the contemporary world have a kind of moral substance which, in reality, they don't. Again, with these cosmopolitan, moral, and historical issues on the table it begins to look as if pacifism is more realistic than just war theory. At least, the aspiration of cosmopolitanism and pacifism is for a world in which these kinds of issues are taken seriously. This would be a world in which borders decrease in importance, a world in which democracy and human rights spread, a world in which autonomy and self-determination are taken seriously, and a world in which violence and war are no longer accepted as a means of resolving conflict.

Reply
Jennifer Kling

There is a lot to think about here! I discuss the coercive element of war—that it creates a structure wherein some people must obey the commands of others to kill or be killed—in my full response to Fiala, and so will not revisit that issue here. However, I do want to take up the questions of both political legitimacy and perspective that Professor Fiala raises. To begin, I disagree that contemporary just war theory is politically agnostic. Recent work on humanitarian intervention (Kling 2018), sovereignty and relationality in the contemporary world (Stacy 2007), just and unjust revolution (Finlay 2017), and the ethics of defensive war (Frowe 2014) all demonstrate just war theorists' increasing concern with issues of political legitimacy, sovereignty, territoriality, and the prevention and suppression of global and regional military conflicts. I acknowledge that the various just war traditions have not always taken up these questions with the urgency that they deserve—but as Professor Fiala would no doubt agree, we should not judge a theory on the basis of its historical adherents. Rather, we should test contemporary just war theory to see if it can meet the challenges posed by cosmopolitan pacifism. As is hopefully apparent, I think it can.

I argue in my initial chapter that a state's rights arise out of, and are dependent on, the rights of individuals within that state. So, if the state in question is not respecting the rights of its members, it is not clear that it has defensive rights of the sort required to justify war. In addition, contemporary just war theory maintains that the only wars that are possibly justified are defensive wars; this takes out of the "possibly justified" picture wars undertaken for revenge or retaliation for historical atrocities. Just war theorists have the conceptual and moral resources to respond to a number of the scenarios that Professor Fiala poses above. Working through each scenario would be complicated, yes, but most large-scale situations are. Just because it would take some time to work through each problem in appropriate detail does not mean that just war theory has no answers here.

Some of the skepticism with which cosmopolitan pacifism views just war theory has to do with perspective. Just war theory does tend to focus on a narrow set of questions—part of my work in this book has been to show that it need not remain so confined. While pacifists see this zoomed-in perspective as a bug, however, it could also be viewed as a feature. It is essential to take up the global perspective at some point and consider what kind of world we want to live in, and how we can go about building systems and institutions to create and support such a world. Yet it is also sometimes essential to focus on the problems in front of us. It does not help those dying at the hands of genocidaires to say that, really, sovereignty is a problematic concept and so the neighboring military is not justified in intervening to stop the slaughter. In order to create the conditions for positive peace, we must first deal with existing wars and military conflicts and their aftermaths. This will involve focusing on, and grappling with, the morally and politically messy situations that are the focus of much of contemporary just war theory.

7. A Continuum of Nonviolence and Violence

Now let's turn briefly to the question of how we define violence and nonviolence and what counts as war. As noted, there is convergence and overlap between just war theory and pacifism. This convergence is especially easy to see when we try to draw a firm line that distinguishes war from non-war, violence from nonviolence. Such a line is difficult to draw because there is a continuum here.

Kling directs us to this issue in her discussion of jus ad vim (the justification of limited violence short of war). Absolute pacifists may simply reject this. But they may also be sympathetic to the attempt to develop non-lethal weapons. And certainly, non-absolutists will be interested in rubber bullets, water cannons, etc. These methods are preferable to killing, just as limited violence is preferable to outright warfare. There are worries about escalation and promiscuous uses of force. But it seems that pacifists and just war theorists can agree that a world with less violence and less lethal violence is better than a world of total war.

We should also admit that some of the nonviolent techniques advocated by pacifists can be destructive and even lethal. Embargoes and boycotts can end up harming people—usually the most vulnerable people in a society. Civil disobedience can cause a riot. And strikes and protests can cause essential goods to become scarce or create a lack of essential services. Pacifists and nonviolentists may try to deny the implications of this by appealing to something like the principle of double effect. The principle of double effect may be employed, for example, as follows: the striking worker is only intending to send a (nonviolent) message; he or she is not intending to cause harm (say if an essential service is disrupted), even though he/she can foresee that such harm may result. But setting the doctrine of double effect aside, it seems that pacifists and nonviolentists should admit that there is a continuum here. In reality it is very difficult to avoid causing harm and to avoid violence entirely. Driving a car can cause harm. And capitalism appears to include what is often called "structural violence."

But—and here is the important point—pacifists and nonviolentists are interested in minimizing violence by imagining creative nonviolent (or less-violent) alternatives. They are especially interested in imagining effective alternatives to the direct and overt violence of war. On the other hand, the proponent of war often simply asserts the *necessity* of violence. Kling puts it this way, more than once, suggesting that just war theorists would prefer non-violent conflict resolution, if possible, but that the just war theorist is willing to affirm violence, "if necessary."

The continental divide that distinguishes just war theory from pacifism runs through the question of necessity and across the continuum of techniques of violence/nonviolence. A line gets drawn somewhere. The just war theorist thinks that violence is necessary in circumstances where the pacifist does not. And the just war theorist is willing to accept certain methods and techniques, while the pacifist is not.

To make this point concrete, consider the issue of torture. In a sense, non-lethal torture is a use of force short of war. Although I have not seen this discussed in the literature of jus ad vim, it might make sense for those interested in minimizing violence to be willing to allow torture—if torture were effective at preventing future violence. If torture were effective in this way, then it may be preferred to outright violence. And here is where again we might find some (admittedly strange) convergence. But such convergence would be short-lived, I argue, because the pacifist is not content to rest easy with such a conclusion. One problem is that there are real-world questions about the effectiveness of torture. Another problem is that exceptional cases tend to become self-reinforcing—and if we were to allow torture in some exceptional circumstances, this might normalize the practice (see Fiala 2006). But more importantly, the pacifist's goal is not simply to justify something like torture and leave it at that. Instead, the pacifist would be interested in imagining effective alternatives—and reconstructing the world so that we keep moving down the continuum toward nonviolence.

Reply
Jennifer Kling

Nonviolent resistance and conflict management and resolution are best. But in extraordinary circumstances, when such resistance and management and resolution fail to stop or ameliorate unjustified aggression, violence may become necessary. Importantly, contemporary just war theory does not rely solely on the claim of necessity to justify violence; as I discuss in my initial chapter, it also relies on the existence of the right to self- and other-defense as a corollary right to our basic autonomy and bodily integrity rights. The right to defense has built-in constraints and limits, such as proportionality, etc. One "bright line" between pacifism and just war theory tends to be—depending on the branch of pacifism in play—that just war theorists think violence is included in the types of actions justifiable in defense, while pacifists think it is not. Another way to say this is that pacifists think nonviolence is a limit on the right to defense. This raises difficult questions about what counts as violence, which I examine in depth in other work (Kling 2022; Kling and Mitchell 2021). This is not the place for such debates though, because our subject, war, is straightforwardly violent. Just war theorists do not deny this, and they agree with pacifism that creative, non-war, and nonviolent solutions should be prioritized. Peacebuilding should be a crucial aspect of just war theory. But just war theorists also think, at the end of the day, that violence, and even the brutal violence of war, is acceptable in certain circumstances. People are allowed to defend themselves and others with violence, and may even sometimes escalate that violence, when nothing else has worked and their and others' lives are threatened. We should never be fully comfortable with this conclusion—just war theorists should not, and I don't think many actually do, justify particular types of violence and then simply "leave it at that" or "rest easy"—but we should recognize this as a valid conclusion for the "unjust meantime" in which we live (Jaggar 2019).

8. Preventative Nonviolence

This brings me to my last point, which is about the importance of imagining ways to prevent war. Kling mentions this briefly in her discussion of jus post bellum. But while this is a minor point of emphasis for just war theory, war prevention is a significant focal point for pacifism. A medical analogy comes to mind here. War is

something like surgery—a "stopgap," as Kling puts it. By the time
we need surgery, many other solutions have been ignored (or have
failed to materialize). In a sense, just war theory is focused on the
narrow question of when surgery is required, while pacifism is
focused on preventative healthcare. It is usually possible to avoid
surgery, if we take proactive care in advance of a crisis. We know
the recipe for health: eat right, get some exercise, minimize stress,
avoid pollution and poisons, etc. The analogy with war works as
follows. We can avoid war if we take proactive care in advance. We
know the recipe for political health: it is what the advocates of
positive peace and cosmopolitanism are focused on. Societies need
to respect the autonomy of persons (including soldiers). Peace
grows when there is a democratic political structure. Societies
should avoid militarism and the growth of the military-industrial
complex. We should work to develop strategies of nonviolent
conflict resolution. We should build cosmopolitan systems of international justice. We should develop strategies of nonviolent
civilian-based defense (as in Sharp 1990). And so on. All of this is
on the table for the critic of war, while the proponent of just war
theory is narrowly focused on the question of when war is justified.
The question of whether war can be justified is like the question of
whether surgery can be justified. It likely can be justified—when the
illness has already gone too far.

Of course, even if a non-absolute pacifist believes that war could
be justified, he may refuse to go along. And here is another divergence. While just war theory sometimes only speaks of war
being "permissible," often this slips over into a claim about the
"necessity" of war. The pacifist avoids this slippage. A non-
absolute pacifist may allow that in some rare case, war could be
permissible. But he will also say that since history tends to show
that war is usually not justifiable, it would be odd to say that war is
necessary, in the sense of being morally required. Rather, if anything is morally required it is that we continue to find ways to
prevent war. And in the concrete emergency, the pacifist will suggest that we should seek alternatives—just as a person for whom
surgery is recommended may prefer to pursue other less-invasive
treatments. But before we reach a crisis point in which we are
confronted with this question, the pacifist will suggest we ought to
engage in a sustained effort to prevent war, so that eventually we
are no longer presented with this terrible choice.

Reply
Jennifer Kling

Throughout, I have agreed with Professor Fiala that preventing war should be a priority. But prevention, contemporary just war theory contends, is not the whole story. We must also consider what to do if and when prevention fails. While Professor Fiala suggests that just war theory's focus on war is somewhat myopic, I contend that this focus reflects a sensitivity to the world in which we find ourselves. To borrow his healthcare analogy, the illness is already that far. Just war theory, rather than bemoaning the fact of emergencies, says "Okay, so what should we do? Let's triage the patient in front of us as best we can, using the guidelines and rules that we've studied and know how to do, and then worry about preventative measures later, once we don't have a patient on the cusp of dying." I think this attitude shows that there is room for both just war theory and pacifism in the world. Just as we need different kinds of doctors (preventative care, routine care, emergency care, etc.) in the world, so too do we need political theorists and activists with different focuses and specializations. Perhaps this might strike some readers as too conciliatory a note to end on, but I think it reflects the deep connections underlying just war theory and pacifism, as well as their divergences.

Chapter 4

Response to Fiala

Jennifer Kling

Contents

In this chapter, Kling responds to Fiala's arguments as he articulated them in Chapter 1. Kling sets out three problems with relying on consequentialist arguments against war, raises concerns about reasoning from religious traditions, questions the need for a unity of means and ends, and emphasizes the importance of non-ideal theory in an imperfect real world that is shot through with violence and injustice. Fiala responds throughout to Kling's comments.

Let me begin my response by agreeing with Professor Fiala that every just war theorist worth their salt would rather pacifism prevail in the world. I wish just war theory were a historical curiosity, something studied in history of philosophy courses—as an outmoded theory that people used to believe—rather than in contemporary political theory and international relations courses. It would be a better world if there were no war, and if war were never needed to defend our, and others', lives and communities.

DOI: 10.4324/9780367809850-6

But sadly, that is not the case. Just war theory has a role to play in our contemporary era, because war is sometimes morally justified in the world as it is today. This is not to say that it should be celebrated; as Fiala notes, both the pacifist and the just war theorist rightly reject bellism (the love or worship of war). But it is to say that sometimes, war is an appropriate last-ditch defensive response to a world shot through with lethal oppression and injustice, mass atrocity, and genocidal violence.

However, this is not to say that anything goes in war. As I wrote in my initial chapter, and as Fiala contends, the goal of both contemporary just war theory and anti-war pacifism is "to shrink the circle of justified violence down toward a vanishing point." The difference is that pacifism strives to erase the circle entirely, while just war theory maintains that some violence can be justified in extraordinary circumstances. The key is that the circumstances must be extraordinary—unlike the realist, the just war theorist does not shrug at violence or see it as inevitable, as a natural part of the world that is either easily justifiable or not subject to moral constraint at all. Stringent moral conditions must be met for violence and war to be justified, both in general and in each particular instance. When those conditions are not met, just war theory joins with pacifism in condemning violence and war as wrong.

This dialogue between Professor Fiala and myself not only brings out important subtleties in the ongoing moral and political debates surrounding war, but also demonstrates one common cause of both pacifism and just war theory: the rejection of Prussian general Carl von Clausewitz's 19th-century realist claim that war is simply politics by other means (Walzer 2006, 79). War represents a fundamental break with ordinary politics, and so should be approached with caution, if at all. It is not merely one means among others, or "the sole art that belongs to him who rules" and who would keep ruling, as Renaissance-era political theorist Niccolò Machiavelli (1469–1527) argues (Machiavelli 1998, chap. xiv). War is horrific and deeply consequential, and so must be treated as a distinct, difficult-to-justify activity that severely disturbs what ought to be the political norm—a just and lasting peace.

In what follows, I offer a few responses to Fiala's arguments, with the goal of helping the reader to imagine counter-arguments and further points of contention. This is not intended as a line-by-line response to Fiala's articulated position in Chapter 1. Rather, I have focused on issues and ideas that I believe warrant further discussion.

I. Weighing Consequences, Side Effects, and the Problem of the Future

Throughout his discussion, Fiala presents a series of strong consequentialist arguments against war, and rightly notes that contemporary just war theory does not often take into consideration the problems of PTSD and moral injury that are suffered by warfighters. Just war theory should take these consequences of war seriously; that should be a part of the transformation of contemporary just war theory that I proposed in the final section of my initial chapter. However, the bad consequences of war, dire as they are, do not—and I suspect cannot—show that war is never justified. Fiala argues that a consequentialist view of war leads to contingent pacifism. There are at least three reasons to think that this argument does not succeed.

First, whenever consequentialist arguments arise in complicated contexts such as war and peace, it is necessary to consider how to weigh the myriad rights, values, harms, and wrongs in play against each other, or whether such weighing is even possible. Consequentialism is relational. It "involves a ratio or comparison of scale between x and y; it implies that x and y stand in a relationship to one another that makes such a comparison appropriate ... . [it] is also normative: it assumes an appropriate correspondence of scale between x and y" (Uniacke 2011, 255). The idea here is complex, but the basic assumption of consequentialism is that every consequence in play—every right, value, harm, or wrong at stake in war—is comparable, such that they can all be weighed against each other to determine the best course of action. Once we compare all of these pros and cons, the thought goes, and so know what would be best overall, we should then act accordingly, to bring about the most good consequences and the fewest bad consequences. The consequentialist contingent pacifist does this weighing and concludes that *not* going to war is most likely to bring about this so-called "best state of affairs."

This might seem like a reasonable way to decide whether war is justified. It tracks how many of us make decisions in everyday life, and it is in general wise to think about the consequences of our choices and actions. The problem though, is that it's not at all clear that it is possible to compare the wide variety and kinds of consequences that are at stake in war. How do we measure the production of severe PTSD against the creation of a liberal democracy?

Does it even make sense to talk about trading off some amount of infrastructure damage for the protection of some individuals' autonomy? For example, would it be acceptable to destroy a building to prevent a war rape? How about two buildings? How do we even begin to make such comparisons? It seems that in each case, both considerations matter—but in different ways, such that we do not want to think about them as being on the same scale of value. This point is sometimes called the **incommensurability of value** or the **incomparability of value**. It is a worry that often arises in political contexts, where several different kinds of rights, values, harms, and wrongs are at stake (Raz 1986). If the incommensurability or incomparability of value is true, then consequentialist arguments—both against and in favor of war—fail, because consequentialism assumes the comparability, or commensurability, of all possible consequences.

But you might disagree with the incommensurability of value. Perhaps it is possible to compare all the consequences of war and trade them off against each other—give up some liberty for some stability there, accept some environmental damage for the implementation of democracy here—in order to discern whether the good outcomes of war could ever outweigh the bad. Notice though, that this moral determination does not distinguish between political and military decision-makers' and warfighters' intended consequences and the unintended side effects of their decisions and actions. This should strike us as strange. Most people would agree that there is a moral difference between what someone means to do and what they inadvertently cause to occur via their otherwise well-intended actions. If I mean to help someone, and in the course of helping, accidentally break their favorite glass, that is different than my deliberately and maliciously breaking their favorite glass. Although in both scenarios, the glass is broken, the moral valence of my actions is different in each case.

This difference depends on there being a distinction between what we intend to happen and what actually does happen. Our actions have side effects. Some of these side effects we can see coming—they are foreseen—and, if they are bad, we have a responsibility to mitigate them to the best of our ability. Warfighters must do their best to ensure that civilians have a chance to evacuate city blocks before surging, because they know that likely side effects of their surge are civilian casualties and other collateral damage. Some side effects we cannot see coming—they are unforeseen. U.S. President Harry Truman did not know that dropping two atomic bombs on Japan would create a collective psychic scar that has spanned generations and influenced Japanese culture, politics, and spirituality. His choice was unjustified and wrong for other reasons, but it does not seem unjustified *because of* this unforeseen, unintended result. To say that this consequence partially makes his action wrong—as consequentialism does—incorrectly morally equates intentions and results. As 20th-century philosopher Bernard Williams (1929–2003) puts it, "Consequentialism is basically indifferent to whether a state of affairs consists in what I do, or is produced by what I do" (Smart and Williams 1973, 93). This indifference leads, Williams concludes, to consequentialism's fundamental absurdity. It puts freedom fighters and oppressors, genocidaires and UN peacekeepers, morally on a par by insisting that all that matters is that good consequences be produced—people's particular intentions, reasons, and agency be damned.

This is the heart of the **integrity objection** to consequentialism. It erases important moral distinctions that should inform our moral judgments. Non-consequentialist just war theory, by contrast, insists that there is a difference between what people intentionally do and the side effects—both foreseen and unforeseen—of their actions. This distinction has at least two roles in discussions of war. For one, when determining whether war is justified, decision-makers should think not just about all the possible and likely consequences of a particular war, but also about whether that war is in accordance with their society's values, ideals, and life and community projects, as well as the constraints of jus ad bellum. For another, when determining what actions in war are justified, military strategists should think about whether those actions are in line with their communal and political values and ideals (such as rule of law and respect for human rights), as well as the constraints of jus in bello, and not just about whether those actions are likely to be effective in achieving the war's aims. Essentially, the point here is that if the integrity objection to consequentialism holds, then consequentialist reasoning is not the right way to frame our moral thinking about war. And thus, it should not lead us to accept contingent pacifism.

My third concern with the consequentialist argument for contingent pacifism is that we don't know the future. Bluntly, humans are bad at predicting what will happen with any level of accuracy or precision, especially as it concerns large-scale social and political issues. As author and futurist Ursula K. Le Guin puts the point rather lyrically, "We live in capitalism. Its power seems inescapable—but then, so did the divine right of kings. Any human power can be resisted and changed by human beings ... we need ... and are missing ... [those] who can see alternatives to how we live now, [who] can see through ... to other ways of being" (Le Guin 2014, no page numbers). The future is radically uncertain. To pretend otherwise, as consequentialist reasoning often does, is to assume a level of foresight, and power, that we simply do not have.

To put the point more philosophically, the world is complex, and at any given time, it is impossible to know with a high degree of certainty either what all of the effects of any particular action will be, or how things are likely to turn out more generally. This is sometimes called the **knowledge problem** for consequentialism. We can make guesses with some degree of probability, yes, but our accuracy levels go down the more wide-ranging and complex the given situation is. And war is a socio-cultural-political activity of enormous complexity and range. So, anyone who is engaging in probabilistic forward-looking risk-reward analyses of war in general, and/or specific wartime actions, is to some extent engaging in false precision. They are claiming to know more about the future than is possible, given human limitations.

To be clear, it is not that we have no ideas about, or knowledge of, the future. As English philosopher John Stuart Mill reminds us, the consequentialist rules of thumb ("if I do x, y is likely to occur: so I should/should not do x") that we use for everyday decision-making are a result of the fact that we do have good general ideas about how the world works and what the effects of our actions are likely to be (Mill 2006). But he also warns against using these everyday rules of thumb to make decisions in unfamiliar contexts. This is because those rules of thumb arise out of our millions of everyday experiences, and so are unlikely to be helpful in navigating unique and extraordinary circumstances. Consequentialist moral reasoning might be a good heuristic for our everyday lives, with which we are intimately familiar—but it is not obviously a good heuristic for thinking through the justification for war, with which many of us are (thankfully) very unfamiliar.

None of this is to say that the consequences of war don't matter. They very clearly do, and we should take account of them when considering whether war is justified. But it is to say that we should be wary of consequentialist reasoning, especially when discussing topics as morally and politically complicated and multi-layered as war. In 1539, Chief Acuera of the Timucua rejected Spanish conquistador Hernando de Soto's argument that the Timucua should submit to his and his army's rule because they could not hope to prevail. Acuera had this to say about such consequentialist reasoning: "As for me and my people, we choose death—yes! a hundred deaths—before the loss of our liberty and the subjugation of our country. Keep on, robbers and traitors: in Acuera and Apalachee we will treat you as you deserve … [with] war, never-ending war" (Acuera 2000, 3).

The Timucua eventually lost to the invaders and, as de Soto predicted, were slaughtered and their surviving people scattered. And perhaps, with the hindsight of history, we can say that such a negative outcome was inevitable. Still, do we really want to conclude, with the consequentialist contingent pacifist, that Acuera and the Timucua's defensive war was therefore unjustified? To do so would be to accept the various consequentialist assumptions discussed in this section, many of which are deeply problematic.

Reply
Andrew Fiala

Kling's points here are important. They are connected with a general critique of consequentialism that cannot be ignored in conversations about ethics. The problem of knowledge (and the challenge of retrospective analysis) are also important philosophical concerns. I tried to acknowledge some of this in my contribution with the World War II example. In retrospect it is not clear that Truman's bombing of Japan was justifiable. But there are things that he didn't know and future consequences he could not predict. The same is true for Kling's example of the Timucua. Agents within history have different priorities and a different vantage point, in comparison with the concerns and perspectives of philosophical critics. And of course, there is the problem of calculating all of the consequences in complex cases such as war. These are among the reasons I do not think that a consequentialist argument in defense of pacifism is entirely persuasive. Consequentialism only produces an open-ended version of contingent or conditional pacifism. But pacifists typically do not merely offer consequentialist arguments. They also bring in deontological considerations as well as the concerns of virtue traditions and religion. I agree with Kling that consequentialism alone is not sufficient to reach a robust pacifist conclusion. But I might also suggest in reply here, that consequentialism is not sufficient either for the justification of war. How do we calculate the utilities with regard to a complex and evolving entity such as war and in light of limitations on knowledge? Furthermore, I also suspect that many who justify war are appealing to different forms of moral justification grounded in ideas about virtue, duty, patriotism, nationalism, and so on. Consequentialism is thus only part of the story.

2. The Perils of Reasoning from Religious Traditions

Of course, not all pacifism is based in consequentialism. As Fiala writes, anti-war pacifism has roots in several religious traditions, including (among others) Buddhism, Christianity, Daoism, and Judaism. He notes that these traditions are complicated, and many of them include both pacifist and just war interpretations. It is worth pointing out though, that none of these venerable traditions include realist interpretations. So, while it is possible to consistently hold to Christian beliefs and pacifism, or Christian beliefs and just war theory, it may be contradictory to hold to Christian beliefs and realism. (The phenomenon of patriotic Christianity, common in the United States, does approach what Fiala refers to as a "moral iteration" of realism. I return to this issue shortly.)

Fiala's discussion of religious traditions and the varying moral views of war that arise from them is quite nuanced and helpful. But there is a worry with turning to religious traditions to justify particular views of war. Once religion is involved, people tend to engage in the no true Scotsman fallacy.

No True Scotsman Fallacy: *Finessing or changing the meaning of a concept or category unilaterally in order to control "what counts" as falling into that concept or category.*

For example, imagine someone saying "All Scotsmen wear kilts." Someone else responds, "Macbeth is Scottish, and he only ever wears pants." The first person could respond, "Ah, but no *true* Scotsman would refuse to wear a kilt. So I'm right: all Scotsmen wear kilts." The implication here is that because Macbeth does not wear kilts, he's not Scottish. But this is fallacious reasoning—the first person, when presented with straightforward counter-evidence to their claim, responds not by admitting their mistake, but by unilaterally changing the boundaries of the category "Scottish" (which is not necessarily linked to kilt-wearing) in order to win the debate. To take a more real-world example of the no true Scotsman fallacy, consider this one: "I don't believe that she's really American. She's anti-gun, and no true American could be."[1]

This fallacy points toward the need, in any discussion or debate, to agree on the definitions of the concepts and categories being used. But part of the nature of religious traditions is that they are **essentially contested concepts**: they contain within themselves conflicting ideas, and so are inherently open to dispute and generative of diverging interpretations (Clarke 1979, 124). Take the following exchange: Andy says that pacifism is an essential part of the Christian tradition (implication: Christians should be pacifists), while Jen says that just war theory is an essential part of the Christian tradition (implication: Christians should be just war theorists). Who is right? As Fiala writes, we both are, because the concept of Christianity itself is essentially contested. And yet, because the nature of religion is such that each person and group has their own interpretation of it, the temptation exists to engage in no-true-Scotsmanning in order to "win" the discussion: "No *true* Christian would support war!" "No *true* Christian would support absolute pacifism!" "All *real* Buddhists are pacifists!" "All *actual* Jews support the Israeli military!" You see how quickly these lines of reasoning spiral toward partisan, us-versus-them dogmatism.

Fiala avoids such fallacious reasoning. However, given this ever-present peril, we would be better off contemplating pacifism and just war theory as independent systems of thought, rather than trying to discern which one better aligns with our preferred religious tradition. While genealogically speaking, both theoretical constructs arise from religious traditions, that is not a sufficient reason to accept either one as true. You should be a just war theorist or a pacifist not because you are a Christian, or a Buddhist, or a Jew, etc., but because you have considered the merits and pitfalls of each position carefully and have determined which you think is more justified and more morally correct.

It is worth pointing out that although religious traditions are essentially contested concepts, this does not mean that just anyone, with just any belief, can appropriately lay claim to being a member of a particular tradition. A Satanist cannot be Hindu. They can *claim* to be Hindu, of course, but they would be wrong. Each religious tradition has boundary markers, such that beliefs that fall outside of those boundaries, or contradict them, disqualify their holders from being members of the tradition.[2] For example, atheists can be culturally Catholic but, due to their atheism, cannot be religiously Catholic (in other words, they are not *Catholic-Catholic*). Realism about war may be such a disqualifying belief for many, if not most, religious traditions. Almost all religious traditions contain universal moral principles and codes of action; realism denies that morality applies to war. So it is difficult, if not impossible, to consistently be both religious and a realist.

Despite this, there is a kind of patriotic Christianity that is rampant in the United States that has many realist elements. Patriotic Christianity usually includes the following key elements: God has blessed the U.S.; because God has blessed us, we are the "good guys" in every conflict in which we're involved; when we are fighting, we are doing God's work; and God will continue to bless the U.S. only so long as we fight to win every conflict. This melding of Christianity with patriotism is toxic and dangerous, as singer-songwriter Bob Dylan recognizes in his incisive song, "With God on Our Side:"

> Oh the First World War, boys
> It closed out its fate
> The reason for fighting
> I never got straight
> But I learned to accept it
> Accept it with pride
> For you don't count the dead
> When God's on your side
>
> ...
>
> But now we got weapons
> Of the chemical dust
> If fire them we're forced to

> Then fire them we must
> One push of the button
> And a shot the world wide
> And you never ask questions
> When God's on your side. (Dylan 1963)

Patriotic Christianity leads to the belief that anything goes in war, so long as it is for the glory and hegemony of the U.S. and by extension, God. Similarly, the only appropriate attitude toward "the troops" (the U.S. military) is uncritical support. While this patriotic Christianity has the veneer of morality—its narrative is that whatever the U.S. does in war is not only right, but also commendable and unquestionable, because it is what God wants—it is actually a form of realism. This is because it takes up the realist attitude, described by Fiala, that "it would be morally wrong, from this point of view, not to do whatever it takes to win." But just because it is your country, and/or your religion, engaging in a military conflict, that does not make that war morally justified, nor does it make any and all actions your side takes in that war justified. Both the pacifist and the just war theorist insist on these crucial points, which all too often get lost when patriotism and religion meld together.

Given this perilous line of thought, which is pervasive in both the U.S. and other cultures and countries, it is all the more important that those concerned to justify war take a long, critical look at their reasons for doing so. Neither religious nor patriotic beliefs can justify war. Only self- or other-defense can possibly justify war, and even then, the circumstances must be extraordinary, such that there is no less lethal and less consequential way to defend people's lives and communities. Those who would justify war must be careful not to be led down the primrose path of national self-interest, religious fanaticism, or an unholy fusion of the two.

Reply
Andrew Fiala

I think that Kling and I agree quite a bit about the need for a nuanced approach to religion. My own approach is agnostic. And I recognize the need to acknowledge diversity within and between religious traditions. Thus, I appreciate Kling's "true Scotsman" warning. It is not clear exactly who counts as a "true Christian" or (to broaden the case a bit) a "true Gandhian." Yes, even the followers of Gandhi have disagreements! But I would like to underline here, in reply to this point, the importance of the idea of a "tradition." There has been some debate in the literature about the difference between the idea of a "just war theory" and a "just war tradition." Philosophers (like myself and, I suspect, Professor Kling) tend to prefer to talk about "theory" rather than "tradition." One reason for this preference is that *theory* seems to imply an objective vantage point from which arguments and truth-claims can be evaluated. *Tradition* is less objective, afflicted by the contingencies of history, textual exegesis, dogmatic pronouncement, debates about what is canonical, and so on. There is a big debate here, which requires further thought. But one point I'd like to emphasize here is that pacifism can be understood in both senses as well: either as a tradition or as a theory. Philosophical defenders of just war theory tend to criticize pacifism as if it is a "theory," i.e., a putatively objective theory that rejects war. Philosophical defenders of what we might call "pacifist theory" do something similar—they focus on principles, arguments, and definitive conclusions. But by invoking the idea of a "pacifist tradition," things get more complicated. As I noted in my contribution, the pacifist tradition includes a variety of disparate thinkers, including thinkers who come from quite different religious traditions. These thinkers are in conversation. And their thinking evolves. In this sense the "true Scotsman" warning holds for accounts of pacifism as well. Who counts as a "true pacifist"? Well, the answer is "it's complicated and evolving."

3. Reconsidering a Unity of Means and Ends

Defenders of pacifism argue that the means used must match the end sought. If our end goal is a just and lasting peace, then we are only justified in using nonviolence to get there. Using violence to achieve peace is generally impermissible, because doing so inevitably sows the seeds of future violent conflict. It also appears to be contradictory: using violent means seems to take you in the opposite direction of your goal, which is a just peace. But this unity argument assumes that there is a linear connection between means and ends, such that at any given moment, we're either moving closer to or further away from the ends we seek. Means and ends are not linear in this way, though; there is not such a straightforward connection between the two as the pacifist position suggests. This is because both means and ends are complicated, and include several aspects that are themselves more or less unified.

Consider the end of a just and lasting peace. Engaging in defensive war to achieve that end does go against negative peace, yes, but it also expresses our commitment to the ideal of positive peace. As Walzer writes, engaging in defensive violence vindicates our desire to live in a world where all people are treated with dignity, where their rights are respected, and where they are able to "freely shape their separate destinies" (Walzer 2006, 72). But that kind of society, and world, "is never fully realized; it is never safe; it must always be defended" (Walzer 2006, 72). The great importance that we attach to the values that are under attack when serious, widespread injustices go unopposed necessitates defense, even to the point of war. Part of what we do when we fight back is fight for the moral character of the world in which we want to live. Ideally, that fight should take a nonviolent form; but sometimes, when all else fails, putting that commitment into practice demands defensive violence.

It is not so clear then, that the means of defensive war always and obviously contradict the end of a just and lasting peace. Furthermore, we need not accept the claim, often included in discussions of using war as a means to achieve peace, that violence inevitably leads to future violence. As we discussed above, we do not know the future. Although the ending of World War I did, in many ways, set up the conditions for World War II to occur, we cannot generalize from that one case to conclude that all wars inexorably create the conditions for more war. That is a very broad conclusion, and even if it turns out to be historically the case, this still does not show that war *necessarily* leads to future war, as Martin Luther King, Jr. implies. It is at least possible that defensive war could lead to a just and lasting peace.

Why think this is possible at all? Because violence, as Megan Mitchell and I have argued in other work, does have a role in political communication (Kling and Mitchell 2019). Although it is true, as Fiala argues, that force does not *rationally* prove anything in the realm of ideas, this does not mean that violence, especially defensive violence, is antithetical to moral and political persuasion. Here, we must bear in mind that people are not purely rational creatures—much as we might wish it to be so, people do not act solely on the basis of what is most rational, or most reasonable. People are subject to ideological infection, which means that they can easily become caught up in ideologies, such as racism, sexism, colonialism, and fascism, which structure their perceptions and conceptualizations of the world, and guide their actions and practices.

Philosopher Sally Haslanger argues that **ideology** consists of more than just a set of shared false beliefs and errors in reasoning. It is best understood as a cultural resource and a source of beliefs that includes, among other things, "a language, a set of concepts, a responsiveness to particular features of things (and not others), [and] a set of social meanings" (Haslanger 2017, 7). It "includes psychological mechanisms—cognitive, conative, perceptual, agentic—that sort, shape, and filter what can be the objects of our attitudes" (Haslanger 2017, 13). These are, as she puts it, "the very tools that our language and culture provide us in order to think" (Haslanger 2017, 7). So, within the context of widespread ideological infection, those fighting for justice will have to engage their interlocutors in ways that are not strictly speaking reasons-giving, but instead involve changing the very terms of the debate (Haslanger 2017, 10). They will have to alter their opponents' perceptions, outside of, or in addition to, reasoned argument, in order to provide them with new conceptual schemas and webs of social meanings, to break them out of their common practices and existing ideologies (Haslanger 2017, 13–15).

Mitchell and I contend that defensive violence, while not in any strict sense reasons-giving, might be a way of changing the terms of the debate. Violence has the potential to shake up people's conceptual schemas and other ideological building blocks which hold in place their oppressive practices (Kling and Mitchell 2021, esp. chap. 4). For example, throwing bottles and bricks at police invading beleaguered Black communities could cause people to question one narrative of police as protectors, and perhaps encourage them to reinterpret the police as occupiers (Kling and Mitchell 2021, chap. 4). Violence is not guaranteed to cause such reconceptualizations and perceptual shifts, but it is not an unfamiliar strategy for trying to break the spell that someone's ideology, and their attendant fears and anxieties, have cast over their best judgment. Violence is literally shocking; it can jar people into seeing the absurdities of their own views and so change their minds.

Defending the killing of a slave-catcher by an escaped enslaved person, Frederick Douglass argues that not only was the killing justified but also that it was likely to be helpful in persuading slaveholders, as well as the public, that slavery was unjustified (Boxill 1995, 718). According to Douglass, slaveholders had ample evidence that enslaved persons were persons who loved liberty. Policies of keeping enslaved persons ignorant and enacting physical and emotional cruelty upon them were the necessary strategies for preventing the exercise of that love (Boxill 1995, 727–730). Fear, however, could cause the slaveholders to revisit that evidence. The aim of attacking slaveholders, Douglass concludes, is not to add evidence that enslaved persons were persons with rights— slaveholders already had sufficient evidence of that—but to convince the slaveholders to pay attention to that evidence. The slaveholders' pride blinded them to enslaved persons' rights because it caused them to believe their own propaganda. They, as well as the general public, began to truly believe themselves superior and thereby invulnerable. Attacks by enslaved persons could undermine slaveholders', and the public's, false pride by producing fear and vulnerability (Boxill 1995, 727–737). The fear and intimidation induced by violence can thus be persuasive; as philosopher of race and political theorist Bernard Boxill concludes in his expansion and defense of Douglass' view, it can "clear their [people's] moral vision" and enable them to see truths they have conveniently ignored or forgotten (Boxill 1995, 727).

Violence has the power to shift and sharpen people's moral vision. This speaks to the role that non-cognitive features such as perception and emotion play in sustaining ideology and through it, widespread oppression and aggression. Breaking through those barriers requires activities that, although persuasive, are not strictly speaking reasons-giving (Kling and Mitchell 2021, chap. 4). Defensive violence thus has the potential to lead to a just and lasting peace. When used appropriately to fight ideological infection, it can bring people back from the brink, not by engaging with them rationally, but by persuading them to reconsider their ideologies and the aggressive actions and practices to which those ideologies give rise.

Does this general argument about the communicative and persuasive power of defensive violence rise to the level of justifying defensive war? That is a tough question, and mirrors many of the difficulties that Fiala considers in his discussion of the "might makes right" fallacy. Each side in a war will tend to think that their use of violence is justified, and might even use the argument provided above as fodder—it would be easy for an aggressor to defend their use of war as a method of persuading the other side out of their dangerous "human rights" ideological infection. Just war theory, like pacifism, must reject this by an appeal to objective moral standards. Some ideologies are bad and wrong (fascism, colonialism, imperialism), and some conceptual schemas are good and right (equality, freedom, human rights). Without this baseline belief, everything is relative, and we fall into Thrasymachus' trap that justice, and rightness, is whatever the strong say it is. But while both pacifists and just war theorists agree that might does not make right, that does not block the possibility of using might to fight for what is right. Ultimately, the unity of means and ends that the pacifist calls for may not always be possible, because sometimes, violence may be required to burn out the ideological infection that is blocking the path to a just and lasting peace.

Reply
Andrew Fiala

This gives me a lot to think about! Professor Kling is probably right that the typical philosophical response to the Thrasymachus problem does not rule out the possibility that (as Kling says) might could be used to fight for what's right. I think my initial presentation is lacking in subtlety on this point. So let's put the pacifist point more carefully and say that while might could be used to fight for what's right, this opens the door to a slippage—as we move from the realm of ideas to the realm of force. But, as Kling suggests, there is no necessary reason that people need to step across that threshold. A wise and virtuous just warrior may say to himself, I am only fighting because I have to defend what is good and true and just. But the pacifist's concern is that there are very few wise and virtuous warriors of that sort. And the general public does not seem to think this way. Of course, this is only a generalization. And perhaps education about justice and virtue would help to eliminate the belief that might makes right, while leaving open the door for the idea that might could be used to fight for what's right.

I'd like to also briefly reply to Kling's fascinating suggestion that violence can be communicative. This is an interesting idea. I do not deny that violence is communicative. But two worries come to mind.

First, what exactly does violence communicate? The pacifist critic will argue that violence does not typically communicate moral truth; rather, it communicates will-to-power, domination, and the rest of what is found in the worry about "victor's justice."

Second, what about war in the contemporary world—what does it communicate? There is no definite answer here. But pacifists worry again about will-to-power, etc. They also tend to argue that war typically communicates in such blunt terms that nuance and subtlety are lost. Instead, there are accusations and recriminations, calls for retaliation and retribution, as well as racist or ethnocentric tropes and stereotypes. Kling suggests that violence can sharpen a person's moral vision. But I might suggest that it can just as easily make things more obscure and give voice to morally suspect ideas.

4. Justice and Injustice in the Real World

War always involves injustice. In the real world, the moral constraints of jus ad bellum and jus in bello, not to mention jus post bellum, are rarely, if ever, met. Contemporary just war theory must grapple with these facts by paying close attention to the experiences of political and military decision-makers and warfighters, in order to understand the personal, social, and political pressures that they face, that lead them to act badly in war. Why did the United States get involved in the Korean war? What were the various factors that led to the Mỹ Lai massacre? There are many different ways to answer these questions, because we can (and should!) consider them through different lenses. The better we can come to grasp the psychological, anthropological, and sociological underpinnings of war, the more we can develop policies, procedures, systems, and institutions that encourage those involved in war to adhere to the spirit of just war theory as well as its current iteration in international law.

I go against many revisionist theorists, who focus on applying the methodology of analytical philosophy to war, when I say that the study of war should not be "purely" philosophical, but rather a collaborative effort that includes practitioners as well as researchers and theoreticians. This is because contemporary just war theory should speak to the reality of war, and it cannot do that if its main focus is working through the permutations of artificial thought experiments and testing the fault lines of ideal theory. This is not to say that such work—exemplified by scholars such as Jeff McMahan, Helen Frowe, and Cécile Fabre—is not important; but it is to say that they defend a more abstract and theoretical form of just war theory, which may be part of the reason for the disconnect seen in the world today between the theory of just war and actual wars (Flisi and Peperkamp 2021). Contemporary just war theory should grapple with the difficulties of our messy, complicated world, and the imperfect warmakers, warfighters, and civilians who populate it. When we take existing social reality as our starting point, we come to see *why* people, communities, and other political groups act as they do. This, in turn, enables us to see the mechanisms by which we might encourage them to operate differently, more in line with the moral frameworks of the various just war traditions.

We cannot snap our fingers and create a just and peaceful world. The world already exists, and it is full of injustice and other imperfections. But in some sense, it is not helpful to sit down and lament the fact that people, communities, and other political groups don't believe, think, and act as our moral theory says they should. Instead, we must work with what we find, in order to make the world a less unjust place, and war less hellish. Working through the realities of tech-based urban warfare and counterinsurgencies in Afghanistan and Iraq, prosecuting war criminals, creating cultural sensitivity and bias trainings for military troops—none of these changes individually will make actual wars fully just, but together they move wars, and warfighting, in the right direction. Defensive wars are sometimes, in extraordinary circumstances, morally justified. The job of the just war theorist is to ensure that only these kinds of wars are fought, and that they are fought as morally as possible. And the best way to do that is by working *with* warmakers and warfighters to create and maintain just pathways through a world that, currently, enables and encourages unjust war.

This is a non-ideal, step-by-step approach to justice. It is not particularly exciting, but it may actually have a chance of succeeding. And more importantly, this non-ideal just war theory works with people rather than running roughshod over them and the values that they hold most dear. As author Terry Pratchett puts it, "only people can build a better world for people. Otherwise it's just a cage" (Pratchett 1991, 305).

A pacifist might respond that war always involves injustice not merely because of how it tends to be practiced in the real world, but also because of the nature of war as a collective activity. As Fiala puts it, war is "fundamentally immoral" because "some individuals command others to kill or be killed" and "some individuals either deliberately subordinate themselves and give up their autonomy or are forced to do so." Fiala is right about the hierarchical nature of war and the chain of command; some autonomy is always lost in war, and this is an injustice. Still, when the choice is between the loss of autonomy for some versus the loss of autonomy for everyone else in a society, it is reasonable to ask whether the loss of autonomy for some is an injustice we should be willing to accept for the sake of protecting the autonomy of everyone else in the society. Consider the ongoing conflict between South and North Korea. The warfighters of the South Korean military have had their autonomy taken from them in precisely the way that Fiala describes, in order to protect their society from becoming like that of North Korea. Their unfreedom is not for nothing—it is for the purpose of promoting more freedom for the rest of the members of their society.

Philosophically, we can put the question thusly: Is doing some amount of injustice acceptable to maintain and promote justice more broadly? The just war tradition says that it is, while lamenting that the aggressive militancy of some political groups necessitates defensive war by others. Again, it would be better if we did not have to make such "greater good" arguments. If there were no aggressors, there would be no need for defense, and thus, no need for the application of just war theory. In line with pacifism, contemporary just war theory agrees that an ounce of prevention is worth a pound of cure. We should do everything possible to avoid war, including working to transform individuals and societies in the ways that both pacifism and non-ideal just war theory suggest.

But, if the extraordinary circumstances arise that necessitate engaging in defensive war, just war theory accepts the subordination
of some individuals to the military chain of command to protect the
freedom, autonomy, and human rights of everyone else.

Of course, you might well respond that a society willing to
produce such injustices is not really concerned with justice at
all, and so does not have the standing to engage in self- or other-
defense. Communist propaganda during the Cold War made precisely this point, lambasting the United States for pushing democratic values abroad while maintaining its brand of domestic
racism. The United States should fix its own house, the Soviet
Union argued, before presuming to comment on other states'
human rights violations (Skrentny 1998, 238–239). And while it is
true that states should always work to be more just domestically, it
would be a mistake to insist that only perfectly just states and
societies may justifiably defend their own or other people with war.

Perfection does not exist in the real world—individuals are imperfect, and thus so are the communities, states, and other political
groups they comprise. Awareness of our own imperfections should
not stop us, though, from trying to do what is right; rather, it
should encourage us to try harder, to act in the best ways that we
know how, to the best of our abilities. Mostly, this should lead
states and other political groups to avoid war whenever possible,
for the sake of justice. But given a world that is shot through with
aggressive militancy, genocidal violence, and mass atrocity, it may
in extreme circumstances lead to justified defensive war.

Reply
Andrew Fiala

I would like to thank Professor Kling for this thought-
provoking debate and commentary. I think we have shown
that pacifists and just war theorists can find common ground.
I must say I agree with much of what Professor Kling says
here. We cannot simply snap our fingers and make the world
less "hellish" (as she puts it). There is work to be done—at
the level of international institutions, domestic political
arrangements, military training, and so on. Pacifists and
just war theorists can work together on much of this.
Indeed, if we want to create a more peaceful world, we

must join together in pursuit of incremental change. Pacifists sometimes wax utopian. There is a place for ideal theory in applied ethics. But until peace dawns, we should also work beside the defenders of the just war tradition to minimize violence and transform military systems from within.

Since our interaction here is a "debate," let me conclude with a more forceful point. Pacifists will say that the work we must do should aim toward a general transformation of the world that includes a critique of nation-states, global economics, social stratification, ecological disaster, gender dynamics, systems of punishment and education, and so on. For the pacifist, the debate about war opens onto further critical conversations about the causes of war, the structures that support war, the psychology of war, and so on. I'm not sure that just war theory goes that far. I wish it did. And I hope that perhaps someday it will.

Notes

1 Thanks to Kiran Bhardwaj for her assistance with this discussion of the no true Scotsman fallacy.
2 What counts as a heresy versus a disqualifying belief is a matter of much debate, especially in the three main Abrahamic religious traditions (Judaism, Christianity, Islam).

Part III

Concluding Arguments

Chapter 5

Summary of the Argument Against War and Conclusion

Andrew Fiala

In this chapter, Fiala sums up his argument that war cannot be justified and provides a final conclusion. He situates his concluding argument by considering concrete historical examples, especially the war in Afghanistan and the War on Terrorism. He concludes that these examples show that might does not make right and that war is not easily justified.

In my final entry in our debate, I would like to return to the basic points I made in the first chapter and apply them once again to the example I began with, in a critical discussion of the war in Afghanistan and the War on Terrorism. This will allow me to make a further critical point with regard to the justification of war in the current global situation. The conclusion to be argued for here is a skepticism toward the justification of the kinds of military force employed in the War on Terrorism. There is some benefit to be obtained in targeted and limited uses of military force—what Kling discusses as "force short of war" (or jus ad vim) in her initial chapter. Some of the methods employed in the War on Terrorism fall under this category, including drone strikes, targeted assassinations, and special forces operations. This is typical of what some scholars call "fourth generation warfare": war that is no longer merely states slugging it out across borders. Fourth generation warfare involves insurgencies and counter-insurgencies, terror attacks and reprisals, international coalitions, and the use of a complex array of weapons and tactics.

DOI: 10.4324/9780367809850-8

The U.S. War on Terrorism is a prime example. It included multiple kinds of attacks in a number of places across the globe. It was fought by a coalition of forces. Sometimes it involved full-scale invasion and occupation (as in Afghanistan and Iraq). In other cases, it involved capture and rendition of terrorist suspects. In some cases, targets were assassinated. In other cases, proxy armies were employed, along with a shifting cast of contractors and local police and military forces. As I argue here, a pacifist analysis of the last 20 years of the War on Terrorism gives us reason for skepticism. As a response to the attacks of 9/11, 20 years of warfare seems disproportionate. Of course, it is true that there has not been another attack as devastating as 9/11 on American soil. So, if that is the marker of success, then we might say "mission accomplished." But at what cost?

The "Costs of War" project at Brown University provides a recent (September 2021) summary of the costs of the War on Terrorism (2021). Totaling deaths from Afghanistan, Iraq, Syria, Yemen, Pakistan, and elsewhere, they estimate that between 897,000 and 929,000 people were killed in the War on Terrorism. This includes over 7,000 American military personnel and 363,000–387,000 civilians. They estimate that 38 million people have been displaced as war refugees (Vine et al 2021). And they estimate the total monetary cost to the United States at $8 trillion ("U.S. Budgetary Costs" 2021). This figure includes an estimate for future veteran care. Speaking of veteran care, we know that many veterans suffer from PTSD and moral injury. Civilians also suffer from these psychological and spiritual harms.

Can these costs of the War on Terrorism be justified? It is difficult to make an absolute judgment about this question—since any judgment must involve counter-factual speculation. What would the world be like if we had not engaged in a 20-year-long War on Terrorism? That's hard to say. But note that this counter-factual judgment should not be understood as a simple either-or proposition. Pacifists and nonviolentists will argue that nonviolent means could have been employed during the past 20 years. The question is not merely what would the world be like if there were no War on Terrorism. Rather, the question is: what would have happened if $8 trillion were spent on nonviolent responses to terrorism? Also, what would the world be like if the creativity, talent, and labor of the millions of people involved in that enterprise were employed nonviolently? As I have argued earlier, there is good empirical evidence that shows that creative, active, and organized non-violence can be effective at promoting positive social change. So let me now return to where I began. Please recall that in the first chapter, I argued that there are a variety of reasons that war cannot be justified. My main argument focused on the following claims:

(1) War produces bad consequences.
(2) War involves bad intentions and actions that are intrinsically evil.
(3) War solves nothing in the realm of ideas.

When these three claims are combined, they provide a powerful critique of war. War tends to produce bad consequences. It tends to involve bad intentions and intrinsic evils. And it does not provide a stable solution to moral, cultural, political, and ideological problems. This skepticism holds for the more traditional (second and third generation) wars of the 19th and 20th centuries. It also holds for the fourth generation wars that are likely to be fought in the 21st century.

I have tried to be careful throughout and avoid dogmatic and absolutist language. As I've said before, it may be possible to imagine a war that does not suffer from these problems. But in reality, most wars fail to avoid these problems.

To make this kind of argument, however, we need historical and empirical data. Pacifism becomes dogmatic when it ignores the real world. But, I submit, there is substantial empirical and historical data to support the claims I have made. As I have noted earlier, this approach—which looks at empirical and historical data—can be described as a kind of "contingent pacifism." It might be that in an ideal world, some wars can be justified. But in the real world, war often violates just war principles.

In my contribution to this debate, I focused often on the Second World War example. This is a useful example because it is often presumed that the Second World War is a paradigm of a just war—and the narrative of the Second World War is familiar (although the memory of this war is fading quickly in the 21st century). In a number of places in my contribution, I have presented reasons to think that the Second World War was not a just war. Atrocities were committed, fueled by racist and ethnocentric thinking. The war also caused massive destruction and dislocation.

Let me now return to the claim that war solves nothing in the realm of ideas. As you'll recall, this is related to the idea that "might does not make right." Well, what about the Second World War? To what extent was it successful "in the realm of ideas"?

One familiar story tells us that the United States and our allies were the good guys and that we established our moral supremacy through our victory in the Second World War. People typically believe that we won because we were the good guys. This is a reassuring narrative. But it is not true.

One problem is that the wars in Europe and Asia did not end as neatly and cleanly as we might imagine. The ensuing Cold War can be considered as part of the problem. Although Germany and Japan were defeated, these victories led fairly quickly to other wars. Germany was divided into armed camps (as was the rest of Europe). And American forces were soon fighting other wars in Asia.

The global tumult that followed in the aftermath of the Second World War included Cold War conflicts between the United States and the U.S.S.R. It also included national liberation movements across the globe, as well as struggles for civil rights and liberation movements within the United States and allied nations.

Pacifists and critics of war will point out that all of this violence is interconnected. One war gives birth to the next. The nationalism (and colonialism) of the 18th and 19th centuries gave birth to the horrors of the First World War, which created conditions that led to the Second World War, which in turn led to the battles of the Cold War, and so on.

Nor is true that the United States was simply "the good guy" in all of this. American military superiority developed as colonial and nationalistic power, which spread at the expense of native peoples displaced at the point of a gun in the 18th and 19th centuries. And victory in the Second World War was achieved, in part, on the backs of those who were treated as second-class citizens (or worse) within the United States. It is well known that Black Americans were discriminated against, even within the American military of that era. And we should not forget the incarceration and dislocation of Japanese Americans. Nor should we forget the ongoing oppression of Native Americans and Pacific Islanders. Our victory in the Second World War occurred despite discrimination and oppression in the United States. We did not win that war because we were moral exemplars. Rather, we won the war because of technological, economic, and military superiority. The moral question of civil rights remained to be confronted in the decades following the Second World War.

Across the globe, in the aftermath of the Second World War, local peoples clamored for liberty and recognition. It was in this context that Gandhi's nonviolent movement for Indian self-rule finally succeeded. Similar struggles for recognition occurred in other colonies and protectorates. But while this was happening, the great powers continued to play games with the lives of people living in Asia, the Middle East, Africa, and Latin America. Subsequent wars were haunted by the legacy of colonialism and the struggle between the West and the rest of the globe: in Korea, in Vietnam, and in the Middle East, including in Iraq and Afghanistan.

And so we come to the War on Terrorism. In a sense, the War on Terrorism—including the wars in Afghanistan and Iraq—was an outgrowth of these prior struggles. Afghanistan became a focal point of Cold War conflict in the 1980s, when Soviet forces invaded and occupied the place. The Cold War also helps to explain the background conditions of the shifting and convoluted structure of alliances and warfare in the Middle East involving Israel, Egypt, Syria, Iran, Iraq, Saudi Arabia, and so on. These background conditions extend back through the 20th century and the "great game" involving British and Russian struggles for power in Asia and the Middle East.

From the pacifist point of view, this long history is important. Wars are not without antecedents. The antecedent of most wars is some other prior war, which creates instability, resentment, anger, hatred, and dislocation. The argument against war includes this broad historical condemnation of the fact that war gives birth to war. When the war-to-war continuum is brought to mind, we discover that it is difficult to sort out the "just cause" and "right intention" of any given war. We thus find that the kind of judgment made by the just war theorist is not as clean and precise as we want to believe.

As American forces pulled out of Afghanistan in August 2021, some commentators said that this 20-year-long conflict was "America's longest war." But was it really? That designation really depends on one's understanding about what counts as war.

Conflicts in Central Asia and the Middle East have extended over the course of generations. And we might also note that American forces were fighting Native American tribes for much longer than 20 years. That war or wars ("The American Indian Wars") lasted for hundreds of years—from the time of the colonies up until the massacre at Wounded Knee in 1890. It is worth pointing out that the end of the American Indian Wars occurred with the establishment of complete military superiority over Native Peoples that included outright massacres (as at Wounded Knee), cultural genocide, and the creation of the reservation system, which is a kind of legal apartheid. My critical point is that this may be what victory looks like: total domination including the extermination of entire cultures.

Now this did not happen in Afghanistan, Iraq, and in the War on Terrorism. American fighting in this region extends widely and across many decades. In Afghanistan, American forces have been engaged in and supporting violence at least since the 1980s, when the United States supported the *mujahideen* resistance against the Soviet Union. The people of that part of the world have been beleaguered by war for 40 years. American forces invaded Afghanistan in full force in 2001 as a response to the terrorist attacks of 9/11. Those terrorist attacks were inspired by Osama Bin Ladin, a Saudi Arabian whose grievances against the United States included a complaint against the first American war in Iraq (the Gulf War of 1991). Twenty years after 9/11, 2001, American forces pulled out, leaving Afghanistan in the hands of the Taliban regime that had been ousted 20 years earlier. But the Taliban survived, holding on in Pakistan and elsewhere.

The Taliban regime is repressive and worthy of criticism. But there are some people in Afghanistan who are simply tired of the fighting and glad to see the Americans leave, as I noted in my opening chapter (Bulos 2021). I also argued at the outset that two of my three arguments give us reason to be skeptical of the justification of the 20-year-long American war in Afghanistan. It is not clear that the result of all this fighting has left the people of Afghanistan better off. The "good guys" committed atrocities along the way. Civilians were killed. And one wonders whether nonviolent methods could not have achieved better and more long-lasting results.

But what about my third concern: about the problem of violence and the "realm of ideas"? What does the case of Afghanistan show us about the question of "might" and "right"? Let me make two points here: one about democratizing wars and another about ongoing instability.

One justification of the wars in Afghanistan (and Iraq) was a "democratizing" argument. The claim was made that we were deposing illiberal and oppressive governments in both Afghanistan and Iraq. This was "regime change" and "nation building." This was in turn connected to a noble and morally significant claim about the defense of human rights including the defense of religious minorities, women, and other oppressed people and groups.

Pacifists should not ignore this important point. Women and minorities were better off, in many cases, when American forces were there to protect their rights. But pacifists may point out, in the aftermath of the American departure from Afghanistan, that this was unstable and unsustainable. It is tragic that under the resurgent Taliban regime, women will be subjected to oppression. But the American military occupation seemed unable to create the kind of liberal and democratic situation that the women of Afghanistan deserve. And here we need to consider that active and creative nonviolence can be more effective at creating lasting change.

So what have we learned about democratizing war, regime change, humanitarian intervention, and nation building after our 20-year occupation of Afghanistan? Well, things do not look good for these ideals. It turns out that in Afghanistan, American military power was propping up a corrupt government and police force, along with a weak and ineffectual military. The Afghan military and political system was either unable or unwilling to defend the more liberal state that the United States had created in Afghanistan once the Americans left. One lesson in all of this is that regime change and democratization foisted upon people by an invading enemy force rarely works.

Democracy cannot typically be imposed from without. It has to grow and develop from within. This does not mean, by the way, that we ought to simply give up on defending human rights and promoting democracy. Rather, the point is that war is not the best tool for promoting democracy. To promote democracy, we would do better to employ nonviolent techniques.

Part of the problem here is summarized in that old saw that "might does not make right." One of the reasons that war and violence are not useful as a technique for creating justice and democracy is that violence provokes reactive counter-violence. Foreign invasions give birth to insurgencies and patriotic resistance. After the invasion, the local population is divided. Some ally themselves with the foreign invaders; others take up arms in resistance. Each views the other with suspicion. It is difficult for lasting social and political institutions to develop organically in such circumstances. War is a blunt instrument for promoting social and political development.

Furthermore, the foreign invaders (the peace-keeping and humanitarian forces) may have to compromise their values along the way. They may have to ally themselves with unsavory allies, and engage in bribery and coercion in order to create regime change. When those sticks and carrots are removed, very little remains in terms of an organic commitment to the values of the new regime. The underlying ideas, values, and commitments of the local people don't simply change overnight because of the presence of a humanitarian force. And when those forces leave, things can quickly fall apart. The corrupt cronies flee the country. The military and the police switch allegiances. And the common people simply want to be left alone.

This is the pacifist lesson to be learned from the War on Terrorism. This is, by the way, an old lesson. Something similar happened when the Soviets released Eastern Europe from their oppressive presence in the late 1980s and early 1990s. Something similar happened in Vietnam in the 1970s when the Americans left. Something similar happened throughout the "great game" and the colonial adventures of the 19th and 20th centuries. The logic of war and violence seems to imply a choice between total domination (as in the case of American victory in the American Indian Wars) or ongoing instability.

This brings me to my final point, which is about ongoing instability and insecurity. A military defeat does not result in the defeated people changing their minds or their allegiances. Instead, it promotes backlash and resistance. The way to change people's minds is through persuasion and logic, science and culture. This requires nonviolent techniques, i.e., arguments, images, narratives, and so on—the basic material of human culture. A phrase often employed to explain this is "winning hearts and minds." One source for this phrase traces it back to John Adams. In a letter from 1818, Adams made a distinction between "the American Revolution" and "the American War." The war involved guns and horses, troops and battles. But the revolution was about ideas. Adams said:

> But what do We mean by the American Revolution? Do We mean the American War? The Revolution was effected before the War commenced. The Revolution was in the Minds and Hearts of the People. A Change in their Religious Sentiments of their Duties and Obligations.
>
> (1818)

This idea of changing minds and hearts is crucial to the project of promoting real regime change and creating a just and lasting peace. Until people's ideas are changed, they will continue to resist ideas they disagree with. And if some foreign invader tries to rule over them, they will refuse to be governed. This is what happened in the American Revolution. The American people changed their hearts and minds and the British were unable to hold onto the colonies through military force. This is what happened during the American Indian Wars. The Native Americans refused to be governed until the American military destroyed their way of life and forced them onto reservations. This is what happened in Afghanistan as the Taliban continued to fight and waited for 20 years to take power again. The people's hearts and minds did not change. And as soon as the foreign occupying forces left, things reverted to the way they were previously.

I realize that I am oversimplifying here. These are complex historical questions that require more than a few paragraphs of discussion. But at the risk of further oversimplification, let me conclude by taking up an obvious objection to the line of thought I am offering here. A realist critic of my pacifist argument may derive another conclusion from the historical examples I've discussed here. There is another option the realist may point out: an option that involves total domination. This is what happened with the American Indian wars—as all Native American resistance was quashed and the tribes were forced onto reservations. This is also what happened in the Second World War when Germany and Japan were defeated, occupied, and transformed into liberal-democratic nations.

The problem is that such wars are immoral either when viewed from the vantage point of just war theory or from the perspective of pacifism. The domination of Native American tribes is no longer viewed as morally defensible. Nor is the firebombing and atomic bombing used in the Second World War viewed as morally defensible. In fact, moral critique of earlier warfare has led to the development of "fourth generation warfare," which aims to use violence in more targeted and morally acceptable ways.

But can such wars be won? Can such wars achieve their humanitarian goals along with the goal of preventing terrorism? I'm not so sure. But again, this is an empirical and contingent point. Perhaps we will get better at targeting violence (and also better at employing less violent or nonviolent means). We should also avoid a false dilemma in thinking about this. The realist may present us with a false dilemma that suggests that there are only two options: total domination that comes at the expense of moral restraint or a weak and ineffectual response hindered by moral limitations. The tradition of nonviolence offers a third option that involves intelligent, creative, and well-funded nonviolent alternatives to war.

The question of war in the 21st century will likely be a continuation of the questions discussed briefly here: about anti-terrorist attacks, humanitarian interventions, democratizing wars, and wars of regime change. Those wars are probably an improvement over the wars of previous centuries. But as I have argued here, there is no good reason to suspect that those wars will be successful. The problem is that might does not make right. A victorious invasion by a foreign country in the name of human rights and democracy is unlikely to win over the hearts and minds of those on the receiving end of violence. In order to change hearts and minds, the means employed must be nonviolent. And so, I conclude in response to the primary question of our debate by stating that war cannot be justified.

Chapter 6

Summary in Defense of Just War Theory and Conclusion

Jennifer Kling

Contents

In this chapter, Kling sums up her argument that war is sometimes justified and provides a final conclusion. She points to the importance of holding to complex moral standards in an imperfect world, situating her argument in the context of the war in Afghanistan and the global challenges of the 21st century. She concludes that might, when it is used in the right way, at the right time, and in the right manner, can open the door to right, and so war is sometimes justified.

In my final contribution to our discussion, I'd like to focus on the state of the debate between pacifism and just war theory and the importance of that debate for our world. Far from being a "philosopher's game," the moral discussion about whether to engage in war or hold hard to nonviolence is essential to who we are and who we decide to be, as individuals, societies, and a global community. As just war traditions around the globe show us, it *matters* what we say about individual and communal defense—is there a right, or even an obligation, to engage in war in defense of ourselves, our

DOI: 10.4324/9780367809850-9

fellows, and our moral values? Or is war always the wrong answer? Is it possible to fight and end a war well? Or does large-scale, sustained, direct violence between organized political groups always involve wicked intentions and lead to bad consequences? Is all war, in the end, immoral?

1. Choosing Where to Stand

As I have argued throughout this book, I think war is sometimes morally justified. It is tricky, of course, because it is almost never the case that the real world lives up to our moral standards. But that should not stop us from setting out and arguing for those standards. Defensive war is morally justified when it is a last-ditch response to unrelenting, serious unjust aggression, and it is fought well when warmakers and warfighters obey the spirit, as well as the rules, of jus in bello. Finally, I maintain that defensive war could be ended well, were the dictates of jus post bellum to be carefully interpreted and followed, in an attempt to create a just and lasting peace.

Professor Fiala and other anti-war pacifists are likely to say, at this point, that the moral standards of just war theory as I have laid them out are simply never followed. Wars, as they are fought in the actual world, aren't just. They may contain moments of moral heroism and justice, yes, but overall, they do not meet or even approximate the ideals of the Western, Chinese, or Native American just war traditions (to say nothing of the Indian just war tradition, which I have not discussed here). Furthermore, wars have a whole host of individual, social, and political bad effects—in part because of bad actors who do not take such consequences into account before they act, but also in part because war is genuinely horrific—including PTSD, moral injury, generational trauma, environmental destruction, the distortion of history, and the glorification of violence and toxic masculinity at the expense of peacemaking and other more sustainable cultural pathways.

This is all true. There will always be bad actors, and there will always be foreseen and unforeseen bad consequences of trying to do what is right. In response to the first point, we shouldn't let the existence of bad actors lead us to abandon our belief in, and our adherence to, moral standards. People commit murder—we don't thereby stop saying or believing that murder is wrong, or retract all of our laws against murder. Instead, we try to hold murderers accountable (both socially and via the law), we teach our children that murder is wrong, and we work to distinguish between murder and defense in the law, so that we don't inadvertently punish people who have acted morally, e.g., who have killed in self-defense or other-defense. Similarly, the existence of unjust wars shouldn't lead us to abandon our moral standards, and related laws, policies, and procedures, around war. Rather, we should determine what it is that makes those wars unjust, maintain that it is possible to follow the constraints of just war theory and the international laws of war, and so hold our warmakers and warfighters to account when they fail to do so. Some warmakers and warfighters are murderers—but this shouldn't lead us to conclude that they are *all* necessarily murderers, simply in virtue of being warmakers and warfighters. I maintain that there is more to it than that; some warmakers and warfighters, when they fight at the right time, in the right way, and for the right reasons, act morally.

In response to the second point, that good actions sometimes— and often do—have bad consequences: this is a reason to try to mitigate those bad consequences to the extent possible, rather than give up on the action in question. Actual wars, even those that are closer to being just, have horrendous effects—but those effects could be ameliorated, softened, or even avoided, were warmakers and warfighters to take the time and effort to do so. For example, warfighters could warn nearby civilians before engaging in targeted air strikes on adjacent military targets. They often won't, I admit, but that should not stop us from saying that they should and, furthermore, that such mitigation efforts are a doable ask. Perhaps I am just less jaded than most, but in my experience, the first step toward getting people and polities to act justly is to convince them that they can, in fact, be better. Simply telling warmakers and warfighters that they are immoral no matter what (even if they are not blameworthy), because of the bad consequences of their war-related actions, is a conversation-stopper. But enjoining them to be concerned about the bad effects of war, and demonstrating the ways in which they have the power to lessen those effects, is likely to lead to positive changes, ones that lessen the horrors of war in practice. (Lest you think I am being overly optimistic, it is these kinds of conversations historically that led to the adoption of international humanitarian law, the development of non-lethal weapons, and the interest, at a policy level, in force short of war and "bloodless" battlespaces such as cyber and space).

The debate between just war theory and pacifism is, to be sure, largely about what political groups are justified in doing in defense of themselves and others. But it is not only about that. It is also about how we should frame these discussions, in recognition that *how* we talk to others—particularly warmakers and warfighters, and those sympathetic to them—is at least as important as what we say. In our conversations and activism, do we cast war into the moral abyss? Or do we work from where we are, with current moral, social, and political understandings of the world, to move the needle toward there being fewer wars, which are more justly fought and ended? Just war theorists, myself included, take the latter approach. The question of where to stand on the spectrum of pacifism, to just war theory, to realism, is not only an abstract moral question, but also a deeply pragmatic and relational one; it has to do with how you think we ought to be, and how you think we are most likely to get there. I think we ought to be, morally, in a place where defensive wars are rare, but recognized as justified in extreme circumstances, and I think we're most likely to get there by working with warmakers and warfighters, rather than maintaining that they are always wrong, all of the time.

2. The Seductive Power of Violence

We should not abandon war as wholly immoral. However, this is not to say that war is always, or even usually, moral; wars are often wrong, either because they are fought for the wrong reasons, or they do not adhere to the constraints of jus in bello, or they aren't ended in ways that are conducive to a just and lasting peace. Consider the U.S.-led coalition's 20-year war in Afghanistan, which ended with the chaotic pull-out of American troops in late August 2021. The Taliban subsequently quickly re-took political control of Afghanistan (as was foreseen by military analysts), leaving many Afghanis fearful that both their human rights will be severely suppressed and that any past help they gave to American and other coalition troops will be ferreted out and punished. It is, to be frank, a humanitarian and political disaster.

As Professor Fiala convincingly argues in his Chapter 5 overall summary, the U.S.-led coalition tried to engage in nation-building in Afghanistan and it didn't work (and perhaps, never could have worked). There are many answers to the question of why the U.S.-led coalition even tried; the one that I want to focus on here is the seductive power of violence. The temptation to engage in violence is strong because it appears to be both easy and final—it's simple to fire a gun, and it purports to end the disagreement. Violence at the level of war is somewhat less easy, but it still holds out the promise of finality: it claims to be able to end the argument (or at least, make it go away) by beating the opponent into submission. In reality though, violence, especially at the level of war, is neither of these things. It is tremendously difficult to convince people to engage in lethal violence against others whom they've never met. This is why military training camps around the world teach not only martial skills, but also pathologize nonviolence as cowardly and emphasize ideologies that dehumanize "the enemy." And even given such training, warfighters experience PTSD and moral injury in high numbers. It is hard to engage in the levels of violence that war demands, and committing such violence has devastating effects on those who do so.

In addition, violence is not final. Twenty years later, and Afghanistan is, politically speaking, roughly where it was at the beginning of the 21st century. Yes, some of the leaders of the Taliban are different, but initial reports suggest that while there are new faces, the group retains its same ideology and ultimate political goals (Terpstra 2021). Violence, as I argue in my initial chapter and in my first response to Professor Fiala, can at best bring people to the negotiating table. Furthermore, some restrained uses of nonlethal violence can clear people's moral vision and undercut their ideologies in ways that make them more open to resolving conflicts and disagreements reasonably, in ways that are amenable to a more just and more peaceful world. That being said, violence cannot solve the problems; it can open a door for discussion, but it cannot take the place of actual conflict resolution. That requires other work, which sadly the U.S.-led coalition failed to do in Afghanistan. Hence, disaster.

It is important to avoid being seduced by the dark side; we should always retain our suspicion of violence. Now, as a just war theorist, I maintain that sometimes, violence is all we have left. When this is the case, it is morally acceptable to use every weapon in our arsenal, subject to jus in bello constraints, to defend ourselves, others, and the world in which we want to live. But this should not be confused with accepting violence as either inevitable or easily justifiable. We must take care to interrogate any proposed uses of martial force—which I would argue did not happen at the start of the Afghan war in 2001—and be critical of our violence-saturated contemporary culture, which tends to see every geopolitical problem as a nail needing a military hammer.

3. The Past and the Future

The history of the world is a history of war. But it is also a history of peace. The oldest surviving peace treaty was signed in 1258 BCE between Ramesses II of Egypt (Ramesses the Great) and Hattušiliš III of the Hittite Empire (now Syria). The peace treaty is extensive, including mutual guarantees against invasion, promises to come to the other nation's aid in case of outside attack, and pledging brotherhood and peace forever (Breasted 1906). Although this is the oldest surviving peace treaty, it is not the first peace treaty ever created; based on extensive analysis of the language, content, and historical context, scholars argue that it essentially follows a semantic and legal pattern that must have been established by still earlier treaties, which unfortunately have been lost to time (Bederman 2001; Klengel 2002). Peace has just as long and storied a history as violent conflict, although it can sometimes be more difficult to see because of the cultural forces that both Professor Fiala and I have discussed. The point is that neither war, nor peace, nor justice is fated, or natural; we cannot read the future of humanity off of its past. We can read possibilities though, and it is the possibility of creating a just and lasting peace that the just war theorist must keep in mind when arguing about the morality of war. Sometimes, the only way out is through.

At the end of the day, it may not be possible to have a world that is altogether without violence. As historian, naturalist, and writer Craig Childs puts it, "Wherever there are humans, there are atrocities" (Childs 2006, 160). But it may be possible to have a world without war, and we should strive for that future. Such striving begins, in my view, by carefully articulating and interpreting our moral standards—the doing of which, I have argued, demonstrates that war is sometimes justified—and extrapolating new views from those moral standards—as we see in current discussions about humanitarian intervention in a globalized world (Allhoff, Evans, and Henschke 2013; Kling 2018) and war's impact on the environment (Woods 2007).

The advent of climate change raises new questions regarding the use of military force: given that it is both human-caused and a threat multiplier, might it be justified for those countries that are hardest hit by climate change to engage in defensive war against the worst climate offenders? (van der Linden 2019). But war itself negatively affects the environment in a variety of ways. This suggests that the victims of climate change are caught in a double bind. Either the use of war in defense is precluded because using traditional warfare to save the environment will necessarily harm the environment, or any war fought over climate change, to be justified, must use very different strategies and weaponry than have been seen in the past, which demands levels of technological investment unavailable to those hit hardest by climate change. As Marcus Hedahl, Scott Clark, and Michael Beggins (2017) argue, these thorny issues call for changes to the very foundations of just war theory.

Such ecological considerations should not lead us to throw out just war theory, though. As I argue in my initial chapter, the various just war traditions are sometimes regarded as old-school and outmoded; but as the previous paragraph shows, the theory is flexible enough to take account of new issues and problems. It can provide us with a nuanced framework for how to think about the intersection of various local, regional, and global considerations. Although it may not have done so in the past, just war theory is able to cast a broad theoretical net, bringing together many different ideas and concerns under its purview. This is possible in part because just war theory insists on a complex moral landscape, which differentiates between people's intentions and the outcomes of their actions, between necessary and unnecessary defense against unjust aggression, and between proportionate and disproportionate responses to occurrent unjust threats and violations. It thus has more resources with which to approach the present and the future, resources that enable moral and political discussion and discernment rather than casting aside all war and military conflict as essentially immoral.

A key element of pacifism is the claim that might does not make right. I agree. But as a just war theorist, I don't stop there—I complicate the discussion by pointing out that might can be a last-ditch way of opening the door to what is right. It can do this either by embodying it, as when people fight back, using whatever weapons they have, against genocide, atrocity, and other kinds of rampant and serious unjust aggression, or by forcing people to the negotiating table, where they can hopefully come to agreements that bring about a more just peace, or by undermining people's oppressive ideologies and giving them new perceptual experiences that could lead them to change their views (aka their hearts and minds). Might does not always do these things, of course, and so I reiterate that it should be avoided whenever possible. War, and violent conflict more generally, is never the first answer. In our current world though, it can do these things, and so war is sometimes a morally justified answer. Ultimately, by thinking through why and when that is true, we garner the intellectual and practical resources that are needed for envisioning, and creating in all its multiplicity, a more just and more peaceful future.

Further Reading

Arguments Against War

The following books are recommended for readers interested in studying the arguments against war and in favor of pacifism and nonviolence (organized chronologically):

- Hauerwas, Stanley. *Should War Be Eliminated?* Milwaukee, WI: Marquette University Press, 1984.
  - A discussion of pacifism and just war theory that is grounded in Christian theology and the Bible, written by an important contemporary theologian.
- Holmes, Robert. *On War and Morality.* Princeton, NJ: Princeton University Press, 1989.
  - In his influential text, Holmes criticizes just war theory, realism, and militarism, while discussing alternatives to war.
- Ruddick, Sara. *Maternal Thinking: Toward a Politics of Peace,* 2nd edition. Boston: Beacon, 1995 (originally 1989).
  - A feminist approach to pacifism that focuses on nonviolence as a maternal virtue. Maternal thinking illuminates the destructiveness of war and the requirements of peace.
- Cady, Duane. *From Warism to Pacifism: A Moral Continuum,* 2nd edition. Philadelphia: Temple University Press, 2010 (originally 1989).
  - Duane Cady, who calls himself a "reluctant pacifist," examines the arguments on all sides of the issue, while providing a critique of the justification of war.
- Fox, Michael Allen. *Understanding Peace: A Comprehensive Introduction.* New York: Routledge, 2014.

- Fox highlights the human capacity for nonviolent cooperation in everyday life and in conflict situations. After
  deconstructing numerous ideas about war and explaining
  its heavy costs to humans, animals, and the environment, he
  turns to evidence for the existence of peaceful societies.
- May, Larry. *Contingent Pacifism: Revisiting Just War Theory.*
  Cambridge: Cambridge University Press, 2015.
  - Larry May appeals to just war arguments, while arguing in
    the direction of pacifism. The book provides an extensive
    account of contingent pacifism.
- Holmes, Robert. *Pacifism: A Philosophy of Nonviolence.*
  London: Bloomsbury, 2017.
  - Robert Holmes is among the most important philosophers
    arguing against the justification of war. In this book, he
    provides an extensive argument in defense of pacifism.
- Fiala, Andrew. *Transformative Pacifism: Critical Theory and
  Practice.* London: Bloomsbury, 2018.
  - This book describes pacifism as a comprehensive normative
    theory, while arguing that pacifism should be understood in
    connection with critical theories such as feminism.

Arguments in Defense of War

The following books are recommended for readers interested in
studying the arguments in defense of war and the just war traditions (organized chronologically):

- Walzer, Michael. *Just and Unjust Wars: A Moral Argument
  with Historical Illustrations,* 4th edition. New York: Basic
  Books, 2006 (originally 1977).
  - Michael Walzer is likely the most important contem-
    porary defender of just war theory. This is one of the
    important books in the revival of just war theory in the
    20th century.
- Teichman, Jenny. *Pacifism and the Just War.* Oxford: Basil
  Blackwell, 1986.
  - This is a widely-cited source that examines the continuum
    including anti-war pacifism, absolute nonviolence, and just
    war theory. It includes a survey with historical references
    and an appendix with quotations from various sources.

- Walzer, Michael. *Arguing about War*. New Haven, CT: Yale University Press, 2004.
  - Extending Walzer's discussion of the justification of war (as a follow-up to Walzer's *Just and Unjust Wars*), with a focus on issues of concern in the 21st century.
- McMahan, Jeff. *Killing in War*. Oxford: Oxford University Press, 2009.
  - In addition to Walzer, Jeff McMahan has become a significant voice thinking about the morality of war. In this book, McMahan offers a critical revision of just war theory.
- Fabre, Cécile. *Cosmopolitan War*. Oxford: Oxford University Press, 2012.
  - This book articulates and defends a cosmopolitan theory of just war. It denies the moral importance of borders, and instead focuses on defending just war from the position that individuals are the locus of moral agency and concern.
- Orend, Brian. *The Morality of War*, 2nd edition. New York: Broadview Press, 2013 (1st edition 2006).
  - Orend blends theory and history to examine the ethics and practice of war and peace in the contemporary world; includes research tools and case studies throughout.
- Frowe, Helen. *Defensive Killing: An Essay on War and Self-Defence*. Oxford: Oxford University Press, 2014.
  - An argument in defense of war based upon the analogy between personal self-defense and war. It offers a revision of the idea of noncombatant immunity.
- Lazar, Seth. *Sparing Civilians*. Oxford: Oxford University Press, 2015.
  - An examination of the claim that killing civilians is worse than killing soldiers, which seeks to vindicate the traditionalist just war theory view instead of revisionist positions.
- Chiu, Yvonne. *Conspiring with the Enemy: The Ethic of Cooperation in Warfare*. New York: Columbia University Press, 2019.
  - An argument in defense of war based on the claim that warfare involves cooperation between enemies to constrain the violence of war. The book explores tensions between the ethic of cooperation and traditional just war theory, and argues for revisions to just war theory.

Historical Sources

For readers interested in the historical sources and background to the contemporary debate, the following primary sources are recommended (organized chronologically):

- Augustine. *Basic Writings of Saint Augustine*. Edited by Whitney J. Oates, 2 vols. New York: Random House, 1948.
  - The first complete articulation of the Western just war tradition, from a Christian perspective. The most complete treatment is in *The City of God*, although Augustine also discusses war in *The Confessions*. These texts were published in the 400s C.E.
- Aquinas, Thomas. *Summa Theologica*. Online Edition Copyright 2017 by Kevin Knight. At New Advent: http://www.newadvent. org/summa/3040.htm.
  - Originally published in 1485, Aquinas focuses on war and peace primarily in II.II, q. 40–64. He draws from Aristotelian philosophy as well as the Christian tradition in defending a nuanced just war position that is similar, but not identical, to Augustine's position.
- Grotius, Hugo. *The Rights of War and Peace*. Edited and with an Introduction by Richard Tuck, from the Edition by Jean Barbeyrac, 3 vols. Indianapolis: Liberty Fund, 2005.
  - An English translation of Grotius' seminal text, originally published in 1625. It forms the foundations of international humanitarian law and defends the rights of individuals and states to secure themselves and their property with war.
- Clausewitz, Carl von. *On War*. New York: Pacific Publishing Studio, 2010 [originally 1832].
  - This unfinished work from the 19th century focuses on war and military strategy from the perspective of Prussian general Carl von Clausewitz. This book defends the realist view of war.
- Tolstoy, Leo. *The Kingdom of God Is Within You*. New York: Cassell, 1894.
  - This is a widely cited account of Christian nonresistance that grounds pacifism in biblical texts. Published at the end of the 19th century.
- James, William. "The Moral Equivalent of War." *Memories and Studies*. New York: Longmans, Green, and Co., 1911.

- Contrasts "pacificism" with militarism, while advocating for a pragmatic "war against war." Aims to stimulate the virtues associated with military service without the destructiveness of war. Published in the early 20th century.
- Addams, Jane. *Essays and Speeches on Peace*. New York: Continuum, 2005.
  - A collection of Jane Addams' pacifist writings and speeches from the 1890s through the 1930s, including a critique of militarism.
- King, Jr., Martin Luther. "My Pilgrimage to Nonviolence." *Stride toward Freedom*. Boston: Beacon, 2010.
  - Seminal text explaining the evolution of King's thinking about nonviolence as active and creative resistance to evil. Originally published in 1958.

Philosophical and Historical Anthologies

For readers interested in philosophical questions about the ethics of war and peace, the following books are recommended (organized alphabetically):

- Allhoff, Fritz, Nicholas G. Evans, Adam Henschke, eds. *The Routledge Handbook of Ethics and War*. New York: Routledge, 2013.
  - This volume includes contemporary authors focused on just war arguments and military ethics.
- Cordeiro-Rodrigues, Luís and Danny Singh. *Comparative Just War Theory: An Introduction to International Perspectives*. New York: Rowman & Littlefield, 2020.
  - This wide-ranging anthology considers questions of war and peace from a number of underrepresented perspectives, including radical, Africana, Islamic, Indian, and South American frameworks.
- Fiala, Andrew, ed. *The Routledge Handbook of Pacifism and Nonviolence*. New York: Routledge, 2018.
  - This volume includes contemporary essays by a range of important authors on a variety of topics related to pacifism and nonviolence.
- Gan, Barry and Robert Holmes, eds. *Nonviolence in Theory and Practice*, 3rd edition. Long Grove, IL: Waveland, 2012.

- This is a collection of key texts focused on nonviolence. With religious texts, historical authors, and contemporary arguments about pacifism, including discussions of applications to a range of contemporary issues.
- Lazar, Seth and Helen Frowe, eds. *The Oxford Handbook of the Ethics of War*. Oxford: Oxford University Press, 2018.
  - An anthology primarily focused on just war arguments, including a number of important contemporary authors.
- May, Larry, Eric Rovie, and Steve Viner, eds. *The Morality of War: Classic and Contemporary Readings*. Upper Saddle River, NJ: Prentice Hall, 2006.
  - An anthology of historical and contemporary texts discussing key issues in just war theory and pacifism. It also includes applications to contemporary issues.
- May, Larry, ed. *The Cambridge Handbook of the Just War*. Cambridge: Cambridge University Press, 2018.
  - This anthology brings together contemporary authors who provide a detailed analysis of just war concepts.
- Twiss, Sumner B. and Ping-Cheung Lo, eds. *Chinese Just War Ethics: Origin, Development, and Dissent*. London: Routledge, 2015.
  - This anthology offers a comprehensive analysis of warfare ethics in early China as well as its subsequent development into the modern period.

Glossary

Absolute Pacifism: An unconditional rejection of war (and/or violence).

Anti-war Pacifism: The rejection of war as almost never justified in the real world. Some anti-war pacifists reject all uses of violence; however, the position is focused on rejecting real-world war and may not include the rejection of other lesser forms of violence.

Bellism: The belief that war is valuable for its own sake, as a way to demonstrate courage, cleverness, strength, and martial skill, and to obtain honor and glory. Sometimes described as the love or worship of war.

Collateral Damage: The bad, regrettable, and unintended consequences of committing an intentional act of war. A description typically used by warmakers and warfighters to excuse unintended but foreseen civilian casualties, harms, and property damage.

Conscientious Objection/Refusal: Refusal to comply with or obey an order. In warfare, this can involve a soldier refusing to obey what they regard as a criminal/immoral order. It can also involve the refusal to serve in the military in cases of conscription.

Consequentialism: An umbrella term for particular moral theories that are concerned with consequences. Broadly, consequentialism states that actions are good insofar as they have good consequences, and bad insofar as they have bad consequences. Consequences are good or bad insofar as they contribute to the creation of the best state of affairs overall.

Consequentialist Argument Against War: War causes widespread destruction and harm. It kills people, disrupts social systems, destroys the environment, and creates instability and terror. These negative consequences cannot be redeemed or outweighed by the positive consequences of war.

Contingent Pacifism: Either rejecting a given war as morally unjustifiable or rejecting a given way of fighting as morally unjustifiable (ex., nuclear-war pacifism rejects nuclear war without necessarily rejecting other forms of warfare).

Defensive War: When states or other political groups fight to repel unjustified outside aggression (invasion or attack).

Deontological Argument Against War: War involves actions that are inherently wrong. It demands that soldiers violate the basic moral rule against killing, and that they give up their autonomy in service to the state. And states that make war are fundamentally corrupt insofar as they focus on power at the expense of justice, care, and other positive values.

Doctrine of Double Effect (DDE): Well-intended actions with harmful side effects are permissible, so long as (a) the action itself is good, (b) the good done by the action outweighs the harm done, (c) the harm isn't the means to the good end, and (d) the harm isn't intended as an end in itself. In context, the DDE stipulates that some collateral damage (the killing or harming of noncombatants or their property) is morally permitted, so long as it is not deliberately intended and is merely a foreseen but accidental secondary effect of a morally legitimate action in war.

Domestic Analogy: An analogue between individuals and polities common in just war theory. It stipulates that just as individuals have the right to defend themselves or others when they are unjustly attacked or threatened, so too do states and other polities have the right to defend themselves or others against unjust aggression.

Essentialism: The position that particular groups of people all have natural inherent or essential traits, in virtue of their membership in that group. For example, an essentialist view of women might say that all women are naturally peacemakers, because that's just part of what it is to be a woman.

Essentially Contested Concept: A concept that contains within itself conflicting ideas, and so is inherently open to dispute and generative of diverging interpretations.

Force Short of War (Jus ad vim): The selective, limited use of military force to achieve particular, pre-determined political objectives. Sometimes, humanitarian interventions fall into this category.

Ideology: A set of concepts, social meanings, beliefs, and ideas that is best understood as a cultural resource that shapes, filters, and sorts our perceptions, attitudes, and reasoning. It is the set of tools that our language and culture provides us with in order to think.

Incommensurability of Value (also called Incomparability of Value): The view that different kinds of considerations cannot be compared or weighed against each other on a single scale of value. In context, this view holds that it is not possible to compare all of the many and varied consequences of war and trade them off against each other to determine whether the good consequences overall outweigh the bad ones.

Integrity Objection to Consequentialism: The contention that consequentialism erases the important moral distinction between what people intentionally do and the side effects of their actions. Put another way, because consequentialism focuses solely on consequences, it fails to consider the moral importance of people acting with integrity.

Isolationist Pacifism: The view that a state or polity should never go to war because that is what minimizes harms for its own members. This position holds that what matters is the consequences for us (the members of the relevant state or polity), rather than the consequences for all.

Jus ad bellum: The justice of going to war. This conceptual category focuses on the moral question of when, if ever, a group may go to war. Traditionally, it is considered to be distinct from jus in bello and jus post bellum, although some contemporary just war theorists challenge this normative and conceptual separation. Typically, jus ad bellum includes thinking about the following: just cause, right intention, legitimate authority, last resort, and macro-level proportionality.

Jus in bello: The justice of fighting a war. This conceptual category focuses on the moral question of what individuals and groups fighting in a war may and may not do. Traditionally, it is considered to be distinct from jus ad bellum and jus post bellum, although some contemporary just war theorists challenge this normative and conceptual separation. Typically, jus in bello focuses on the following: the principle of discrimination, fair treatment of prisoners, micro-level proportionality, and avoiding intrinsically evil means.

Jus post bellum: The justice of transitioning from war to peace. This conceptual category focuses on the moral question of establishing justice after war. Traditionally, it is considered to be distinct from jus ad bellum and jus in bello, although some contemporary just war theorists challenge this normative and conceptual separation. Typically, jus post bellum includes the following: avoiding revenge and punitive damages, providing closure, and ensuring a just peace that ameliorates future conflict.

Just war myth: The claim that people have an ideologically biased view of history, in which the interpretation of the historical record has been warped by pro-war and militaristic propaganda to support the view that at least some wars have been justly entered into, justly fought, and justly ended.

Just War Position: The claim that war can be morally justified, when certain stringent, normative conditions are met.

Just War Traditions: Developed conversations in histories of thought oriented toward defending and explaining the Just War Position. In describing just war thinking as a set of "traditions," some authors point out that people's thinking about war develops in light of changing cultural norms, philosophical and religious ideas, new forms of political organization, and emerging technologies.

Knowledge Problem for Consequentialism: The contention that it is impossible to know with a high degree of certainty either what all of the effects of any particular action will be, or how things are likely to turn out more generally. This makes it difficult, if not impossible, to use consequentialist reasoning to calculate the right course of action.

Last Resort: A just war principle within the jus ad bellum category. It states that violence should be a last resort, meaning that nonviolent and possibly violent alternatives to war should be employed before going to war.

LAWS: Lethal autonomous weapons systems.

Means-Ends Problem: The view that for a course of action to succeed in attaining its goal, the means taken to achieve that goal, or end, must match the nature of the end. In context, the means-ends problem for just war theory is that the theory claims that it is possible to use the means of war to achieve the end of peace. However, the concern is that the nature of war is antithetical to the nature of peace, which means that the theory is self-defeating.

Might Does Not Make Right: A common pacifist slogan that stands for the idea that the more powerful party does not necessarily have justice on its side. Overpowering your opponent does not show that your ideas are better. Having the power to do something does not mean you have the right to do that thing.

Militarism: A political, economic, and cultural system that is grounded on military power, including extensive defense and arms industries as well as a standing military.

Moral Equality of Combatants: The claim that, so long as the warfighters on all sides adhere to jus in bello constraints, they are all acting morally correctly. This is despite the fact that they are trying to kill each other, and despite the fact that at least some of them must be fighting for the unjust, or wrong, side. This claim is usually, although not always, accepted by traditionalists and rejected by revisionists.

Moral Injury: A result of transgressive acts that one has committed or participated in and supported, which violate one's conscience or sense of self.

Nation-Building: The creation, from the outside, of self-sustaining political, social, and economic institutions within a state or polity that will permit and encourage competent governance, social stability, and economic growth.

No True Scotsman Fallacy: Finessing or changing the meaning of a concept or category unilaterally in order to control "what counts" as falling into that concept or category.

Noncombatant Immunity: The idea associated with just war thinking that persons who are not involved in fighting (i.e., noncombatants) should not be intentionally targeted (see *Principle of Discrimination*).

Non-Lethal Weapons (NLW): Violent weapons that stun, immobilize, and otherwise render individuals nonthreatening and disperse crowds without killing. Examples include rubber bullets, stun guns and tasers, kinetic nets, chemical agents, water and sound cannons, and directed energy weapons.

Non-Resistance: The idea that people should never return evil for evil, which can also mean that people should never use violence even in self-defense or in defense of another; associated with Tolstoy and other 19th-century pacifists.

Nonviolent Resistance: A range of alternatives to violence and war for seeking peace. Examples include strikes, work slow-downs, economic sanctions, legal sanctions, the creation of safe passages and havens, sit-ins, die-ins, and media campaigns. This idea is associated with the philosophies and strategies of Mohandas K. Gandhi and Martin Luther King, Jr. Advocates of nonviolent resistance may be pacifists who reject war. But defenders of war will typically argue that war should be a last resort, taken up only after nonviolent methods fail (see *Last Resort*).

Pacifist Position: The claim that war is wrong. Large-scale, sustained, direct political violence cannot be morally justified.

Pacifist Traditions: As in the Just War Traditions, pacifist traditions are conversations about why war is wrong that develop over time and in light of cultural, philosophical, religious, political, and technological changes. There are diverse pacifist traditions that reflect different cultural and historical backgrounds. But typically, pacifist traditions hold that there should be a unity of means and ends, and that peace should be pursued by nonviolent means (see also *Means-Ends Problem* and *Nonviolent Resistance*).

Pluralism: An approach to moral judgment that allows for more than one argument or theory to be employed. These divergent theories/arguments could be conflicting (and incommensurable) or they could provide overlapping consensus.

Political Sovereignty: The right of a state or polity to make and implement its own laws, policies, and procedures, and more broadly, to run itself, free from undue outside or external interference.

Post-Traumatic Stress Disorder (PTSD):   Psychological damage resulting from experiencing traumatic events.

Preemptive War: When states or other political groups fight to block or prevent threatened outside invasion or attack.

Principle of Discrimination (also called the Principle of Noncombatant Immunity):   Warfighters must always discriminate between military targets and civilian targets (both objects and people), and may intentionally attack only military targets. Noncombatants are morally immune from intentional attack.

Principle of Non-Refoulement: International humanitarian law that refugees cannot be returned to their country of origin if doing so will place them in renewed danger of persecution and/or death.

Proportionality: Cost-benefit analysis applied in the context of war in two ways: either with regard to macro-level considerations about going to war (i.e., at the level of jus ad bellum) or within a given war, with regard to specific tactics/ actions (i.e., in relation to jus in bello).

Realism: Fiala defines realism as the claim that moral judgment does not apply in war, i.e., that anything goes in war so long as it is effective for bringing about victory. Kling defines realism as the idea that war is easily or always morally justified, or that war is outside of the moral realm altogether.

Refugee: A person who has been forced to flee their country of origin due to either (1) well-founded fears of persecution on the basis of their social identity (international law), or (2) forcible displacement by war or violent conflict (international norm).

Responsibility to Protect (R2P):   A global political commitment based on three broad pillars of action:

- **Pillar 1:**   Every state has the responsibility to protect its populations from the four mass atrocity crimes (genocide, ethnic cleansing, war crimes, and crimes against humanity).
- **Pillar 2:**   The wider international community has the responsibility to encourage and assist individual states in meeting that responsibility.
- **Pillar 3:**   If a state is manifestly failing to protect its populations, the international community must be prepared to take appropriate collective action in a timely and decisive manner and in accordance with the UN Charter.

Revisionist Just War Theory: Just war theorists who maintain that jus ad bellum and jus in bello are conceptually connected, such that warfighters on the unjust side of a war act wrongly when they fight, even if they follow jus in bello constraints. Revisionists often also question other aspects of traditional Western just war theory (such as the principle of noncombatant immunity).

Revolution: The rejection, by people within the relevant state or polity, of the current regime's political authority and an attempt to replace it. (This term covers civil war as well.)

Right Does Not Make Might: A cautionary slogan that stands for the following claims: those who have justice on their side do not always prevail. Sometimes unjust parties win. Those who do have justice on their side are not thereby justified in doing whatever they want in pursuit of justice.

Territorial Integrity: The right of a state or polity to maintain its recognized territory and territorial boundaries.

Toxic Masculinity: The collection of traits traditionally associated with men and masculinity—such as violence, anger, aggression, the will to power and dominance, martial skill, and an obsession with social and political hierarchical status—which is harmful to men, women, and society overall.

Traditionalist Just War Theory: Just war theorists who maintain that jus ad bellum and jus in bello are conceptually separate, such that it is possible for warfighters to fight well, or justly, even when the war doesn't meet the standards of jus ad bellum. Traditionalists generally argue in favor of the basic tenets of traditional Western just war theory while expanding on and reinterpreting certain aspects of them.

Transformative Pacifism: A critical pacifist theory that digs deeply into psychological, social, cultural, economic, and political sources of violence, seeking to criticize violence in all aspects of life while hoping to transform the world so there is less war and more peace.

War: Fiala defines war as large-scale, sustained, and direct political violence. Kling adds that war is such violence between organized political groups.

War Crime: An action done in wartime that violates international legal agreements governing the rules of war or that violates basic moral principles governing warfighting (such as those principles found in jus ad bellum, jus in bello, and jus post bellum). War crimes include torturing or enslaving prisoners, deliberately attacking noncombatants, and also genocide and ethnic cleansing.

Warism: The assumption that war is easily morally justifiable in theory and that wars have been justified in historical reality. This view is generally dismissive of pacifism.

Bibliography

Acuera. "With Such a People I Want No Peace." In *Great Speeches by Native Americans*, edited by Bob Blaisdell, 3. New York: Dover Publications, Inc., 2000.

Adams, John. "From John Adams to Hezekiah Niles, 13 February 1818." Founders Online, National Archives. https://founders.archives.gov/documents/Adams/99-02-02-6854

Addams, Jane. "Democracy or Militarism." In *Jane Addams's Essays and Speeches on Peace*. London: Continuum, 2005.

Allhoff, Fritz, Nicholas G. Evans, and Adam Henschke, eds. *The Routledge Handbook of Ethics and War*. New York: Routledge, 2013.

American National Conference of Catholic Bishops. "The Challenge of Peace." 1983. http://www.usccb.org/upload/challenge-peace-gods-promise-our-response-1983.pdf

Andrew, Barbara. "The Psychology of Tyranny: Wollstonecraft and Woolf on the Gendered Dimension of War." *Hypatia: A Journal of Feminist Philosophy* 9, no. 2 (1994): 85–101.

Anscombe, G.E.M. "War and Murder" and "Mr. Truman's Degree." In *Ethics, Religion, and Politics*. Minneapolis, MN: University of Minnesota, 1981.

Anselm. "Monologion." In *Anselm of Canterbury: The Major Works*, translated by Brian Davies and G.R. Evans. Oxford: Oxford University Press, 1998.

Aquinas, Thomas. *Summa Theologica: Literally Translated by Fathers of the English Dominican Province*, 2017. Online Edition Copyright 2017 by Kevin Knight. At New Advent: http://www.newadvent.org/summa/3040.htm

Aristotle. *Nicomachean Ethics*. Cambridge, MA: Harvard University Press, 1934. At Perseus: http://www.perseus.tufts.edu/hopper/text?doc=Perseus:text:1999.01.0054

Aristotle. *Politics*, translated by Benjamin Jowett. New York: Digireads.com, 2017.

Augustine, *Epistle to Boniface*. From *Nicene and Post-Nicene Fathers, First Series*, Vol. 1, edited by Philip Schaff. Buffalo, NY: Christian Literature Publishing Co., 1887. At New Advent: http://www.newadvent.org/fathers/1102189.htm

Augustine. *City of God*. From *Nicene and Post-Nicene Fathers, First Series*, Vol. 2, edited by Philip Schaff. Buffalo, NY: Christian Literature Publishing Co, 1887. At New Advent: http://www.newadvent.org/fathers/120119.htm

Badru, R.O. "An African Philosophical Account of just War Theory." *Ethical Perspectives* 26, no. 2 (2019): 153–181.

Ballou, Adin. *Christian Non-Resistance*. London: Charles Gilpin, 1848.

Bazelon, Emily. "From Bagram to Abu Ghraib." *Mother Jones*, March/April 2005. https://www.motherjones.com/politics/2005/03/bagram-abu-ghraib/

Bederman, David J. *International Law in Antiquity*. Cambridge: Cambridge University Press, 2001.

Berenbaum, Michael. *The World Must Know*. Washington, DC: United States Holocaust Museum, 2006.

Black Hawk. "Black Hawk's Surrender Speech." 1832. https://s3.amazonaws.com/oh.oercommons.org/media/editor/47/Black_Hawks_Surrender_Speech.pdf

Boersema, David. "Positive Peace." In *The Routledge Handbook of Pacifism and Nonviolence*, edited by Andrew Fiala. New York: Routledge, 2018.

Boxill, Bernard R. "Fear and Shame as Forms of Moral Suasion in the Thought of Frederick Douglass." *Transactions of the Charles S. Peirce Society* 31, no. 4 (1995): 713–744. doi:https://www.jstor.org/stable/40320570

Brady, Michael and Miranda Fricker, eds. *The Epistemic Life of Groups: Essays in the Epistemology of Collectives*. Oxford: Oxford University Press, 2016.

Bray, Mark. *Antifa: The Anti-Fascist Handbook*. Brooklyn, NY: Melville House, 2017.

Breasted, James Henry. "Treaty with the Hittites." In *Ancient Records of Egypt: Historical Documents from the Earliest Times to the Persian Conquest*, Vol. III, 163–175. Chicago, IL: University of Chicago Press, 1906.

Brunstetter, Daniel and Megan Braun. "From *Jus Ad Bellum* to *Jus Ad Vim*: Recalibrating our Understanding of the Moral use of Force." *Ethics & International Affairs* 27, no. 1 (2013): 87–106.

Bulos, Nabih. "In Afghanistan's War-Torn Countryside, America's Exit Means One Thing: Peace." *Los Angeles Times*, September 17, 2021. https://www.latimes.com/world-nation/story/2021-09-17/afghanistan-countryside-us-exit-means-peace-taliban

Cady, Duane. *From Warism to Pacifism: A Moral Continuum*, 2nd edition. Philadelphia: Temple University Press, 2010.

Cady, Duane. "Warism and the Dominant Worldview." In *The Routledge Handbook of Pacifism and Nonviolence*, edited by Andrew Fiala. New York: Routledge, 2018.

Chenoweth, Erica and Maria J. Stephan. *Why Civil Resistance Works: The Strategic Logic of Nonviolent Conflict*. New York: Columbia University Press, 2011.

Childs, Craig. *House of Rain: Tracking a Vanished Civilization across the American Southwest*. New York: Back Bay Books, 2006.

Chiu, Yvonne. *Conspiring with the Enemy: The Ethic of Cooperation in Warfare*. New York: Columbia University Press, 2019.

Christenson, Kit. *Nonviolence, Peace, and Justice: A Philosophical Introduction*. Peterborough, ON: Broadview Press, 2010.

Clarke, Barry. "Eccentrically Contested Concepts." *British Journal of Political Science 9*, no. 1 (1979): 122–126. doi:10.1017/S0007123400001654

Coady, C.A.J. "Terrorism, Morality, and Supreme Emergency." *Ethics* 114, no. 4 (2004): 772–789. doi:10.1086/383440

Coi, Giovanna. "The War in Afghanistan—by the Numbers." *Politico*, August 19, 2021. https://www.politico.eu/article/war-afghanistan-numbers-costs-taliban-migration-europe-refugees/

Cooper, Ryan. "American Atrocities Doomed the Afghanistan Occupation." *The Week*, August 30, 2021. https://theweek.com/afghanistan-war/1004297/atrocities-in-afghanistan

"Costs of War." Costs of War Project. Watson Institute for International and Public Affairs, Brown University, September 2021. https://watson.brown.edu/costsofwar/figures/2021/WarDeathToll

Davidovic, Jovana. "What Do We Owe Refugees: 'Jus Ad Bellum' Duties to Refugees from Armed Conflict Zones and the Right to Asylum." *Journal of Global Ethics* 12, no. 3 (2016): 347–364.

Delmas, Candice. *A Duty to Resist: When Disobedience Should Be Uncivil*. New York, NY: Oxford University Press, 2018.

Dickinson, Goldsworthy Lowes. *The Choice Before Us*. New York: Dodd, Mead, and Co, 1917.

Dower, John. *War Without Mercy: Race and Power in the Pacific War*. New York: Pantheon, 1986.

Dubois, Laurent. *Avengers of the New World: The Story of the Haitian Revolution*. Cambridge, MA: Belknap Press of Harvard University Press, 2004.

Dylan, Bob. *With God on our Side*. Warner Bros. Inc, 1963.

Edwards, Robert. *White Death: Russia's War on Finland 1939–40*. London: Weidenfeld & Nicolson, 2006.

Emerick, Barrett. "The Limits of the Rights to Free Thought and Expression." *Kennedy Institute of Ethics Journal* 31, no. 2 (2021): 133–152. https:// philarchive.org/archive/EMETLO-2v2

Emonet, Sgt Maj Florian. "The Importance of Ethics Education in Military Training." *NCO Journal*, November 16, 2018.

Fabre, Cécile. "Cosmopolitanism, Just War Theory and Legitimate Authority." *International Affairs* 84, no. 5 (2008): 963–976.

Fabre, Cécile. *Cosmopolitan Peace*. Oxford: Oxford University Press, 2016.

Fee, Chester Anders. *Chief Joseph: The Biography of a Great Indian*. Indiana: Wilson-Erickson, Inc., 1936.

Fiala, Andrew. *Practical Pacifism*. New York: Algora Publishing, 2004.

Fiala, Andrew. "A Critique of Exceptions: Torture, Terrorism, and the Lesser Evil Argument." *International Journal of Applied Philosophy* 20, no. 1 (2006): 127–142.

Fiala, Andrew. *The Just War Myth*. Lanham, MD: Rowman and Littlefield, 2008.

Fiala, Andrew. *Public War, Private Conscience*. London: Continuum/ Bloomsbury, 2010.

Fiala, Andrew. "Just War Ethics and the Slippery Slope of Militarism." *Philosophy in the Contemporary World* 19, no. 1 (2012), 92–102.

Fiala, Andrew. *Against Religions, Wars, and States: Enlightenment Atheism, Just War Pacifism, and Liberal-Democratic Anarchism*. Lanham, MD: Rowman and Littlefield, 2013.

Fiala, Andrew. "Contingent Pacifism and Contingently Pacifist Conclusions." *Journal of Social Philosophy* 45, no. 4 (2014), 463–477.

Fiala, Andrew. *Secular Cosmopolitanism*. New York: Routledge, 2016.

Fiala, Andrew. "Moral Injury and Jus Ad Bellum." *Essays in Philosophy* 18, no. 2 (2017, Special Issue on Moral Psychology and War): 281–294. doi:10.7710/1526-0569.1585

Fiala, Andrew. "Pacifism." In *The Stanford Encyclopedia of Philosophy* (2018 revision), edited by Edward N. Zalta, 2018a. https://plato.stanford.edu/entries/pacifism/

Fiala, Andrew. "The Pacifist Tradition and Pacifism as Transformative and Critical Theory." *The Acorn* 18, no. 1 (2018b): 5–28.

Fiala, Andrew. *Transformative Pacifism*. London: Bloomsbury, 2018c.

Fiala, Andrew. *Nonviolence: A Quick Immersion*. New York: Tibidabo, 2020.

Fiala, Andrew. "Peace as Intrinsic Value: The Pacifist Intuition and Intuitive Pacifism." *Peace & Change* 47, no. 2 (2021): 152–169.

Finlay, Christopher J. *Terrorism and the Right to Resist: A Theory of Just Revolutionary War*. New York: Cambridge University Press, 2017.

Fischer, J.M., M. Ravizza, and D. Copp. "Quinn on Double Effect: The Problem of 'Closeness'." *Ethics* 103, no. 4 (1993): 707–725.

Fisher, Roger. "Preventing Nuclear War." *The Bulletin of the Atomic Scientists* 37, no. 3 (1981): 11–17.

Fitz-Gibbon, Jane Hall. "Of Course, God Is a Man! Masculinist Justifications of Violence and Feminist Perspectives." In *Pacifism, Politics, and Feminism: Intersections and Innovations*, edited by Jennifer Kling, 80–95. Leiden, Netherlands: Brill Rodopi, 2019.

Flisi, Ilaria and Lonneke Peperkamp. "Reports from Abroad: An Interview with Dr. Lonneke Peperkamp on Just War Theory and Space Wars." Blog of the APA, 2021. https://blog.apaonline.org/2021/08/02/reports-from-abroad-an-interview-with-dr-lonneke-peperkamp-on-just-war-theory-and-space-wars/

Francis (Pope). "Homily of His Holiness Pope Francis." September 13, 2014. https://w2.vatican.va/content/francesco/en/homilies/2014/documents/papa-francesco_20140913_omelia-sacrario-militare-redipuglia.html

Freedman, Lawrence and Efraim Karsh. *The Gulf Conflict 1990–1991: Diplomacy and War in the New World Order*. New Jersey: Princeton University Press, 1993.

Fregosi, Paul. *Dreams of Empire: Napoleon and the First World War, 1792–1815*. London: Hutchinson, 1989.

Frowe, Helen. *Defensive Killing: An Essay on War and Self-Defence*. Oxford: Oxford University Press, 2014.

Galliott, Jai, ed. *Force Short of War in Modern Conflict*. Edinburgh: Edinburgh University Press, 2019a.

Galliott, Jai. "An Introduction to Force Short of War." In *Force Short of War in Modern Conflict*, edited by Jai Galliott, 1–10. Edinburgh: Edinburgh University Press, 2019b.

Galtung, Johan. "Violence, Peace, and Peace Research." *Journal of Peace Research* 6, no. 3 (1969): 167–191.

Galtung, Johan. *Peace by Peaceful Means*. London: Sage, 1996.

Gandhi, Mohandas K. *Collected Works*, Vol. 1–98. New Delhi: Publications Division Government of India, 1999. https://www.gandhiashramsevagram.org/gandhi-literature/collected-works-of-mahatmagandhi-volume-1-to-98.php

Gay, William. "The Military-Industrial Complex." In *The Routledge Handbook of Pacifism and Nonviolence*, edited by Andrew Fiala. New York: Routledge, 2018.

Goldman, Emma. *Anarchism and Other Essays*. New York: Dover Publications, 2012.

Gossman, Patricia. "How US-Funded Abuses Led to Failure in Afghanistan." *Human Rights Watch*, July 6, 2021. https://www.hrw.org/news/2021/07/06/how-us-funded-abuses-led-failure-afghanistan#

Grotius, Hugo. *The Rights of War and Peace*. New York: M. Walter Dunne, 1901. At Liberty Fund: https://oll.libertyfund.org/titles/553#Grotius_0138_258

Harsch, Ernest. "OAU Sets Inquiry into Rwanda Genocide." *Africa Recovery* 12, no. 1 (1998): 4.

Haslanger, Sally. "Racism, Ideology and Social Movements." *Res Philosophica* 94, no. 1 (2017): 1–22. doi:10.11612/resphil.1547

Hedahl, Marcus, Scott Clark, and Michael Beggins. "The Changing Nature of the Just War Tradition: How Our Changing Environment Ought to Change the Foundations of just War Theory." *Public Integrity* 19, no. 5 (2017): 429–443. doi:10.1080/10999922.2017.1278667

Heldke, Lisa. "Do You Mind if I Speak Freely? Reconceptualizing Freedom of Speech." *Social Theory and Practice* 17, no. 3 (1991): 349–368. http://www.jstor.org/stable/23557428

Hill, Thomas E. *Virtue, Rules, and Justice: Kantian Aspirations*. Oxford: Oxford University Press, 2012.

Hobbes, Thomas. *Leviathan*. Edited by Richard Tuck. Cambridge: Cambridge University Press, 1991.

Holmes, Robert. "Pacifism for Non-Pacifists." *Journal of Social Philosophy* 30, no. 3 (1999): 387–400.

Holmes, Robert. *The Ethics of Nonviolence: Essays by Robert Holmes*, edited by Predrag Cicovacki. London: Bloomsbury, 2013.

Holmes, Robert. *Pacifism: A Philosophy of Nonviolence*. London: Bloomsbury, 2017.

Holmes, Robert. "Pacifism and the Concept of Morality." In *The Routledge Handbook of Pacifism and Nonviolence*, edited by Andrew Fiala. New York: Routledge, 2018.

Homer. *Iliad*. Lattimore Translation. Chicago: University of Chicago Press, 2011.

Human Rights Watch. *World Report 2020: Somalia*. New York: Human Rights Watch, 2020.

Jaggar, Alison M. "Thinking about Justice in the Unjust Meantime." *Feminist Philosophy Quarterly* 5, no. 2 (2019). doi:10.5206/fpq/2019.2.7283.

James, William. "A Moral Equivalent of War." In *Memories and Studies*, edited by William James. New York: Longmans, Green and Co., 1911.

Johnson, James Turner. *Just War and the Restraint of War*. Princeton, NJ: Princeton University Press, 1981.

Johnson, James Turner. "Just War: As It Is and As It Was." *First Things*, January 2005. https://www.firstthings.com/article/2005/01/just-war-as-it-was-and-is

Johnson, Rebecca. "'Jus Post Bellum' and Counterinsurgency." *Journal of Military Ethics* 7, no. 3 (2008): 215–230.

Kant, Immanuel. *Perpetual Peace* in *Kant: Political Writings*, edited by H.S. Reiss. Cambridge: Cambridge University Press, 1991.

Kaplan, Shawn. "Are Novel *Jus Ad Vim* Principles Needed to Judge Military Measures Short of War?" In *Force Short of War in Modern Conflict*, edited by Jai Galliott, 213–237. Edinburgh: Edinburgh University Press, 2019.

Katchadourian, Haig. "Is the Principle of Double Effect Morally Acceptable?" *International Philosophical Quarterly* 28, no. 1 (1988): 21–30.

Kaurin, Pauline. "With Fear and Trembling: An Ethical Framework for Non-Lethal Weapons." *Journal of Military Ethics* 9, no. 1 (2010): 100–114. doi:10.1080/15027570903523057

King, Jr. Martin Luther. "The Quest for Peace and Justice." Nobel Lecture. December 11, 1964. https://www.nobelprize.org/prizes/peace/1964/king/lecture/

King, Jr. Martin Luther. "A Christmas Sermon on Peace." In *The Trumpet of Conscience*, 67–78. New York: Harper & Row, 1967.

King, Jr. Martin Luther. *A Gift of Love: Sermons from Strength to Love and Other Preachings*. Boston: Beacon Press, 2012.

Klengel, Horst. *From War to Eternal Peace: Ramesses II and Khattushili III*. Toronto: Canadian Society for Mesopotamian Studies, 2002.

Kling, Jennifer. "Justifying the State Right of Self-Defense." In *The State Right of Self-Defense: A Claim in Need of Justification*. PhD Dissertation: UNC-Chapel Hill, 2015. https://cdr.lib.unc.edu/concern/dissertations/bz60cx27s

Kling, Jennifer. "Humanitarian Intervention and the Problem of Genocide and Atrocity." In *The Routledge Handbook of Pacifism and Nonviolence*, edited by Andrew Fiala, 154–167. New York: Routledge, 2018.

Kling, Jennifer. "Engaging in a Cover-Up: The "Deep Morality" of War." In *Pacifism, Politics, and Feminism: Intersections and Innovations*, edited by Jennifer Kling, 96–116. Leiden, Netherlands: Brill Rodopi, 2019a.

Kling, Jennifer. "The U.S. Military Needs to Budget: Decreasing Military Spending in the 21st Century." In *Ethics, Left and Right: The Moral Issues that Divide Us*, edited by Bob Fischer. Oxford: Oxford University Press, 2019b.

Kling, Jennifer. *War Refugees: Risk, Justice, and Moral Responsibility*. Lanham: Lexington Books, 2019c.

Kling, Jennifer. "Wealth, Violence, and (in)Justice: Refugees, Robin Hood, and Resistance." In *Peaceful Approaches for a More Peaceful World*, edited by Sanjay Lal. Leiden, Netherlands: Brill Rodopi, 2022.

Kling, Jennifer and Megan Mitchell. "Bottles and Bricks: Rethinking the Prohibition Against Violent Political Protest." *Radical Philosophy Review* 22, no. 2 (2019): 209–237.

Kling, Jennifer and Megan Mitchell. *The Philosophy of Protest: Fighting for Justice Without Going to War*. New York: Rowman & Littlefield International, 2021.

Knickmeyer, Ellen. "Costs of the Afghanistan War, in Lives and Dollars." *AP News*, August 16, 2021. https://apnews.com/article/middle-east-business-afghanistan-43d8f53b35e80ec18c130cd683e1a38f

Knight, Franklin W. "The Haitian Revolution." *The American Historical Review* 105, no. 1 (2000): 103–115.

Laozi. *Daodejing: A Philosophical Translation*, translated by Roger T. Ames and David L. Hall. New York: Ballantine Books, 2003.

Lau, D.C., H.C. Wah, and C.F. Ching, eds. *A Concordance to the Mengzi*. ICS Series. Hong Kong: Commercial Press, 1995.

Lazar, Seth. "Authorization and the Morality of War." *Australasian Journal of Philosophy* 94, no. 2 (2016): 211–226. doi:10.1080/000484 02.2015.1050680

Lazar, Seth. "Just War Theory: Revisionists Versus Traditionalists." *Annual Review of Political Science* 20, no. 1 (2017): 37–54. doi:10.1146/annurev-polisci-060314-112706

Lazar, Seth. "War." In *The Stanford Encyclopedia of Philosophy*, edited by Edward N. Zalta, 2020. https://plato.stanford.edu/archives/spr2020/entries/war/

Lazar, Seth and Helen Frowe, eds. *The Oxford Handbook of the Ethics of War*. Oxford: Oxford University Press, 2018.

Le Guin, Ursula K. "Speech in Acceptance of the National Book Foundation Medal for Distinguished Contribution to American Letters." The National Book Foundation Medal for Distinguished Contribution to American Letters, November 19, 2014. https://www.ursulakleguin.com/nbf-medal?rq=National%20Book%20Foundation%20Medal

Lewis, Colin and Jennifer Kling. "Justified Revolution in Contemporary American Democracy: A Confucian-Inspired Account." In *The Crisis of American Democracy*, edited by Leland Harper, 167–192. New York: Vernon Press, 2022.

Li, Chenyang. "The Confucian Ideal of Harmony." *Philosophy East and West* 56, no. 4 (2006): 583–603. http://www.jstor.org/stable/4488054.

Lo, Ping-cheung. "The Art of War Corpus and Chinese Just War Ethics Past and Present." *Journal of Religious Ethics* 40, no. 3 (2012): 404–446. doi:10.1111/j.1467-9795.2012.00530.x

Locard, Henri. "State Violence in Democratic Kampuchea (1975–1979) and Retribution (1979–2004)." *European Review of History* 12, no. 1 (2005): 121–143. doi:10.1080/13507480500047811

Locke, John. *Letter Concerning Tolerance*. In *Classics of Modern Political Theory*, edited by Steven M. Cahn. New York: Oxford University Press, 1997.

Locke, John. *Two Treatises of Government and a Letter Concerning Toleration*. New Haven: Yale University Press, 2004.

Machiavelli, Nicolo. *The Prince*, translated by W.K. Marriott. Project Gutenberg, 1998. https://www.gutenberg.org/files/1232/1232-h/1232-h.htm#chap14

Mallow, Sean L. "Harry S. Truman and the Decision to Use the Atomic Bomb." In *A Companion to Harry S. Truman*, edited by Daniel S. Margolies. Malden, MA: Wiley Blackwell, 2012.

Masakowski, Yvonne R., ed. *Artificial Intelligence and Global Security: Future Trends, Threats and Considerations*. Warrington, UK: Emerald Publishing Limited, 2020.

May, Larry. *Contingent Pacifism: Revisiting Just War Theory*. Cambridge: Cambridge University Press, 2015.

May, Larry, ed. *The Cambridge Handbook of the Just War*. Cambridge: Cambridge University Press, 2018.

McMahan, Jeff. "Revising the Doctrine of Double Effect." *Journal of Applied Philosophy* 11, no. 2 (1994): 201–212.

McMahan, Jeff. *Killing in War*. Oxford: Oxford University Press, 2009.

McMahan, Jeff. "Pacifism and Moral Theory." *Diametros* 23 (2010): 44–68.

McPherson, Lionel K. "The Costs of Violence: Militarism, Geopolitics, and Accountability." In *To Shape a New World: Essays on the Political Philosophy of Martin Luther King, Jr*, edited by Tommie Shelby and Brandon M. Terry, 253–266. Cambridge, Massachusetts: Harvard University Press, 2018.

Meisels, Tamar. "Fighting for Independence: What can Just War Theory Learn from Civil Conflict?" *Social Theory and Practice* 40, no. 2 (2014): 304–326.

Mill, John Stuart. "Utilitarianism." In *The Blackwell Guide to Mill's Utilitarianism*, edited by Henry R. West. Massachusetts: Blackwell Publishing Ltd, 2006.

Mills, Charles W. *The Racial Contract*. Ithaca, N.Y: Cornell University Press, 1997.

Morgenstern, George. *Pearl Harbor: The Story of the Secret War*. New York: Devin Adair, 1947.

Morrow, Paul. "Contingent Pacifism." In *The Routledge Handbook of Pacifism and Nonviolence*, edited by Andrew Fiala. New York: Routledge, 2018.

Noddings, Nel. *The Maternal Factor: Two Paths to Morality*. Berkeley: University of California Press, 2010.

Orend, Brian. "Jus Post Bellum." *Journal of Social Philosophy* 31, no. 1 (2000): 117–137.

Parekh, Serena. *Refugees and the Ethics of Forced Displacement*. New York: Routledge, 2017.

Peach, Lucinda J. "An Alternative to Pacifism? Feminism and Just War Theory." *Hypatia* 9, no. 2 (1994): 152–172. http://www.jstor.org. libproxy.uccs.edu/stable/3810175

Perry, James. *Arrogant Armies: Great Military Disasters and the Generals Behind Them*. New York: John Wiley & Sons, Inc., 2005.

Pinker, Steven. *The Better Angels of Our Nature*. New York: Penguin, 2011.

Plato. *Laws*. Cambridge, MA: Harvard University Press, 1967. At Perseus: http://www.perseus.tufts.edu/hopper/text?doc=Perseus:text:1999.01. 0166

Pratchett, Terry. *Witches Abroad*. New York: HarperTorch, 1991.

Quinn, Warren S. "Actions, Intentions, and Consequences: The Doctrine of Double Effect." *Philosophy & Public Affairs* 18, no. 4 (1989): 334–351.

Rawls, John. *The Law of Peoples*. Cambridge, MA: Harvard University Press, 1999.

Rawls, John. "Fifty years after Hiroshima." In *Collected Papers*, 565–572. Cambridge, MA: Harvard University Press, 1999.

Raz, Joseph. *The Morality of Freedom*. New York: Clarendon Press, 1986.

Reitberger, Magnus. "License to Kill: Is Legitimate Authority a Requirement for Just War?" *International Theory* 5, no. 1 (2013): 64–93. doi:10.1017/ S1752971913000122

Rodin, David. *War and Self-Defense*. Oxford: Oxford University Press, 2002.

Roosevelt, Theodore. *The Strenuous Life*. New York: Century, 1901.

Roosevelt, Theodore. *America and The World War*. New York: Charles Scribners, 1915.

Roosevelt, Theodore. "Wake Up America" (Speech of July 27, 1917). In *Newer Roosevelt Messages*, Vol. 3, edited by William Griffith. New York: The Current Literature Publishing Company, 1919.

Rousseau, Jean-Jacques. *The Social Contract and Discourses*. London and Toronto: J.M. Dent and Sons, 1923. At Liberty Fund: https://oll. libertyfund.org/titles/638

Russell, Bertrand. "The Future of Pacifism." *The American Scholar* 13, no. 1 (1943): 7–13.

Ryan, Cheyney. "The Pacifist Critique of the Just War Tradition." In *The Routledge Handbook of Pacifism and Nonviolence*, edited by Andrew Fiala. New York: Routledge, 2018.

Ryan, Cheyney. "Pacifism." In *The Oxford Handbook of Ethics of War*, edited by Seth Lazar and Helen Frowe. Oxford: Oxford University Press, 2018.

Sawyer, Ralph D. *The Seven Military Classics of Ancient China*. New York: Westview, 2007.

Schweitzer, Albert. *The Philosophy of Civilization*. Amherst: Prometheus, 1923/1987.

Sharp, Gene. *Civilian-Based Defense*. Princeton: Princeton University Press, 1990.

Sharp, Gene. *Waging Nonviolent Struggle: 20th Century Practice and 21st Century Potential*. Boston: Porter Sargent, 2005.

Sharp, Gene, M.S. Finkelstein, and T.C. Schelling. *The Politics of Nonviolent Action*, 3 Volumes. Manchester, NH: Porter Sargent, 1973.

Singer, Peter. "Famine, Affluence, and Morality." *Philosophy & Public Affairs* 1, no. 3 (1972): 229–243. http://www.jstor.org.libproxy.uccs.edu/stable/2265052

Sitting Bull. "The Life My People Want Is a Life of Freedom." In *Great Speeches by Native Americans*, edited by Bob Blaisdell, 169–170. New York: Dover Publications, Inc., 2000.

Skrentny, John David. "The Effect of the Cold War on African-American Civil Rights: America and the World Audience, 1945-1968." *Theory and Society* 27, no. 2 (1998): 237–285. http://www.jstor.org/stable/657868

Smart, J.J.C. and Bernard Williams. *Utilitarianism: For and Against.* Cambridge: Cambridge University Press, 1973.

Smith, Matthew Noah. "Rethinking Sovereignty, Rethinking Revolution." *Philosophy & Public Affairs* 36, no. 4 (2008): 405–440.

Stacy, Helen. "Humanitarian Intervention and Relational Sovereignty." In *Intervention, Terrorism, and Torture: Contemporary Challenges to Just War Theory*, edited by S.P. Lee, 89–104. New York: Springer, 2007.

Steffen, Lloyd. *Ethics and Experience.* Lanham, MD: Rowman and Littlefield, 2012.

Steinbeck, John. *Once There Was a War.* New York: Penguin Books, 2007.

Sterba, James. *Justice for Here and Now.* Cambridge: Cambridge University Press, 1998.

Sterba, James. "The Most Morally Defensible Pacifism." In *Pazifismus: Ideengeschichte, Theorie und Praxis*, edited by Barbara Bleisch and Jean-Daniel Strub. Bern: Haupt Verlag, 2006.

Stinnet, Robert. *Day of Deceit: The Truth about FDR and Pearl Harbor.* New York: Free Press, 2001.

Sundstrom, Ronald. "Frederick Douglass." In *The Stanford Encyclopedia of Philosophy*, edited by Edward N. Zalta, 2017. https://plato.stanford.edu/entries/frederick-douglass/

Tecumseh. "Sleep Not Longer, O Choctaws and Chickasaws." In *Great Speeches by Native Americans*, edited by Bob Blaisdell, 50–53. New York: Dover Publications, Inc., 2000.

Temam, Edgar I. "The 'Might Makes Right' Fallacy." PhD Dissertation: University of Oregon, 2014. https://scholarsbank.uoregon.edu/xmlui/bitstream/handle/1794/18310/Temam_oregon_0171A_10887.pdf?sequence=1&isAllowed=y

Terpstra, Niels. "The 'new' Taliban regime in Afghanistan: Different Methods but the Same Political Goal." *The Conversation*, September 6, 2021. https://theconversation.com/the-new-taliban-regime-in-afghanistan-different-methods-but-the-same-political-goal-166793

Thoreau, Henry David. "On Civil Disobedience." In *Thoreau: Walden and Other Writings*. New York: Modern Library, 2000.

Tiwald, Justin. "A Right of Rebellion in the Mengzi?" *Dao* 7, no. 3 (2008): 269–282. doi:10.1007/s11712-008-9071-z

Tolkien, J.R.R. *The Lord of the Rings*. New York: Ballantine Books, 1973.

Tolstoy, Leo. *What I Believe*. New York: Gottsberger, 1886. At Nonresistance.org: http://www.nonresistance.org/docs_pdf/Tolstoy/What_I_Believe.pdf

Tolstoy, Leo. *The Kingdom of God is Within You*. 1894. At Project Gutenburg: http://www.gutenberg.org/files/43302/43302-h/43302-h.htm

Tolstoy, Leo. "Letter to a Hindu." 1908. At Project Gutenburg: http://www.gutenberg.org/files/7176/7176-h/7176-h.htm

Truman, Harry S. *Where the Buck Stops: The Personal and Private Writings of Harry S. Truman*. Boston, MA: New Word City, 2018.

Twiss, Sumner B. and Ping-Cheung Lo, eds. *Chinese Just War Ethics: Origin, Development, and Dissent*. London: Routledge, 2015.

UNHCR. *Global Trends: Forced Displacement in 2018*. Geneva: UNHCR, 2019.

Uniacke, Suzanne. "Proportionality and Self-Defense." *Law and Philosophy* 30, no. 3 (2011): 253–272. http://www.jstor.org/stable/41486983

United Nations. *2005 World Summit Outcome [A/RES/60/1]*. Geneva: United Nations, 2005.

"United Nations Security Council Resolution 678." Geneva: United Nations, 1990.

United States National Holocaust Museum. "Documenting the Numbers of Victims of the Holocaust and Nazi Persecution." 2020. https://encyclopedia.ushmm.org/content/en/article/documenting-numbers-of-victims-of-the-holocaust-and-nazi-persecution

"U.S. Budgetary Costs." Costs of War Project. Watson Institute for International and Public Affairs, Brown University, September 2021. https://watson.brown.edu/costsofwar/figures/2021/BudgetaryCosts.

U.S. Defense Department. *Military and Security Developments Involving the Democratic People's Republic of Korea: A Report to Congress*. U.S. Department of Defense, 2015.

van der Linden, Harry. "Climate Change Mitigation and the U.N. Security Council: A Just War Analysis." In *Pacifism, Politics, and Feminism: Intersections and Innovations*, edited by Jennifer Kling, 117–136. Leiden, Netherlands: Brill Rodopi, 2019.

Vine, David, Cala Coffman, Katalina Khoury, Madison Lovasz, Helen Bush, Rachael Leduc, and Jennifer Walkup. "Creating Refugees: Displacement Caused by the United States' Post-9/11 Wars." *Costs of War Project*. Watson Institute for International and Public Affairs, Brown University, August 19, 2021. https://watson.brown.edu/costsofwar/files/cow/imce/papers/2021/Costs%20of%20War_Vine%20et%20al_Displacement%20Update%20August%202021.pdf

Walzer, Michael. *Arguing about War*. New Haven, CT: Yale University Press, 2004.

Walzer, Michael. *Just and Unjust Wars: A Moral Argument with Historical Illustrations*, 4th edition. New York: Basic Books, 2006.

Wasserstrom, Richard. "On the Morality of War: A Preliminary Inquiry." In *Military Ethics*, edited by C.A.J. Coady and Igor Primoratz. New York: Routledge, 2016.

Weigel, George. "Moral Clarity in Time of War." *First Things*, January 2003.

White, Matthew. "War, Massacres, and Atrocities of the 20th Century." 1999. http://users.erols.com/mwhite28/war-1900.htm

Wilde, Oscar. "A Woman of No Importance." In *Complete Works of Oscar Wilde*, edited by Robert Baldwin Ross. New York: Bigelow, Brown & Co., 1921.

Woods, Mark. "The Nature of War and Peace: Just War Thinking, Environmental Ethics, and Environmental Justice." In *Rethinking the Just War Tradition*, edited by Michael W. Brough, John W. Lango, and Harry van der Linden, 17–34. New York: SUNY Press, 2007.

Woolard, Fiona. "Double Effect, Doing and Allowing, and the Relaxed Nonconsequentialist." *Philosophical Explorations* 20, no. 2 (2017): 142–158. doi:10.1080/13869795.2017.1356355

World War Two Museum. "Worldwide Deaths in World War II." N.D. https://www.nationalww2museum.org/students-teachers/student-resources/research-starters/research-starters-worldwide-deaths-world-war

Yoder, John Howard. *The Politics of Jesus*, 2nd edition. Grand Rapids, MI: Eerdmans, 1994.

Yoder, John Howard. *Christian Attitudes to War, Peace, and Revolution*. Grand Rapids, MI: Brazos, 2009.

Zhang, Ellen Y. "Weapons are Nothing but Ominous Instruments: The *Daodejing*'s View on War and Peace." *Journal of Religious Ethics* 40, no. 3 (2012): 473–502. doi:10.1111/j.1467-9795.2012.00532.x

Index

Daoism 75, 105, 110
Day, Dorothy 139
death ix, 3–4, 19, 21–22, 61, 83;
    choice of 75; cycle of 75; from
    genocide 91; of innocents 15;
    and resources 83; minimization
    of 97; nonviolence and 95,
    127–28; power of 98; threats of
    99; tolls 62n4, 76, 88–89,
    104, 176
DDE see Doctrine of Double Effect
de-escalation see diplomacy;
    escalation; nonviolence
defeat 41–42, 74, 78, 111–12,
    182–83
defense spending see militarism;
    military industrial complex
defensive war xii, 42, 78, 83–84,
    89; climate change and 191;
    domestic analogy and 80; ethics
    of 145–46; international law and
    64; invasion and 158, 170–71;
    jus in bello and 186; justification
    for 167, 188; lasting peace and
    164; see also just war theory; war
dehumanization 46, 189;
    see also realism; us vs. them
democracy 26, 144–45, 154–55,
    181, 184
deontological arguments 5–6, 18,
    22–24, 39, 61; and exceptions
    43; as moral framework 77–78;
    and noncombatants 25, 159;
    obedience and 26; rights and
    76–77; see also human rights
Desert Shield 98
Desert Storm 98
destruction ix, 4, 18, 22, 35;
    ecological 113, 118, 186; of
    infrastructure 21; as lesser evil
    41; mutually assured xv; as
    means of peace 109; of political
    authority 87; as violence of war
    55, 61, 75, 101, 110, 177;
    weapons of mass 19
dignity 81, 87, 95, 108; of the
    group 77; right to 89, 119, 164;
    social safety nets and 111; state

sovereignty and 94;
    see also rights
diplomacy 84–85, 98, 109, 128;
    see also negotiation; nonviolence
discrimination 44, 79, 102–4, 113;
    see also consequentialism; jus in
    bello; see also jus post bellum
displaced persons x, 87–88;
    see also refugees
Doctrine of Double Effect (DDE)
    23, 24, 26, 117, 200; challenges
    to 25; intent 147;
    see also collateral damage;
    combatants; noncombatants
dogmatism 5, 7–8, 18–19, 24, 177;
    Tolstoy and 33–34; tradition
    and 163
domestic analogy 12–15, 80–81,
    93, 121n1, 143
domestic politics xv, 81, 141
domestic violence see violence
domination 30, 38, 52, 107, 168,
    180–84
Douglass, Frederick 119, 166
draft see conscription
drones 4, 25, 62n4, 102
duty 18, 39, 144, 159; moral 26,
    93–94; peace as 54

Egypt 190
Eisenhower, Dwight 56
emancipation 66, 88–89, 119
embargo xv, 16, 22, 123
encroachment 82, 94
enemy ix, 14, 30, 47, 181;
    battlespaces 104; depravity of
    43; Othering of 46, 103, 189;
    soldiers 15; treatment of the 44,
    110; weakness as 57
environment xi, 15, 18, 77, 155,
    186, 190–91; respect for 143
escalation xiv–xv, 46, 85, 103, 147
ethics xii, 6, 8, 158; applied 172;
    care 48, 135–36; of defensive
    war 145; and killing 23; military
    99; see also virtue ethics
ethnic cleansing 91–92, 205, 206;
    see also genocide

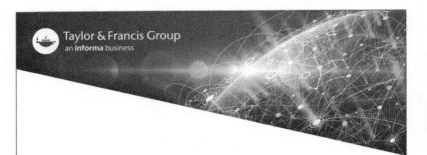

Made in the USA
Las Vegas, NV
18 August 2023

76239421R00144